Everyday Spanish

a basic text & workbook
for introductory spanish

Elliot Glass
Chairperson, Department of Foreign Languages and Literatures
Queensborough Community College

Ricardo Diez
Department of Modern Languages
Brooklyn College

Nancy Liberti
Department of Foreign Languages and Literatures
Queensborough Community College

Warren Bratter
Department of Languages and International Studies
Adelphi University

AVERY PUBLISHING GROUP INC.
Wayne, New Jersey

Photograph Credits:

Photographs on pages 12, 14, 65, 97, 102, 214, 253, 258, 273, 275, 300 and 341 by Elliot Glass.

Photographs on pages 22, 69, 70, 144, 250 and 280 by Alexine Curtis.

Photographs on pages 120, 122 and 296 from *Bilingual Education*, Avery Publishing Group, Inc.

Photographs on pages 157, 186 and 207 by Steven Friedman.

Photograph on page 324 courtesy of the *American Educator Magazine*, Washington, D.C.

Cover design by Martin Hochberg and Rudy Shur.

Printed in the United States of America

10 9 8 7 6 5 4 3

Contents

*This book is dedicated to
the memory of Enrique Ledesma
whose loyal friendship, intelligence, smile, and wit
brightened our days.*

Acknowledgements

We would like to express our appreciation to all our colleagues who class-room-tested the preliminary edition of *Everyday Spanish*. Their unflagging encouragement helped make this first edition possible.

We wish to thank especially Dr. Carlos Esturo and Dr. Carmen Esteves for their thoughtful revisions of all the *Lecturas*. We would also like to extend our gratitude to Professors Delphine Fernández McLean, David Altabé, and Bertha Gervasio for critically reviewing the text. For the long and tedious hours spent in producing the audio tapes for the text, we extend our hearty thanks to Professors Jaime Quiroga and Paul Sullivan. This book could not have been completed on time without the steady patience and tenacity of Joan Winant and Sue Nahmias.

A special commendation goes to Dr. Enrique Ledesma for the many hours he devoted to the final editing and revising of the entire manuscript.

Finally, we would like to acknowledge our greatest debt to Rudy Shur, our Publisher. His patience and forbearance have been exemplary.

Preface

With the considerable growth of the Hispanic community in the United States during the past two decades, it has become necessary to update the approach to the teaching of Spanish. What is now required is not the "guided tour" approach, but the teaching of the actual Spanish that is used in the large Hispanic communities of the United States. Courses such as Spanish for Hospital Personnel, Spanish for Teachers, and Business Spanish have become popular because they are necessary for dealing with Hispanics in everyday life. In order to meet the demands of this new approach, we have written *Everyday Spanish: A Basic Textbook*, which combines the best of a basic Spanish textbook with the real life situations that call for an ability to communicate in Spanish.

In *Everyday Spanish* we attempt to integrate three key elements into the teaching of Spanish. First, we build upon a clear understanding of both English and Spanish grammar. To this we add a variety of workbook exercises. Finally, we introduce the students to practical vocabulary and phrases used in various professional settings. No text or phrase book provides as comprehensive an approach to the fundamentals of teaching practical Spanish.

Each chapter opens with a third person narrative (*Lectura*) and closes with a dialogue (*Diálogo*). The focus in both is on grammatical concepts covered in the chapter and on career-oriented vocabulary and phrases. Both narratives and dialogues complement each other through the story line that gives cohesion and an overall context to the sixteen chapters. This story line centers on the everyday experiences and problems of a Chilean immigrant, José García, and his family as they begin to adjust to life in the United States. Consistent with the practical nature of the text, we have introduced "popular language" in both the dialogues and narratives. It is our intention to provide the means for the student to become familiar with what he will really hear in daily life.

By following the experiences of the García family, we are taken through numerous real life learning situations. These scenes depict some of the most common job situations in which Spanish may be used: Health Services, Education and Educational Administration, Insurance, Law Enforcement, Legal Counseling, and Community Services.

In short, *Everyday Spanish* can be used effectively in basic Spanish courses as well as in career-oriented language courses which emphasize the use of Spanish in everyday life.

Introduction

Students who have a knowledge of the grammar of their own language are able to master a second language much faster and more thoroughly than those who don't. In the preliminary lesson, therefore, we review some basic principles of English grammar. By learning this section first, the student will be able to understand the concepts in the following chapters with ease and, thereby, move more quickly from conceptual material to practical vocabulary.

Grammar is Coming Back

For centuries the study of grammar was an essential part of a primary school education. For a variety of reasons over the past thirty-five years, the emphasis on grammar has all but disappeared from the grade school curricula. It is only now, with reports about poor verbal skills and the functional illiteracy of many high school graduates, that there has been a new importance placed on grammar. Paradoxically, many college students learn the grammar of their native language when studying a foreign language, and they readily agree that had they known English grammar before embarking on their study of the foreign language, they would have been able to learn and master the new language faster and easier.

"I just want to speak the language."

A frequent comment made by students is that they "just want to speak the language." This is a task that would, in most cases, require a 48-hour-a-week total-immersion course over a period of several months. This kind of course, despite its emphasis on oral skills, still includes grammar lessons, because, as we all know, it is not enough just to speak a language. We should speak it so that others will understand exactly what we want to say and what we mean.

Since most students have neither the time nor the money to take total-immersion courses, the next best way to learn a language is to study its design and learn the vocabulary that would be most useful.

The Language Code: Grammar

Grammar is not a disease. It is a code that allows us to see an overall design of how a language works. Once we understand.the various components (the grammatical terms) that make up the code, then we can see clearly similarities and differences between our language and the one we are studying. The grammar of a language gives us a blueprint of that language so that we can put words and phrases together in a meaningful way.

English Grammar: A Means to an End

When we have learned how to read the blueprint of our own language, then we will be better equipped to see how a second language works. The first section of *Everyday Spanish* is designed to familiarize the student with the basics of English grammar so that the terms, definitions, and concepts that are found in the sections dealing with the various professions will be readily understood. In this way, having gained an understanding of the grammatical concepts and terms, more time can be dedicated to learning the professional vocabulary.

Chapter 1
A Short Review of English Grammar

As we indicated in our introduction, studies have shown that a better knowledge of the grammar of one's native language is useful and at times necessary if one hopes to master the skills required to communicate effectively in a second language. In this chapter we take a look at grammatical terms and at the structure and patterns found in English.

THE ARTICLE

The first part of speech we will look at is the **article**. In English, as in most languages, the article can be divided into two categories: the definite article and the indefinite article. The **definite article** is *the* and the **indefinite article** is *a* or *an*.

Definite Article	*Indefinite Article*
the book	*a* book
the hour	*an* hour

THE NOUN

In the above examples, we see two nouns following the articles. Both **book** and **hour** are called nouns. A **noun** is a word used to name a person, place, or thing.

THE ADJECTIVE

If you want to describe the **book** or the **hour**, you add an **adjective**:

the *good* book	a *good* book
the *odd* hour	an *odd* hour

The term **adjective** is applied to words that modify—limit the meaning of—or describe a noun or a word that takes the place of a noun (a pronoun). Adjectives encompass a big category. For example, *this, that, these, those* are called **demonstrative adjectives**:

this good book	*that* odd hour
these good books	*those* odd hours

Adjectives that show possession are called **possessive adjectives**:

my good book(s)	*your* odd hour(s)
our good book(s)	*his* odd hour(s)
her good book(s)	*their* odd hour(s)

Adjectives that ask questions are called **interrogative adjectives** (think of interrogate or interrogation):

Which good book(s)?	*What* odd hour(s)?

Adjectives that follow the verb *to be* (I *am*, you *are*, he/she/it *is*, we *are*, you *are*, they *are*) are called **predicate adjectives**.

The book is *good*.	Your hours are *odd*.
My book is not *good*.	Which hours are *odd*?
This book is *good*.	Those hours are *odd*.

Notice that we have included more than one adjective in all but the first sentence.

VERBS

A verb is a word that indicates an action or expresses a state of being. The verb *to be* which we have just mentioned is a verb that expresses a state of being. It does not convey an action. The verbs *to fall* and *to pass*, on the other hand, do express an action. Let's add these verbs to some of the phrases that we illustrated earlier:

My good book *falls* from the shelf.
Their busy hours *pass* quickly.

THE TENSES

Verbs not only tell us about a state of being or action; they also tell us *when* something existed or happened. Verbs tell us whether the action or state of being *is taking place, takes place habitually, has taken place, had taken place, used to take place, took place, will take place,* or *would take place.* The term **tense** so often used in grammar books simply denotes the time frame of the verb. Let's take a look at possible time frames for verbs.

Present Tense

If the action or state of being takes place in the present, then we use the **present tense**:

The hours *pass* quickly.
The books *fall* from the shelf.

We also use the **present tense** if we are describing something which is universally true or something that happens habitually:

Water *freezes* at 32 degrees.
John always *calls* at noon.

Present Progressive Tense

If the action is ongoing or in progress at the time the speaker is describing it, we use the **present progressive tense**:

> The hours *are passing* quickly.
>
> Watch out! The books *are falling*!

Simple Past or Preterite Tense

If the action or state of being *took place*, we use the **simple past** or **preterite**. In English, the simple past has many irregular verb forms (*saw, went, ate, swam, ran, was/were, drank*, etc.).

> The hours *passed* quickly.
>
> The books *fell*.

Imperfect or Past Progressive Tense

If an action or state of being *used to take place, would take place*, or *was taking place*, we use the **imperfect** or **past progressive tense**:

> The hours *used to pass* quickly when I *was working* hard.
>
> When I *would slam* my door, the books *would* always *fall*.

Future Tense

If the action or state of being *will take place*, the **future tense** is used. The future in English is formed by adding *will* to the verb.

> The hour *will pass* quickly.
>
> Those books *will fall* soon.

Periphrastic Future

The **periphrastic future** refers to our using the present progressive of the verb *to go* to express a future tense:

> The hour *will pass* quickly. *becomes* The hour *is going* to pass quickly.
>
> Those books *will fall* soon. *becomes* The books *are going* to fall soon.

Conditional Tense

When an action or state of being *would take place* if another condition is met, the tense is called the *conditional.*

> The hour *would pass* quickly, if you *would work* harder.
>
> If you *would fix* the shelf, the book *would* not *fall*.

While the spelling of *would* is exactly the same in both the conditional and the past progressive tenses, there should be no confusion here because one refers to an action in the past and the other refers to an action in the future. The conditional tense is often used after hypothetical clauses or statements of conditions contrary to fact.

> If I were you (*condition contrary to fact*), I **would do** it.
>
> If she had the money (*hypothetical*), she **would be** happy.

THE MYSTERIOUS PARTICIPLE

For some reason the word **participle** often frightens people. It seems that many of us have heard teachers talk about *dangling participles* and *participial phrases*, and it is perhaps because we never quite understood how a participle could dangle that we now have no idea what a participle is. Well, it is simply a word formed from a verb that has the qualities of both a verb and an adjective. In English there are two types of participles:

1. Present Participle

The **present participle** always ends in *-ing*. Using our examples, *take, pass,* and *fall,* we can form present participles by adding *-ing*: tak*ing*, pass*ing*, fall*ing*.

2. Past Participle

The **past participle** in English is often spelled exactly the same as the simple past or preterite verb form (**passed, bought, looked**); however, there are many irregular past participles which are not at all similar (**taken, fallen, seen, gone, eaten, run**).

Functions of the Participles

The participle can function as an **adjective**.

> The **talking** doll broke. (*talking* modifies the noun *doll*)
>
> The money **taken** was his. (*taken* modifies the noun *money*.)

The participle can also function as a **verb** following some form of either the verb "to be" or "to have."

> The books are/were **falling**.
>
> The books have/had/will have/would have **fallen**.

In the first sentence (*The books are/were falling.*), we see that the present participle is combined with some form of the verb **to be** (**am, is, are, was, were,** etc.). As we have seen, this combination forms the present progressive and past progressive tenses.

In the second sentence (*The books have/had/will have/would have fallen.*), we see that the participle is combined with some form of the verb **to have**. The various combinations are labeled in accordance with the tense of the helping verb **to have**.

> **Present Perfect:**
> I have **fallen**, you have **fallen**, he has **fallen**, etc.
>
> **Past Perfect:**
> I had **fallen**, you had **fallen**, he had **fallen**, etc.

Future Perfect:

I will have *fallen*, you will have *fallen*, he will have *fallen*, etc.

Conditional Perfect:

I would have *fallen*, you would have *fallen*, he would have *fallen*, etc.

Perfect, in grammatical terms, means that the action expressed by the verb is seen as completed. **Perfect** = complete, finished, ended. The participle in its perfect form does not change.

Present, Past, Future, and Conditional refer to the period of time expressed by the verb, *to have.*

THE PASSIVE VOICE

A reference to the *passive voice* is not a reference to someone speaking in a low or fading voice. It refers to another use of the past participle. When a form of the verb **to be** is used with a *past participle*, the result is the *passive voice*:

> The books *are taken* by John.
> The books *were taken* by John.
> The books *have been taken* by John.
> The books *had been taken* by John.

By making **John** the subject of all of the above sentences (*John takes/took/has taken/ had taken the books.*), we perform an act of grammatical wizardry—we transform the sentences from the passive voice to the active voice. In the active voice the subject acts upon the verb: John (*the actor*) takes (*action*) the books (*the object*). In the passive voice, the subject is acted upon and we have a passive description of an event.

PAST PARTICIPLE VS. PRETERITE OR SIMPLE PAST

We mentioned earlier that the past participle is often spelled the same as the simple past or preterite (*returned, bought, sold,* etc.), and this similarity in spelling has caused great havoc in our speaking correct English. Since we know that so many simple past or preterite forms are the same as the past participles, we sometimes tend to use one in place of the other even when the past participle form is completely different from the preterite or simple past. We hear, for example:

> "I have went."   *instead of* **I have gone.**   *or* **I went.**
> "He seen."   *instead of* **He has seen.**   *or* **He saw.**

This confusion is most often made with the irregular preterites and participles. One of the ways to correct this is to do a lot of reading; another is to get a college English grammar handbook or a dictionary and look up irregular preterites and past participles.

THE INFINITIVE

We have seen that the different forms of the verb indicate different time periods: *present, future, past,* etc. But we have not spoken about the form of the verb that is *timeless,* the verb that simply names the action without telling us anything about the subject or about the tense (*when*). This form is called the **infinitive**. The infinitive in English is preceded by *to.*

to run	to read
to be	to pass
to jump	to fall

Infinitives have a restricted usage. They can never be used as the main verb and are frequently used after conjugated verbs. What are conjugated verbs? Let's take a minute to clarify the term "conjugate." When you *conjugate* a verb, you simply arrange the forms of the verb to match the changes in person, number (singular or plural), and tense. As an example, we will conjugate two verbs: the regular verb "to jump" and the irregular verb "to be."

to be				to jump		
Singular				**Singular**		
	Subject Pronoun	Conjugated Verb			Subject Pronoun	Conjugated Verb
1st person	I	am		1st person	I	jump
2nd person	you	are		2nd person	you	jump
3rd person	he/she/it	is		3rd person	he/she/it	jump**s**
Plural				**Plural**		
1st person	we	are		1st person	we	jump
2nd person	you	are		2nd person	you	jump
3rd person	they	are		3rd person	they	jump

For regular English verbs in the present tense the letter **s** in the third person singular is the only distinguishing feature in the conjugation. But it is, indeed, an important one. One of the most common errors in spoken English is the omission of this third person singular **s**. All of us have heard people say, "It don't matter." If we remove the contraction, we see that we are really saying, "It *do not* matter." Obviously, it should be, "It doesn't matter."

As one learns a language, one must learn to conjugate verbs—to add proper endings to indicate person, number, and tense. It is interesting to note that the English tense system has few variations. Look at the tense system of any regular verb (like *jump, sing, work*) and you will see little or no variation with the person and number:

I jumped.	I used to jump.	I will jump.
You jumped.	You used to jump.	You will jump.
He jumped.	He used to jump.	He will jump.
We jumped.	We used to jump.	We will jump.
All of you jumped.	All of you used to jump.	All of you will jump.
They jumped.	They used to jump.	They will jump.

Because of this lack of variation, the subject pronoun or noun must always be there. In other languages the conjugated form of the verb often tells us who the subject is, and, therefore, the subject pronouns are not required and often are omitted.

Now before we go astray, let's return to the infinitive and its dependence on a conjugated verb. While an infinitive can be the subject of a sentence (*To dine here is a delight.*), most infinitives will be found following a conjugated verb:

> I want *to go*.
> They hope *to win*.
> She intends *to sing*.

AUXILIARY OR HELPING VERBS

Auxiliary verbs are not verbs that come to your rescue if you have a problem speaking. They are verbs that help to form tenses when combined with main verbs, or they help the main verb express an action or make a statement. The verbs *to have, to be, to do, may, can, must,* and *will* are some of the most common helping verbs.

The verb *to do* is used to ask a question or to show emphasis:

> *Do* you understand?   We *do* learn!
> *Did* she go?   They *did* go!

The verb *to have* is used with the past participle to form the **perfect tenses:**

> I *have* fallen.   (present perfect)
> I *had* fallen.   (past perfect)
> I *will have* fallen.   (future perfect)
> I *would have* fallen.   (conditional perfect)

The verb *to be* is used with present participles to form the **progressive tense** and with the past participle to form the **passive voice:**

> The book *is falling*.   (present progressive)
> The book *was falling*.   (past progressive)
> The books *are read* by me.   (passive voice)

The verb *may* and its past tense *might* and the verb *can* and its past tense *could*, unlike the above three verbs, cannot ever stand alone without a main verb:

> The books *may fall*.
> They *might fall* later.
> She *can learn*, but they *could* not *learn*.

Must and *will* also require a main verb all of the time.

We *must go* now.

The books *will fall* quickly.

PRONOUNS

In several places in our discussion we have used the term *pronoun* and it is time to focus on this important part of speech. *Pronouns* take the place of *nouns*.

Personal pronouns take the place of specific persons or things. *I, you, he, she, it, we, you,* and *they* are the personal pronouns. When they provide a subject for a sentence or phrase, they are called **subject pronouns**.

Indefinite pronouns refer to vague or nonspecific persons, things, or quantities:

No one is here.

Something is wrong.

The more, the merrier.

Possessive pronouns denote ownership: *mine, yours, his, hers, ours, theirs.*

Reciprocal pronouns *(each other, one another)* indicate the relationship between individual members of a plural subject. For example,

They see each other and we write to one another.

Reflexive pronouns are used when the object of the verb refers back (flexes back) to the subject:

He washes **himself** and they bathe **themselves**.

The key to the reflexive pronouns is the *-self* or *-selves* which must always be present.

Object Pronouns stand for objects of the verb, be they persons or things. There are direct and indirect object pronouns. **The direct object**, the initial receiver of the action, answers the question *whom* or *what.*

For example:

(Whom)	They see *John*.	*John* is the **direct object noun**.
	They see *him*.	*Him* is the **direct object pronoun**.
(What)	María has *the books*.	*Books* is the **direct object noun**.
	María has *them*.	*Them* is the **direct object pronoun**.

Direct Object Pronouns

Singular	*Plural*
me	us
you	you
him	them (*objects/persons*)
her	
it (*objects*)	

The Indirect Object can be identified because it answers *to whom* or *for whom* the action is done.

For example:

(to whom)	He gives the money *to John*.	*John* is the **indirect object noun**.
	He gives the money *to him*.	*Him* is the **indirect object pronoun**.
(for whom)	We buy the books *for Jane*.	*Jane* is the **indirect object noun**.
	We buy the books *for her*.	*Her* is the **indirect object pronoun**.

One of the confusing things about indirect object pronouns in English is that sometimes they are not preceded by the prepositions *to* and *for* and, therefore, appear to be direct object pronouns.

He gives me the money.	We buy her the books.
He gives the money *to me*.	We buy the books *for her*.

If you are in doubt about whether you have a direct object or indirect object pronoun, you should first see if it answers *to whom* or *for whom* the action is done. If there is still doubt, then rearrange the sentence and insert the prepositions *to* or *for* accordingly.

Indirect Object Pronouns

	Singular		*Plural*
	me		us
	you	to/for	you
to/for	him		them (*objects/persons*)
	her		
	it (*object*)		

Direct and Indirect Object Pronoun Combinations

Whenever we use direct and indirect object pronouns in the same sentence, the direct object pronoun goes before the indirect object pronoun.

	Direct Object	*Indirect Object*
John gives	*it*	*to them*.
We bring	*them*	*to her*.

PREPOSITIONS

Speaking of prepositions, we should mention that a preposition relates a noun or pronoun to some other word in the sentence with regard to *time, place, position,* or *direction.*

I saw him *at* noon.	*(time)*
Hang your coat *in* the closet.	*(place)*
They go to school *from* here.	*(direction)*
The books are *on* the table.	*(position)*

LARGER UNITS

Prepositions link words together and form larger units. The two larger units which tend to cause students some difficulty are **clauses** and **sentences**. First let us look at the clauses.

CLAUSES

A **clause** is any group of words that contains a verb and its subject. Clauses may stand alone or function as a dependent part of the complete sentence. If they serve as part of a complete sentence, they do not convey a complete thought. Let us examine two kinds of clauses:

Main/Independent Clauses

If a clause makes an independent statement, a statement that expresses a complete thought, then it is a **main** or **independent clause**.

> ***He gives me the money*** when I ask him.

Dependent Clauses

If a clause must depend on another clause to complete a thought, then it is a **dependent** or **subordinate clause.**

> He gives me the money ***when I ask him.***

Dependent clauses are often introduced by: *since, as, when, because, who, that,* or *which*.

Now let's look at three kinds of dependent clauses: *adjective clauses, adverbial clauses,* and *noun clauses.*

1. An **adjective clause** functions like an adjective. It modifies a noun or pronoun in the sentence:

> The monument   ***which was constructed last year***   has collapsed.
> *(noun)*   *(adjective clause)*

> Anyone   ***who has seen it***   can tell you what happened.
> *(pronoun)*   *(adjective clause)*

2. An **adverbial clause** functions as an adverb by modifying (a) *a verb*, (b) *an adjective*, or (c) *another adverb*.

| The child | **cried** | ***when the dog appeared.*** |
| | (verb) | (adverbial clause) |

| I am | **sorry** | ***that he is ill.*** |
| | (adjective) | (adverbial clause) |

| He runs more | **quietly** | ***than I do.*** |
| | (adverb) | (adverbial clause) |

3. A **noun clause** functions as a noun in a sentence. It can serve as the *subject* or *object* of the verb.

| ***What John wants*** | is a better job. |
| (subject) | |

| Please tell him that | ***I will be late.*** |
| | (object) |

THE SENTENCE

Now that we have an idea of what clauses are about, let us turn to the sentence. A **sentence** is another word for an independent clause.

There are three kinds of sentences: ***declarative, exclamatory,*** and ***interrogative.***

1. The **declarative sentence** primarily conveys information (it makes a declaration) and ends with a period. It is a statement.
2. The **exclamatory sentence** expresses a strong emotion on the part of the speaker and ends with an exclamation point.
3. The **interrogative sentence** asks a question and ends with a question mark.

MOODS

Sentences and clauses reflect the speaker's attitude toward what is said. The different verb forms that indicate this attitude are called ***moods***. In English we have the ***indicative, imperative,*** and ***subjunctive moods.***

1. **The Indicative Mood**

   If the speaker states a fact or asks a factual question, then the sentence is in the **indicative mood** (something is indicated).

   > He buys the books.

2. **The Imperative Mood**

   If the speaker expresses a command, request, or gives instructions, then the sentence is in the **imperative mood**.

   > Buy the books!

3. The Subjunctive Mood

If the speaker expresses a condition, hypothesis, contingency, possibility, wish, etc., rather than actual fact, then the sentence is in the **subjunctive mood**.

> If I *were* you, I would buy the books.
>
> It is important that he *be* there at 5:00.
>
> It is possible that she *may* buy the books.

Now that you have gone through our brief introductory grammar, we hope that you have a better understanding of grammatical concepts and will be able to recognize and identify them when you examine an English sentence. Your knowledge of English grammar will give you an enormous advantage in your study of Spanish since the grammatical terms used are almost identical in both languages.

Un restaurante puertorriqueño

REVIEW

The exercises below are designed to improve your familiarity with the terms and concepts we have just covered. If you get any wrong, go back and study the concept or term until you have a thorough understanding of it.

Match the term with the definition:

a. noun   _____ Used with the verb **to have** to form the perfect tenses.

b. pronoun   _____ If a speaker expresses a condition, hypothesis, contingency, or any nonfactual statement.

c. adjective   _____ *the*

d. infinitive   _____ Adjectives that distinguish one item from other items in the same class.

e. simple past   _____ Used to name a person, place, or thing.

f. passive voice   _____ *a* or *an*

g. demonstrative adjectives   _____ Adjectives that ask questions.

h. past progressive or imperfect   _____ Words that modify or describe a noun or pronoun.

i. dependent clause   _____ The action or state of being is taking place now.

j. past participle   _____ The action or state of being *used* to take place, would take place in the past, or was taking place.

k. reflexive pronoun   _____ The form of the verb that is *timeless*. In English, this form is preceded by *to*.

l. indirect object   _____ They take the place of nouns.

m. subjunctive mood   _____ Is used when the object of the verb refers to the same person as the subject.

n. indefinite article   _____ The secondary receiver of the action of the verb. It answers *to whom* or *for whom* it is done.

o. interrogative adjective   _____ *to be* + past participle.

p. present tense   _____ An action that took place or did take place. Sometimes called the preterite.

q. definite article   _____ A group of words which contain a subject and verb but which must depend on another clause to complete the thought.

Un restaurante chino-cubano

Chapter 2
The Spanish Sound System, Punctuation, and Capitalization

Before we focus in on Spanish grammar, we must master the sounds and sound combinations found in Spanish. In English, when we put stress on the wrong syllable (*dé-sert* vs. *de-sért*), we change the meaning of the word. Likewise in Spanish, when an accent is misplaced (*hablo* [I speak] vs. *habló* [he spoke]), or when we improperly pronounce a word or combination of words, we will not communicate *our intended idea*. Since a student must be familiar with the sound system, the punctuation, and capitalization of a language in order to make unimpeded progress in learning that language, this chapter should be reviewed thoroughly before beginning the actual text, which starts with Chapter 3.

Sounds of the Spanish Language

SPANISH VOWELS

	English Sound	*Spanish Sound*
a	c*a*r, *a*h	Ana, llamar
e	s*e*t, m*e*t	Elena, beber
i	rout*i*ne, *e*at	Ignacio, vivir
o	*o*ught, R*o*se	Rodolfo, como
u	tr*u*e, s*oo*n	Ursula, su

All Spanish vowels are pronounced clearly and distinctly. Their sound is constant and does not vary in length when pronounced in a stressed or unstressed syllable. The simple vowel sound is produced in Spanish by keeping the tongue, lips, and jaws in a fixed position. Avoid the glide sound or slur resulting from moving the tongue, lips, and jaws to form the vowel sounds in English.

For example: tea / té

EJERCICIOS. Repeat after your instructor:

a	Adela, Clara, mamá, papá, ala
e	Pepe, Teresa, ese, este, café

i	Isabel, Israel, visita, lista, así
o	Paco, Ramón, oso, oro, loco
u	Jesús, Raúl, suyo, usted, un

THE ALPHABET

There are 30 letters in the Spanish alphabet. Some letters occur only in words of foreign origin; for example, *k* (kilómetro, krausismo) and *w* (wagneriano, watercloset). Some letters do not exist in English; for example, *ch, ll,* and *rr* (in Spanish they are considered single consonants).

a	(a)	**Panamá, ala, andar**
b	(be)	Pronounced like *boy*: **beber, baña, buscar**
c	(ce)	(1) Before *e* and *i, c* is pronounced like *s* in *sin* in Spanish America and in southern Spain, as in **Cecilia, Cirilo.**
		In northern and central Spain, the *c* is pronounced like *th* in *thin*: **ciento, ciudad.**
		(2) Before *a, o, u* and ***consonants***, it is pronounced like *c* in *cork*: **casa, cosa, curar, claro, crema.**
ch	(che)	Pronounced like *ch* in *China*: **chasco, chico, chiste.**
d	(de)	Pronounced like the hard, dentalized *d* in *dog* when it is the first letter of a word: **diente, Darío, dulce.**
		In all other instances, it assumes a less dentalized and often softer pronunciation approximating the English *th* sound in *this*: **verdad, pared, Ricardo.**
e	(e)	**él, Elsa, entre**
f	(efe)	Pronounced the same as in English: **Francisco, teléfono.**
g	(ge)	(1) Before *e* and *i* the sound is soft and is pronounced like *h* in *hat*: **gente, gesto, legión.**
		(2) Before *a, o, u* and consonants the sound is hard and is pronounced like *g* in *go*: **gastar, gordo, Gustavo.**
h	(hache)	Is silent (not pronounced): **hasta, hoy, hospital.**

i	(i)	**indio, idea, sí**
j	(jota)	There is no exact equivalent in English. It is a hard guttural pronunciation of the **h** sound: **Juan, José, jefe.**
k	(ka)	Pronounced like *k* in *Kremlin*: **kilómetro, Alaska, kilogramo.**
l	(ele)	Pronounced like *l* in *let*: **Luis, lista, lavar.**
ll	(elle)	Pronounced like *y* in *yes* in most parts of South America and in some parts of Spain. In other parts of Spain it is pronounced like the *ll* sound in *million*: **calle, llamar, caballero.**
m	(eme)	Pronounced the same as in English: **maestro, mamá, mesa.**
n *ñ*	(ene)	(1) Pronounced the same as in English: **ni, Nerón, nene.** (2) Pronounced like *ny* in *canyon*: **doña, uña, niña.**
o	(o)	Pronounced like *o* in *obey*: **Olga, oso, todo.**
p	(pe)	Pronounced like *p* in *past*: **Pedro, pasta, apartar.**
q	(ku)	Pronounced like *k* in *Kansas*: **queso, quizás, querer.**
r	(ere)	Pronounced like *r* in *or*: **motor, oro, traer.** If the *r* is in initial position, the sound is hard: **Roberto, radiador, rotor.**
rr	(erre)	The same as when *r* is in initial position: **berro, barrer, barrio.**
s	(ese)	Pronounced like *s* in *Susan*: **sin, sé, salsa.**
t	(te)	Pronounced like *t* in *tip*: **traer, Tomás, tener.**
u	(u)	Pronounced like *oo* in *moon*: **Perú, untar, uno.**
v	(be)	Pronounced like the Spanish *b*: **Virgilio, vino, ver.**

w	(doble ve)	Pronounced like w in *Wilson*: Wilfred, Wisconsin, whisky.

x	(equis)	Pronounced like x in *exact* before vowels: **examen, existir.**
		Pronounced like s in *so* before consonants: **experimento, externo.**

y	(i griega)	Pronounced like y in *yes*: Yucatán, ya
		(exception: when y appears alone meaning *and*, then it is pronounced like the vowel *i).*

z	(zeta)	(1) Pronounced like s in *sip* in Spanish America.
		(2) Pronounced like *th* in *thin* in Spain, **except** in southern Spain where it is pronounced the same as in Spanish America: **zumbar, zorra, luz.**

LINKING

In the spoken language, words should be linked since they usually appear in groups (phrases). Linking occurs mainly as follows:

1. If a word ends in a *vowel*, and the next word begins with the *same vowel*, then the sounds blend into one.

   Luis compra allí.   **Ella va a casa.**   **Luis salió hoy.**

2. If a word ends in a *consonant* and the next word begins with a *vowel*, the two sounds are blended into one syllable.

   Juan anda apurado.   **El quiere comprar eso.**   **¿Quieres helado?**

3. If two successive vowels are a combination of a strong vowel *(a, e,* or *o)* and a weak vowel *(i, u)* or two weak vowels, they are linked, and thus form a *diphthong*, which is pronounced as one syllable.

   Luis *(vs. fe-o* or *mío).* The written accent dissolves the diphthong.
   Fuerte, Diego *(vs. dí-a).*

ACCENTUATION

1. Words ending in a *vowel* or with n or s are stressed on the next to the last syllable: **punto, coma, Carmen, casas.**

2. Words ending in a consonant, except n or s, are stressed on the last syllable: **usted, verdad, hablar.**

3. The written accent is used to indicate that a syllable is stressed in a way different from the general rules: **mío, débil, lección.**

   or to distinguish words different in meaning but similar in spelling:

él	he	**té**	tea	**sí**	yes
el	the	**te**	you/to you	**si**	if

EJERCICIOS. Pronounce after your instructor:

a	arar, acá, halar, hallar, caminar
b	bestia, burro, bulto, bastante, baranda
c	clase, hacer, cantar, coser, concepción
d	dedo, dedal, Madrid, Darío, ladrón
e	feo, egoísta, educar, eléctrico, elástico
f	familia, falso, faltar, farsa, fatal
g	ligero, grande, ágil, gustar, gastar
h	hondo, ahorcar, alcohol, hinchar, hacer
i	infantil, individuo, inducir, indiferencia
j	jabón, Jaime, jirafa, joya, juez
k	kaiser, kantiano, kilociclo, kerosina
l	lápiz, lindo, labor, lente, luz
m	María, mesa, madrina, mal, metal
n	no, nombre, noche, nada, novela
ñ	ñandú, uña, ñoño, señor, señora
o	ojo, ocasión, ocioso, occidente, ocurrir
p	pesar, pero, para, pan, papá
q	que, quien, quiere, quinto, quitar
r	radical, atrás, orar, traer, ladrón
rr	arrastrar, cigarro, barril, derrumbar, carril
s	sabor, sacar, tras, después, sin
t	tratar, tener, detrás, tierra, tiempo

u	usar, Luis, uva, pluma, uno
v	venir, atravesar, vaca, avaro, vicio
w	wagneriano, watt, water-closet, whisky
x	examen, existir, extra, extraer
y	yo, yunta, yarda, yeso, yoga
z	zafra, zafar, empezar, rezar, azul

PHONETIC VARIATIONS

Many Spanish-speaking people do not articulate all of the vowels and consonants in words. One of the most common omissions is the *s* sound. **Los libros** might be pronounced **Loh libroh**. In the question, **¿Cómo está usted?** (How are you?), you might hear: **¿Cómo ehtá uhté?** This pronunciation is not considered standard.

Another common omission is the *d* sound when it is in final position: **usted** becomes **uh**te; libertad (liberty) becomes **libertá**.

Often when the *d* sound is between the vowels *a* and *o*, it is not pronounced; instead of hearing **he terminado**, you might hear **he termina-o**.

Sometimes two sounds are omitted. Instead of hearing **para mí** (for me) or **para él** (for him), you might hear **pa-mí** or **pa-él**.

Two not so common occurrences are the pronunciation of the *r* as an *l* and the pronunciation of the double or trilled *r* as *j*. For example, the infinitive **comer** (to eat) would be pronounced **comel** and the name **Roma** would be pronounced **Joma**.

Careful speakers of Spanish will make sure to articulate all sounds clearly and, thereby, avoid any confusion.

CAPITALIZATION

Spanish *does not capitalize* any word in the following categories, unless it is used as the first word of a sentence:

(1) the pronoun I: **yo**;
(2) names of languages: **alemán** (German);
(3) names of days of the week and months of the year:
   martes (Tuesday), **junio** (June);
(4) adjectives denoting nationality: **ruso** (Russian).

Spanish *does capitalize* the following:

(1) proper names: **Juan Valera, María Elena Gómez.**

(2) the first letter of the title of a book, play, article, etc.

La rebelión de las masas	*The Rebellion of the Masses*
La vida es sueño	*Life is a Dream*

(3) abbreviations:

usted	**(ustedes)**	you	*becomes*	**Ud.**	**(Uds)**	*or* **Vd. (Vds.)**
señor	**(señores)**	Mister	*becomes*	**Sr.**	**(Sres.)**	
señorita	**(señoritas)**	Miss	*becomes*	**Srta.**	**(Srtas.)**	
señora	**(señoras)**	Mrs.	*becomes*	**Sra.**	**(Sras.)**	

(4) the first letter of a sentence:

La casa es grande.   The house is large.

PUNCTUATION

The rules of punctuation in English and Spanish are the same except for the following:

1. An inverted question mark (¿) is placed at the point where the question begins, which may not necessarily be at the beginning of the sentence:

    Hola María, ¿cómo está usted?   Hi Mary, how are you?

2. An inverted exclamation point (¡) precedes an exclamatory phrase, a command, or an emphatic statement; it is placed at the point where the exclamation begins, which may not necessarily be at the beginning of the sentence:

¡Qué horror!	How terrible!
¡Cálmese!	Calm down!
¡No me diga!	You don't say!

3. A dash (—) is used to indicate a change of speaker:

--**Buenos días, señor García.**	Good day, Mr. García.
—**Buenos días, señora Jiménez.**	Good day, Mrs. Jiménez.

Una vista de la ciudad

Capítulo 3
La agencia de empleo*

Lectura

El señor y la señora García **buscan**	are looking
empleo en la **ciudad** de Nueva York. Ellos	city
caminan muchas **cuadras desde**	walk / blocks from
el tren subterráneo **hasta** la agencia de empleo.	to
Entran en la agencia y **hablan con** una	They enter / they speak with
recepcionista.	
La recepcionista **ayuda** mucho.	helps
Los García† **llenan un cuestionario**;	fill out
después llenan tres más	
y, por fin, **firman** cuatro documentos.	they sign
Luego hablan con una **consejera**.	Then / counselor
Ella **contesta sus preguntas**.	answers their questions
Desgraciadamente, la consejera	Unfortunately
desea más documentos.	wishes
Los García **necesitan regresar** mañana	need to return
con el resto de la documentación.	

* employment
† Los García translates as Mr. and Mrs. García.

La gramática

NOUNS AND DEFINITE ARTICLES

In Spanish the definite article and the noun can be masculine or feminine. The masculine definite article is *el* in the singular and *los* in the plural. Masculine nouns generally end in *o* in the singular and *os* in the plural.*

	Definite Article		Noun	
Singular	el	the	cuestionario	questionnaire
Plural	los	the	cuestionarios	questionnaires

The feminine definite article is *la* in the singular and *las* in the plural. Feminine nouns generally end in *a* in the singular and *as* in the plural.*

Singular	la	the	agencia	agency
Plural	las	the	agencias	agencies

In general, when nouns end in a vowel, add *s* to form the plural; when they end in a consonant, add *es*. For nouns that end in stressed vowels, one usually adds *es* to form the plurals: **rubí** (ruby), **rubíes**.

Masculine		Feminine	
el hombre	the man	la tarde	the afternoon
los hombres	the men	las tardes	the afternoons
el estado	the state	la cuadra	the block
los estados	the states	las cuadras	the blocks
el papel	the paper	la mujer	the woman
los papeles	the papers	las mujeres	the women

* Some common exceptions are:
  el día, los días (the day, the days); **la mano, las manos** (the hand, the hands),
  and many nouns ending in *ma* —
  el electrocardiograma, los electrocardiogramas, el telegrama, los telegramas, el programa, los programas, el poema, los poemas.

EJERCICIOS. Give the plural of the following nouns:

1. el documento — _los documentos_
2. la referencia — _las referencias_
3. el nombre (the name) — _los nombres_
4. la dirección (the address)* — _las direcciones_
5. el estado — _los estados_
6. la ciudad (the city) — _las ciudades_
7. el teléfono — _los teléfonos_
8. la posición (the position) — _las posiciones_
9. el tren — _los trenes_
10. la profesión — _las profesiones_
11. el cuestionario — _los cuestionarios_
12. la mujer — _las mujeres_
13. el doctor — _los doctores_
14. la calle (the street) — _las calles_
15. el obrero (the male worker) — _los obreros_
16. la cuadra — _las cuadras_
17. el señor — _los señores_
18. la casa — _las casas_
19. el hospital — _los hospitales_
20. la experiencia — _las experiencias_
21. el empleo — _los empleos_
22. la oficina (the office) — _las oficinas_
23. el contrato (the contract) — _los contratos_
24. la tarde (the afternoon) — _las tardes_
25. la pregunta (the question) — _las preguntas_
26. la carta (the letter) — _las cartas_
27. el director — _los directores_

* *ción* nouns which have an accent over the ó in the singular, do not retain the written accent in the plural.

25

NOUNS THAT REFER TO PERSONS

Nouns that refer to persons are masculine or feminine according to the sex of the person. If a masculine noun ends in *o*, drop the *o* and add *a* to form the corresponding feminine form; if the masculine noun ends in a consonant, then add *a* to form the feminine.

el puertorriqueñ*o*	the Puerto Rican man
la puertorriqueñ*a*	the Puerto Rican woman
el supervisor	the male supervisor
la supervisor*a*	the female supervisor

EJERCICIOS.

Change the masculine article and noun to the corresponding feminine form:

1. el colombiano — *la colombiana*
2. el doctor — *la doctora*
3. el puertorriqueño — *la puertorriqueña*
4. el supervisor — *la supervisora*
5. el dominicano — *la dominicana*
6. el argentino — *la argentina*
7. el señor — *la señora*
8. el profesor — *la profesora*
9. el empleado (male employee) — *la empleada*
10. el obrero — *la obrera*
11. el mexicano — *la mexicana*
12. el consejero (male counselor) — *la consejera*
13. el hermano (the brother) — *la hermana*
14. el primo (the male cousin) — *la prima*
15. el muchacho (the young man) — *la muchacha*
16. el cubano — *la cubana*
17. el hispano (the Hispanic man) — *la hispana*

THE INDEFINITE ARTICLE: *a* or *an*

The indefinite article, like the definite article, agrees with the noun in gender (masculine/feminine) and number (singular/plural). **Un** is the masculine indefinite article and **una** is the feminine indefinite article.

Masculine		*Feminine*	
un cuestionario	a questionnaire	una agencia	an agency
un hospital	a hospital	una estudiante	a student (female)
un hombre	a man	una mujer	a woman
un puertorriqueño	a Puerto Rican man	una puertorriqueña	a Puerto Rican woman

The plurals **unos** and **unas** are translated as *some*.

unos cuestionarios	some questionnaires	unas agencias	some agencies

EJERCICIOS. Supply the indefinite singular and plural articles.

		Singular	Plural
1.	el documento	*un*	*UNA documentos*
2.	la muchacha	*UNO*	*UNOS muchachas*
3.	la experiencia		*experiencias*
4.	el obrero		*obreros*
5.	la mujer		*mujeres*
6.	el doctor		*doctoras*
7.	la supervisora		*supervisoras*
8.	el colombiano		*colombianos*
9.	la ciudad		*ciudades*
10.	el tren		*trenes*
11.	la calle		*calles*
12.	el primo		*primos*
13.	la mexicana		*mexicanas*
14.	el cuestionario		*cuestionarios*
15.	la oficina		*oficinas*
16.	el profesor		*profesoras*
17.	el estado		*estados*

18. el hermano   _____   _____

19. el consejero   _____   _____

20. la tarde   _____   _____

21. el contrato   _____   _____

EJERCICIOS.

Insert the corresponding article.

Definite

1. _____ teléfono

2. _____ doctoras

3. _____ direcciones

4. _____ empleadas

5. _____ mujeres

6. _____ nombres

7. _____ muchachos

8. _____ documentación

9. _____ mexicana

10. _____ señor

11. _____ posición

12. _____ cheque

13. _____ nombre

14. _____ trenes

15. _____ profesión

16. _____ doctor

17. _____ empleo (employment)

18. _____ ciudad

Indefinite

1. _____ hospital

2. _____ cubana

3. _____ agencia

4. _____ nombre

5. _____ autobús

6. _____ calle

7. _____ hispano

8. _____ posición

9. _____ hermano

10. _____ tarde

11. _____ director

12. _____ argentina

13. _____ empleado

14. _____ cuadra

15. _____ experiencia

16. _____ contrato

17. _____ carta

18. _____ estado

Definite	Indefinite
19. _____ autobús	19. _____ oficina
20. _____ tren	20. _____ colombiano
21. _____ supervisor	21. _____ mexicano
22. _____ calle	22. _____ papel

EJERCICIOS. Translate into Spanish.

1. some contracts _____

2. the supervisor _____

3. a state _____

4. some experiences _____

5. the Argentine man _____

6. a train _____

7. some buses _____

8. the streets _____

9. a woman worker _____

10. some Puerto Rican women _____

11. the women doctors _____

12. a young man _____

13. some telephones _____

14. the female employee _____

15. a male professor _____

16. some offices _____

17. a city _____

18. some addresses _____

19. the Mexican man _____

20. a bus _____

CONTRACTIONS:

---
de + el = del / a + el = al

The prepositions *de* (of, from, about, than) and *a* (to, at, for, after) contract when combined with the definite article **el**.

La agencia **del** estado   The agency of the state

El camina **al** parque.   He walks to the park.

EJERCICIOS.

1. La dirección _____ *(of the)* cubano.   3. El camina _____ *(to the)* hospital.

2. El empleado _____ *(of the)* estado.   4. El camina _____ *(to the)* autobús.

LOS VERBOS: *–AR*

The Infinitive

The infinitive is the basic or general form of the verb. It simply names the action, making no distinction as to person or tense. In Spanish, the infinitive ends in *-ar, -er,* and *-ir:*

habl**ar** to speak   com**er** to eat   viv**ir** to live

Present Indicative of *–ar* Verbs

The present indicative mood describes a fact or action that takes place regularly or that is taking place now. It is formed by dropping the final two letters of the infinitive (*-ar, -er,* or *-ir*) and adding a personal ending to what remains (the stem). To form the present indicative of regular *-ar* verbs, drop the *-ar* from the infinitive and add the appropriate personal ending (*-o, -as, -a, -amos, -áis,* or *-an*) to the stem of the verb.

---
habl**ar** to speak

Subject Pronoun		Stem	+	Personal Ending	
yo	I	habl	+	*o*	I speak, I am speaking, I do speak
tú	you	habl	+	*as*	You speak (familiar form), you are speaking, you do speak
usted	you	habl	+	*a*	You speak (formal or polite form), you are speaking, you do speak
él	he	habl	+	*a*	He speaks, he is speaking, he does speak
ella	she	habl	+	*a*	She speaks, she is speaking, she does speak
nosotros	we	habl	+	*amos*	We speak, we are speaking, we do speak
nosotras	we	habl	+	*amos*	We speak (feminine), we are speaking, we do speak
vosotros*	you	habl	+	*áis*	You speak (plural familiar form), you are speaking, you do speak
ustedes	you	habl	+	*an*	You speak (formal or polite form), you are speaking, you do speak
ellos	they	habl	+	*an*	They speak, they are speaking, they do speak
ellas	they	habl	+	*an*	They speak (feminine), they are speaking, they do speak

* In all subsequent conjugations, the **vosotros/as** form will not be used because of its infrequent usage in Latin American countries.

30

2. Nosotros **pagamos** mensualmente (mon
   (las compañías, la agencia de desemple

   _____

   _____

   _____

   _____

3. Los obreros **desean** la oportunidad de
   (la secretaria, el señor Martínez, yo, ell

   _____

   _____

   _____

   _____

4. Yo **necesito** más información y más do
   (el supervisor, tú, los García, tú y yo)

   _____

   _____

   _____

   _____

5. La señora García **llena** todos los cuestic
   (yo, Ricardo y Pablo, nosotras, la direct

   _____

   _____

   _____

   _____

ily).

o [unemployment agency], yo, él).

_____

_____

_____

_____

rabajar (opportunity to work).
os)

_____

_____

_____

_____

umentación.

_____

_____

_____

_____

narios.
ra)

_____

_____

_____

_____

EJERCICIOS. Fill in the appropriate form of the verb:

1. usar, necesitar   Yo _____ la computadora (computer).

2. ayudar, trabajar, desear   Nosotros _____ mucho.

                                    Ellos _____ poco.

3. firmar, necesitar, llenar   Tú _____ el contrato.

                                    Los Martínez _____ el cuestionario.

4. escuchar, buscar, mirar   Ellas _____ las noticias (the news).

                                    Usted _____ al reportero.

5. esperar, ganar, hablar   Ella _____ mucho.

                                    Tú y yo _____ poco.

EJERCICIOS. Fill in the appropriate form of the verb.

1. Ellos siempre (always) (ayudar) _____ .

2. El señor García (buscar) _____ empleo.

3. Ustedes (contestar) _____ las cartas.

4. Yo (conversar) _____ con los dominicanos.

5. Tú (desear) _____ más noticias.

6. Ella siempre (escuchar) _____ la radio.

7. Nosotros (esperar) _____ el contrato.

8. Los clientes (firmar) _____ los documentos y los contratos.

9. El empleado (ganar) _____ mucho dinero (a lot of money).

10. Tú (hablar) _____ muy bien (very well).

11. Los puertorriqueños (llenar) _____ los cuestionarios.

12. Los García (llevar) _____ unos paquetes (some packages).

13. Ustedes siempre (mirar) _____ la televisión.

14. El y yo (necesitar) _____ auxilio/ayuda (help).

15. La compañía (pagar) _____ muy bien.

16. ¿Qué (what) (pasar) _____ ahora (now)?

17. El señor García y la señora García (solicitar) _____ empleo.

18. Generalmente yo (tomar) _____ un taxi.

19. Los consejeros (trabajar) _____ hoy (today).

20. Nosotras (usar) _____ la computadora todos los días (every day).

21. Tú y yo (ayudar) _____ mucho.

MAKING A SENTENCE NEGATIVE IN SPANISH:

In order to make a Spanish sentence negative, place **no** before the conjugated verb:

Subject	+	**no**	+	verb	+	. . .
Pedro	+	**no**	+	habla		español.
Los obreros	+	**no**	+	trabajan		hoy.

Pedro **no** habla español.   Peter does *not* speak Spanish.
Los obreros **no** trabajan hoy.   The workers do *not* work today.

EJERCICIOS. Put each sentence in the negative.

1. Yo firmo los documentos.

    _____

2. El señor Rodríguez y yo trabajamos aquí (here).

    _____

3. El llena los cuestionarios y ella toma toda (all) la información.

    _____

4. Nosotros contestamos las cartas.

    _____

5. Tú necesitas más preparación (more skills).

_____

6. Ustedes esperan la respuesta (answer).

_____

7. Yo paso los exámenes (the exams).

_____

8. El empleado firma el contrato.

_____

9. Unos colombianos esperan el autobús.

_____

10. Nosotros solicitamos empleo.

_____

11. Ella conversa con los empleados.

_____

ASKING A QUESTION IN SPANISH

One way to ask a question in Spanish is to place the conjugated verb before the subject:

¿Verb + Subject?

¿Habla Pedro español?
¿Trabajan los obreros hoy?

Another way to ask a question is simply to have the intonation rise at the end of the statement:

¿Subject + Verb?

¿Pedro habla español?
¿Los obreros trabajan hoy?

EJERCICIOS. Change the statement into a question.

1. Tú llevas las cartas.

   _____

2. Tú no tomas la información.

   _____

3. Ellos contestan las preguntas.

   _____

4. María necesita auxilio/ayuda.

   _____

5. Ustedes esperan la respuesta.

   _____

6. Unos puertorriqueños conversan con la supervisora.

   _____

7. La colombiana habla inglés.

   _____

8. Usted busca empleo hoy.

   _____

9. Pedro y Luis ganan mucho dinero aquí.

   _____

10. Ella no lleva la carta.

    _____

11. Ellos no pagan la cuenta (bill).

    _____

12. El desea más preparación.

    _____

EJERCICIOS. Translate into Spanish.

1. The man works a lot. The men work every day.

   _____

2. He does not speak. She answers the questions.

   _____

3. Do the workers fill out the questionnaires?

   _____

4. Some Colombian men and a Colombian woman want more information.

   _____

5. Some States use all the questionnaires.

   _____

6. You (tú) want a lot, and you earn little.

   _____

7. Does he listen to the news? The employees do not work today.

   _____

8. The Garcías do not take a taxi. They wait for a bus.

   _____

9. Do we answer the telephone?

   _____

10. She passes the exam and signs the contract every year (_todos los años_)

    _____

11. Today we look for employment.

    _____

12. Do I pay monthly? They pay the bills every year.

    _____

13. The women doctors help a lot; they speak Spanish.

   _____

14. The women counselors always answer the letters.

   _____

15. We do not use the computer today.

   _____

INTERROGATIVES

Interrogatives alert the listener or the reader that a question will follow. Some common interrogatives are:

¿Qué?	What?	**¿Dónde?**	Where?	**¿Cómo?**	How?
¿Cuándo?	When?	**¿Por qué?**	Why?	**¿Con quién?**	With whom?
¿Quién?	Who?				

The above follow the formula:

¿Interrogative + Verb + Subject . . . ?

¿Qué usan ustedes?	¿Dónde trabaja él?	¿Cómo ayudas tú?
¿Cuándo estudia él?	¿Por qué firma ella?	¿Con quién habla María?

When the interrogative **¿Quién?** (Who?) is used, the formula is:

¿Interrogative + Verb + Object . . . ?

¿Quién necesita los documentos?

¿Quién solicita empleo?

All interrogatives require accents. Without the accent the meaning may change. For example:

¿Qué?	What?
. . . **que** . . .	who, which, that
¿Qué paga él?	What does he pay?
El hombre **que** trabaja aquí necesita documentos.	The man who works here needs documents.
¿Por qué?	Why?
porque	because
¿Por qué trabajas tú?	Why do you work?
Porque necesito dinero.	Because I need the money.

EJERCICIOS.
Fill in the blank space with the appropriate form.

1. (Who) ¿ _____ trabaja todos los días?

2. (Why) ¿ _____ no caminan ellos ahora?

3. (What) ¿ _____ necesitamos hoy?

4. (Where) ¿ _____ trabaja ella?

5. (How) ¿ _____ llevas el paquete?

6. (Who) ¿ _____ mira la televisión?

7. La mujer, (who) _____ trabaja aquí, ayuda mucho.

8. Necesitamos las referencias (because) _____ buscamos empleo.

9. (When) ¿ _____ estudian ellas?

10. (With whom) ¿ _____ caminas todos los días?

11. (Why) ¿ _____ no toman ustedes el tren?

12. (Where) ¿ _____ entramos?

Los García buscando empleo

39

Diálogo

Señor García	—	¿Habla usted español?
Señora Richards	—	Sí, ¡**cómo no!** ¿Necesita usted ayuda?
Señor García	—	Sí, por favor. **Soy radiólogo** y busco empleo en Nueva York.
Señora Richards	—	**Pues,** siéntese aquí, por favor. **Primero** usted necesita llenar el cuestionario A-1 (ah uno). **Luego** necesita firmar el documento A-5 (ah cinco).
Señor García	—	Lleno el documento A-8 (ah ocho), ¿no?*
Señora Richards	—	No, por favor, **solamente** el documento A-5. Ah, señor García, usted habla inglés, ¿verdad?*
Señor García	—	**Bueno,** hablo **bastante** y todos los días miro la televisión, escucho la radio, y converso con **los vecinos.**
Señora Richards	—	Muy bien. ¡**Espere** un minuto! Necesito hablar con **el jefe.** (*Ella habla con el jefe.*) Señor García, por favor, **regrese mañana.**
Señor García	—	Muy bien. **Adiós.**
Señora Richards	—	**Hasta mañana.**

VOCABULARIO DEL DIALOGO

¡cómo no!	of course
soy radiólogo†	I am a radiologist
pues	well
primero	first
luego	then

* End questions like "don't you," "haven't they," and "aren't we," usually translate as **no?** at the end of the sentence. **Verdad,** which means "right" or "true," conveys a similar meaning.

† The uses of the verb *ser* (to be) will be discussed in detail in capítulo 5. The verb *ser* is conjugated below:

yo	***soy***	I am	nosotros	***somos***	we are
tú	***eres***	you are			
usted		you are	ustedes		you are
él	***es***	he is	ellos	***son***	they are
ella		she is	ellas		they are

bueno	used at beginning of a sentence, it means "well," "all right," "OK"
solamente	only
bastante	enough
los vecinos	the neighbors
espere	wait (command)
el jefe	the boss
regrese mañana	return tomorrow
adiós	goodbye
hasta mañana	until tomorrow
hasta luego	until then
hasta la vista	until I see you again

PREGUNTAS SOBRE EL DIALOGO

1. ¿Quién (Who) busca empleo en Nueva York?

   _____

2. ¿Qué (What) cuestionario necesita llenar?

   _____

3. ¿Qué documento necesita firmar?

   _____

4. ¿Habla el señor García inglés?

   _____

5. ¿Con quién (With whom) conversa el señor García todos los días?

   _____

Vocabulario del capítulo

COGNATES OR NEAR COGNATES

adicional

la agencia

el autobús

la burocracia

la compañía

la computadora

el contrato

el cuestionario

la directora

el doctor

la documentación

el documento

el examen

la experiencia

la familia

el hospital

la información

la oficina

la oportunidad

la posición

la preparación

la profesión

el profesor

la radio

la recepcionista

la referencia

el reportero

el resto

la secretaria

el supervisor

el taxi

el teléfono

la televisión

VOCABULARIO

el argentino	the Argentine man	**la consejera**	counselor (female)
la argentina	the Argentine woman	**la cuadra**	block
aquí	here	**el cubano**	Cuban man
la ayuda	help	**la cubana**	Cuban woman
el auxilio	aid	**la cuenta**	bill
bien	well	**de**	from, of
la calle	the street	**desde . . . hasta**	from . . . to
la carta	the letter	**desgraciadamente**	unfortunately
el cartero	the mailman	**después**	after
el colombiano	Colombian man	**el día**	day
la colombiana	Colombian woman	**el dinero**	money
la ciudad	the city	**la dirección**	address
con	with	**el dominicano**	Dominican man
el consejero	counselor (male)	**la dominicana**	Dominican woman

el empleo	employment, job	muy	very
el empleado	employee (male)	la noche	night
la empleada	employee (female)	el nombre	name
en	in	las noticias	news
español	Spanish	el obrero	worker (male)
generalmente	generally	la obrera	worker (female)
el hermano	brother	el papel	paper
la hermana	the sister	el paquete	package
el hispano	Hispanic male	pero	but
la hispana	Hispanic female	la planilla	form
el hombre	man	poco	little
hoy	today	la pregunta	question
inglés	English	el primo	cousin (male)
luego	then	la prima	cousin (female)
la máquina	machine	el puertorriqueño	Puerto Rican man
mañana	tomorrow	la puertorriqueña	Puerto Rican woman
más	more	la respuesta	answer
mensualmente	monthly	el señor	gentleman / Mr.
el mexicano	Mexican man	la señora	lady / wife / Mrs.
la mexicana	Mexican woman	siempre	always
el muchacho	young man	el subterráneo	subway
la muchacha	young woman	la tarde	afternoon
mucho	much, a lot	todo/a	all
la mujer	woman	el tren	train
el mundo	world	y	and

FRASES

todos los días	every day	todas las noches	every evening
todas las tardes	every afternoon	todos los años	every year

Vocabulario adicional

SOME COMMONLY USED COMMANDS

Singular Command/Usted Form:

¡Siéntese!	Sit down!
¡Espere un minuto!	Wait a minute!
¡Regrese mañana!	Return tomorrow!
¡Cálmese!	Calm down!

¡No se preocupe!	Don't worry!
¡Firme aquí!	Sign here!
¡Perdóneme!	Pardon me!
¡Hable despacio!	Speak slowly!
¡Llene el cuestionario!	Fill out the questionnaire!
¡Ayúdeme!	Help me!

Plural Command/Ustedes Form:

If you are addressing more than one person, simply add **n** to the verb:

¡Siéntense!	¡Firmen aquí!
¡Esperen un minuto!	¡Perdonen!
¡Regresen mañana!	¡Hablen despacio!
¡Cálmense!	¡Llenen el cuestionario!
¡No se preocupen!	¡Ayúdenme!

Be polite! Add *por favor* (please) to your commands.

EJERCICIOS. Translate into Spanish.

1. Please sit down! ¡ _____ usted!

2. Sign here, please! ¡ _____ ustedes!

3. Please don't worry! ¡ _____ usted!

4. Calm down, please! ¡ _____ ustedes!

5. Speak slowly, please! ¡ _____ usted!

6. Help me! ¡ _____ ustedes!

7. Please return tomorrow! ¡ _____ usted!

8. Wait a minute, please! ¡ _____ ustedes!

9. Pardon me, please! ¡ _____ ustedes!

10. Fill out the questionnaire! ¡ _____ usted!

11. Sit down, please! ¡ _____ ustedes!

12. Please sign here! ¡ _____ usted!

LOS NUMEROS

cero	zero	treinta	thirty
uno*	one	treinta y uno	thirty-one
dos	two	treinta y dos, etc.	thirty-two, etc.
tres	three		
cuatro	four	cuarenta	forty
cinco	five	cuarenta y uno	forty-one
seis	six	cuarenta y dos, etc.	forty-two, etc.
siete	seven		
ocho	eight	cincuenta	fifty
nueve	nine	sesenta	sixty
diez	ten	setenta	seventy
		ochenta	eighty
once	eleven	noventa	ninety
doce	twelve		
trece	thirteen	cien(to)**	one hundred
catorce	fourteen	doscientos/as	two hundred
quince	fifteen	trescientos/as	three hundred
diez y seis / dieciséis†	sixteen	cuatrocientos/as	four hundred
		quinientos/as	five hundred
diez y siete/ diecisiete	seventeen	seiscientos/as	six hundred
		setecientos/as	seven hundred
diez y ocho/ dieciocho	eighteen	ochocientos/as	eight hundred
		novecientos/as	nine hundred
diez y nueve/ diecinueve	nineteen	mil	one thousand
		dos mil	two thousand
veinte	twenty	cien mil	one hundred thousand
veinte y uno/ veintiuno	twenty-one		
veinte y dos, veintidós	twenty-two	un millón	one million
veinte y tres/ veintitrés, etc.	twenty-three, etc.		

*uno drops the o when followed by a masculine noun: un libro = one book; veintiún libros = twenty-one books; treinta y un libros = thirty-one books.

† In Spanish, y is used between the tens and units; however, when it is replaced by i, the z changes to c and the appropriate accents are added to dós, -trés, and séis.

** The to of ciento is dropped before nouns and the numbers mil and millones. The full form is used when it is followed by a number smaller than itself.

LOS DIAS DE LA SEMANA

el lunes	(on) Monday	**el viernes**	(on) Friday
el martes	(on) Tuesday	**el sábado**	(on) Saturday
el miércoles	(on) Wednesday	**el domingo**	(on) Sunday
el jueves	(on) Thursday		

The days of the week require the definite article **el**, except when you say **hoy es** (today is) or **mañana es** (tomorrow is).

Hasta el domingo	until Sunday
Hoy es lunes	Today is Monday.

The article also translates as *on* when referring to a given day:

Yo necesito ayuda *el* lunes.	I need help *on* Monday.

The days of the week that end in **s** have the same form for singular and plural.

el lunes	on Monday
los lunes	on Mondays

sábado and **domingo** add an **s**.

los sábados	on Saturdays

LAS ESTACIONES DEL AÑO

el invierno	winter
la primavera	spring
el verano	summer
el otoño	autumn

LOS MESES DEL AÑO

enero	January	**julio**	July
febrero	February	**agosto**	August
marzo	March	**septiembre**	September
abril	April	**octubre**	October
mayo	May	**noviembre**	November
junio	June	**diciembre**	December

YO SOY — I am
Tu Eres → you are
usted es → you are
EL — he is
DE — from
y — and

WRITING THE DATE

To the question

¿Cuál es la fecha de hoy?

one should answer:

Hoy es + day + numerical date + de + month

Hoy es martes, (el) seis de febrero.

Hoy es sábado, (el) veinte y dos de abril.

The only exception here is for the first day of the month — **el primero** is used to express the first of every month:

Hoy es viernes, (el) primero de mayo.

LETTER HEADINGS

For letter headings use the formula:

City + number + de + month + de + year

México, 4 de agosto de 1984

Bogotá, 1 de mayo de 1985

EJERCICIOS — Los números.

Add the following:

1. *Ejemplo:* Siete más (+) cinco son (are) **doce.**

2. Diez y seis más cuatro son _____

3. Ocho más once son _____

4. Quince más veinte y cinco son _____

5. Nueve más trece son _____

Subtract the following:

1. *Ejemplo:* Veinte menos (−) quince son **cinco.**

2. Diez y ocho menos ocho son _____

3. Cincuenta menos seis son _____

4. Diez y nueve menos siete son _____

5. Veinte y dos menos cuatro son _____

Multiply the following:

1. *Ejemplo:* Cuatro multiplicado (×) por cinco son **veinte**.

2. Dos por once son _____

3. Seis por seis son _____

4. Cinco por ocho son _____

5. Diez por tres son _____

Divide the following:

1. *Ejemplo:* Cuarenta y cinco entre (÷) cinco son **nueve**.

2. Cincuenta entre diez son _____

3. Noventa entre diez son _____

4. Diez y ocho entre seis son _____

5. Sesenta y seis entre once son _____

MAS EJERCICIOS

Write the following dates:

January 28 _____

February 6 _____

March 11 _____

July 4 _____

August 15 _____

Capítulo 4
La entrevista

Lectura

El señor García **tiene** una **entrevista**   has / interview
con la **jefa** de la administración de   head (woman)
un hospital municipal. El señor García
llega al hospital unos minutos antes de   arrives
la **cita**. El **ve** que el hospital es un   the appointment / sees
edificio viejo; sin embargo las   old building / nevertheless
facilidades técnicas son **nuevas**. El   new
camina **por los pasillos** y **se da cuenta**   through the halls / realizes
que **hay** muchos hispanos que **trabajan**   there are / work
allí. Muchos de los pacientes hablan
español también. El señor García **quiere**   wants
trabajar en **este** hospital porque él **se siente**   to work / this / feels
muy cómodo en **este ambiente** hispano.   very comfortable / this atmosphere

La gramática

POSITION OF THE ADJECTIVE

In English, adjectives (modifying words) that limit and/or describe a noun go before the noun they modify:

Limiting	Descriptive	Noun
three	old	hospitals
some	red	machines
many	Puerto Rican	doctors
several	Dominican	nurses

In Spanish, limiting adjectives precede the noun and descriptive adjectives follow the noun:

Limiting	Noun	Descriptive
tres	hospitales	viejos
unas	máquinas	rojas
muchos	doctores	puertorriqueños
varias	enfermeras	dominicanas

AGREEMENT WITH NOUNS

All adjectives must agree in *number* (singular/plural) with the nouns they modify. Add *s* to form the plural of adjectives that end in a vowel and *es* to adjectives that end in a consonant:

los hospitales viej*os*	the old hospitals
las máquinas roj*as*	the red machines
los técnicos jóven*es*	the young technicians
las máquinas azul*es*	the blue machines

All adjectives must agree in *gender* (masculine/feminine) with the nouns they modify. Adjectives ending in *o* are masculine. The *o* is changed to *a* to form the feminine:

el hospital viej*o*	los hospitales viej*os*
la máquina viej*a*	las máquinas viej*as*
el médico colombian*o*	los médicos colombian*os*
la enfermera cuban*a*	las enfermeras cuban*as*

SOME COMMON DESCRIPTIVE ADJECTIVES

hábil	able, capable	difícil	difficult
incapaz*	incompetent	fácil	easy
fuerte	strong	bueno	good
débil	weak	malo	bad

* To form the plural of nouns and adjectives ending in *z*, change the *z* to *c* and add *es:* incapaces.

rico	rich	largo	long
pobre	poor	corto	short
alto	tall	delgado	thin
bajo	short	gordo	fat
		ancho	wide
rojo	red	joven‡	young
blanco	white	viejo	old
negro	black		
pequeño	small	peligroso	dangerous
grande	large	seguro	safe

EJERCICIOS. Put the appropriate ending on the adjective in parenthesis.

1. el papel (*blanco*) _____

2. los cuestionarios (*largo*) _____

3. la carta (*largo*) _____

4. los médicos (*joven*) _____

5. las referencias (*excelente*) _____

6. las enfermeras (*eficiente*) _____

7. los enfermeros (*eficiente*) _____

8. los mexicanos (*hábil*) _____

9. las peruanas (*hábil*) _____

10. el equipo (*público*) _____

11. la institución (*público*) _____

12. los obreros (*fuerte*) _____

13. las obreras (*fuerte*) _____

14. los hombres (*peligroso*) _____

15. las mujeres (*rico*) _____

16. la consejera (*alto*) _____

17. los consejeros (*alto*) _____

18. los documentos (*importante*) _____

‡ In the plural **joven** requires an accent: **jóvenes**.

19. la compañía (*grande*) _____

20. las ciudades (*grande*) _____

21. los empleos (*difícil*) _____

22. las respuestas (*difícil*) _____

23. los empleados (*pobre*) _____

24. las supervisoras (*bueno*) _____

25. la droga (*malo*) _____

26. las cartas (*largo*) _____

27. los papeles (*corto*) _____

28. los doctores (*malo*) _____

29. las calles (*ancho*) _____

EJERCICIOS. Translate the word in parenthesis, making sure that the adjective agrees with the noun it modifies.

1. los documentos (old) _____

2. muchos hombres (intelligent) _____

3. pocos médicos (poor) _____

4. unos ecuatorianos (rich) _____

5. las drogas (dangerous) _____

6. los contratos (public) _____

7. las referencias (bad) _____

8. muchas ciudades (small) _____

9. pocas mujeres (tall) _____

10. unos autobuses (public) _____

11. los puestos (difficult) _____

12. unas familias (large) _____

13. muchos enfermeros (good) _____

14. muchas doctoras (efficient) _____

15. pocos técnicos (good) _____

ADJECTIVES OF NATIONALITY

For adjectives of nationality ending in a consonant, add *a* to form the feminine:

    el doctor español   la doctora español*a*

Add *s* to form the feminine plural and *es* to form the masculine plural:

    los doctores español*es*   las doctoras español*as*

EJERCICIOS. Change the article, noun, and adjective to the feminine.

1. el profesor ecuatoriano   _____

2. el director mexicano   _____

3. los supervisores cubanos   _____

4. el médico puertorriqueño   _____

5. los profesores españoles   _____

6. el obrero colombiano   _____

7. el supervisor dominicano   _____

8. los profesores argentinos   _____

9. el administrador peruano   _____

10. los médicos chilenos   _____

11. el doctor boliviano   _____

THE POSSESSIVE ADJECTIVE

In Spanish, possessive adjectives agree in gender and number with the nouns they modify. That is, they agree with the thing possessed and not the possessor.

English	Spanish		
my	mi(s)	mi casa/mis casas	mi auto/mis autos
your	tu(s) (familiar)	tu casa/tus casas	tu auto/tus autos
your	su(s) (polite)	su casa/sus casas	su auto/sus autos
his/her/its	su(s)	su casa/sus casas	su auto/sus autos
our	nuestro/a(s)	nuestra casa/nuestras casas	nuestro auto/nuestros autos
your	vuestro/a(s) (familiar)	vuestra casa/vuestras casas	vuestro auto/vuestros autos
your	su(s)	su casa/sus casas	su auto/sus autos
their	su(s)	su casa/sus casas	su auto/sus autos

There may be times when it is not clear to whom **su** or **sus** is referring. In those instances, use *de* before the appropriate subject pronoun.

Unclear Reference

su(s) casa(s)	his house(s)
su(s) casa(s)	her house(s)
su(s) casa(s)	your house(s)
su(s) casa(s)	their house(s)
su(s) casa(s)	your house(s)

Clear Reference

la(s) casa(s)	*de*	él
la(s) casa(s)	*de*	ella
la(s) casa(s)	*de*	usted
la(s) casa(s)	*de*	ellos/ellas
la(s) casa(s)	*de*	ustedes

EJERCICIOS. Fill in the blank spaces with the appropriate possessive adjective.

1. (her) _____ hermano

2. (his) _____ hermanas

3. (his) _____ abogado

4. (her) _____ abogadas

5. (your) _____ agencia

6. (their) _____ cuestionario

7. (her) _____ hospital

8. (his) _____ oficina

9. (your) _____ papeles

10. (their) _____ máquinas

11. (his) _____ cheque

12. (her) _____ supervisor

13. (their) _____ carta

14. (his) _____ oportunidades

15. (your) _____ referencias

16. (their) _____ computadora

17. (her) _____ nombre

EJERCICIOS. Translate the following using both possessive adjectives and the clarifying form.

1. her checks _____ _____

2. his family _____ _____

3. his questionnaire _____ _____

4. her brother _____ _____

5. their address _____ _____

6. your references _____ _____

7. his opportunity _____ _____

8. her packages _____ _____

9. your answers   _____   _____

10. their lawyer   _____   _____

11. his position   _____   _____

12. your nurse   _____   _____

13. her letters   _____   _____

14. their money   _____   _____

15. your machines   _____   _____

16. his advisers (male)   _____   _____

17. your contract   _____   _____

18. his name   _____   _____

19. her street   _____   _____

20. his books   _____   _____

21. their houses   _____   _____

22. your family   _____   _____

LOS VERBOS: —ER

To form the present indicative of regular **-er** verbs, remove the **-er** from the infinitive and add the personal endings (**-o, -es, -e, -emos, -en**) to the stem of the verb.

---
aprend**er**   to learn

Subject Pronoun	Stem	+	Personal Ending	
yo	aprend	+	**o**	I learn, I am learning, I do learn
tú	aprend	+	**es**	you learn, you are learning (familiar), you do learn
usted	aprend	+	**e**	you learn, you are learning (polite), you do learn
él	aprend	+	**e**	he learns, he is learning, he does learn
ella	aprend	+	**e**	she learns, she is learning, she does learn
nosotros/as	aprend	+	**emos**	we learn, we are learning, we do learn
ustedes	aprend	+	**en**	you learn, you are learning, you do learn
ellos	aprend	+	**en**	they learn, they are learning, they do learn
ellas	aprend	+	**en**	they learn (feminine), they are learning, they do learn

STEM CHANGING -*ER* VERBS

Some verbs change their stem vowels from *e* to *ie* and from *o* to *ue*. These changes occur in the present tense only and in all but the **nosotros** and **vosotros** forms.

querer *(ie)* to wish, to want			
yo	qu**ie**ro	nosotros	queremos
tú	qu**ie**res		
usted		ustedes	
él	qu**ie**re	ellos	qu**ie**ren
ella		ellas	

poder *(ue)* to be able, can			
yo	p**ue**do	nosotros	podemos
tú	p**ue**des		
usted		ustedes	
él	p**ue**de	ellos	p**ue**den
ella		ellas	

entender *(ie)* to understand			
yo	ent**ie**ndo	nosotros	entendemos
tú	ent**ie**ndes		
usted		ustedes	
él	ent**ie**nde	ellos	ent**ie**nden
ella		ellas	

volver *(ue)* to return			
yo	v**ue**lvo	nosotros	volvemos
tú	v**ue**lves		
usted		ustedes	
él	v**ue**lve	ellos	v**ue**lven
ella		ellas	

TWO IRREGULAR –*ER* VERBS

tener to have			
yo	**tengo**	nosotros	**tenemos**
tú	**tienes**		
usted		ustedes	
él	**tiene**	ellos	**tienen**
ella		ellas	

ver to see			
yo	**veo**	nosotros	**vemos**
tú	**ves**		
usted		ustedes	
él	**ve**	ellos	**ven**
ella		ellas	

VERB LIST (some commonly used -*er* verbs)

aprender	to learn	**comprender**	to understand
beber	to drink	**entender***(ie)*	to understand
creer	to believe	**leer**	to read
comer	to eat	**ofrecer***	to offer

* Verbs ending in **cer** change the **c** to **zc** in the first person singular (yo form) in the present tense: **ofrezco, ofreces, ofrece,** etc.; **conocer** (= *to know)* also follows this pattern.

56

poder*(ue)*	to be able	**tener que**	to have to / must
querer*(ie)*	to wish / to want	**vender**	to sell
responder	to answer	**ver**	to see
tener	to have	**volver***(ue)*	to return

EJERCICIOS ORALES. Insert the proper form of the verb.

1. Yo **veo** el documento.
   (Juan y María, tú, ella, usted)

_____

_____

_____

_____

2. Nosotros no **entendemos** las preguntas (the questions).
   (yo, tú, ellas, el cliente)

_____

_____

_____

_____

3. José y Juan **beben** chocolate.
   (ella, ustedes, tus amigos, él y yo)

_____

_____

_____

_____

4. (Yo) **puedo** aprender fácilmente (easily).
   (ella, tú, José y María, nosotros)

   _____

   _____

   _____

   _____

5. El **tiene** que volver a la ciudad.
   (yo, el avión, nosotros, ellas)

   _____

   _____

   _____

   _____

6. Ella **vuelve** a casa (home) temprano (early).
   (nosotros, Perla, Juan y ella, yo)

   _____

   _____

   _____

   _____

EJERCICIOS. Fill in the appropriate form of the verb.

1. aprender, comer   Nosotros _____ mucho.

2. querer, vender   Yo _____ café con leche.

3. volver, responder   Tú _____ inmediatamente.

4. aprender, leer   Usted _____ inglés y español.

5. entender, comprender   Ella y él _____ la materia (the material).

6. comer, beber   Ella _____ muy poco (very little).

7. tener, querer   Ustedes _____ la dirección del jefe.

8. ofrecer, conocer   Ellos _____ toda clase de servicio.

9. ver, entender   Ellas _____ a los oficiales.

Give the appropriate form of the verb in parenthesis.

1. Los oficiales (aprender) _____ mucho todos los días.

2. La amiga de María (beber) _____ mucho café en la cafetería.

3. (creer) ¿ _____ tú las noticias?

4. Mis amigos no (comprender) _____ la tarea (the assignment).

5. Ellos (entender) _____ todo (everything).

6. Yo no (leer) _____ libros técnicos.

7. ¿Qué (ofrecer) _____ ellas en el verano?

8. Ellos (poder) _____ llenar el cuestionario oficial.

9. Pablo no (querer) _____ sus servicios.

10. El burócrata (responder) _____ por correo (by mail).

11. Tus hermanos (tener) _____ mucho dinero ahora.

12. Nuestra máquina no (vender) _____ bebidas (drinks) alcohólicas.

13. (ver) ¿ _____ los García el edificio alto (tall building)?

14. ¿Cuándo (volver) _____ ellos a la ciudad?

15. Los amigos de él (comer) _____ platos criollos.*

SENTENCE GENERATORS

In Spanish, as in English, many conjugated verbs can be followed by an infinitive:

English	*Spanish*
He **wishes (desires)** to work.	El desea trabajar.
She **needs** to fill in the questionnaire.	Ella necesita llenar el cuestionario.
They **want** to sign the papers.	Ellos quieren firmar los papeles.
We **are able** to learn a lot.	Nosotros podemos aprender mucho.
I **hope** to eat soon.	Espero comer pronto.

* **Criollo** has had a variety of meanings since its introduction into the Spanish lexicon. While it was used originally to designate the sons and daughters of Spaniards born in the New World, today the term **criollo** is used especially in the Caribbean to describe anyone or anything native to a country. Thus, one might see a restaurant in an Hispanic neighborhood advertising **comidas criollas.**

We should now add to this category **tener que** + **infinitive**, which translates as *must* or *has/have to.*

I **must** (have to) work a lot.　　　　Yo <u>tengo que</u> trabajar mucho.

She **has to** sign the contract.　　　Ella <u>tiene que</u> firmar el contrato.

By combining conjugated forms of **necesitar, esperar, desear, tener que, poder,** and **querer** with infinitives, we are able to generate a great many useful sentences.

A "Sentence Generator"

Below is what we might call a "sentence generator." Notice that there are five steps required to generate a sentence. In the illustration we see that the operator has pushed the **yo** button, the **NO** or negative button, the **poder** button (*puedo*), the **hablar** infinitive button, and **ahora** (the adverb of time). The important thing to remember is that once you have selected the subject and made the conjugated verb agree with it, then you can generate many sentences by simply selecting different infinitives and adverbs. Also, the number of possible sentences increases with different subjects and different conjugated verbs.

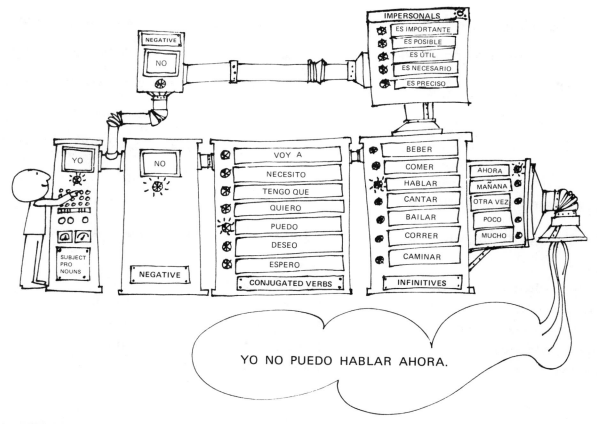

EJERCICIOS.
Generate your own sentences using the above sentence builders and infinitives.

1. _____

60

2. _____

3. _____

4. _____

5. _____

6. _____

7. _____

8. _____

9. _____

EJERCICIOS. Translate into Spanish.

1. I want to drink chocolate.

   _____

2. She has to return on Monday.

   _____

3. We need to fill out the questionnaire.

   _____

4. You are able to understand everything.

   _____

5. They want (desire) to read the technical books.

   _____

6. He does not want to drink coffee.

   _____

7. Do you need to have money?

   _____

8. I am not able to respond now.

   _____

HERE, THERE, and OVER THERE

acá and **aquí** = here

Acá tends to be less precise than **aquí**.

allí, ahí, and **allá** = there

In Latin America **allí** and **allá** are used interchangeably.

MORE INTERROGATIVES

¿Cuál?	Which?	**¿Cuánto/-a?**	How much?
¿Cuáles?	Which ones?	**¿Cuántos/-as?**	How many?

¿cuál + singular verb . . . ?	**¿cuáles + plural verb . . . ?**
¿Cuál es su libro? Which is your book?	**¿Cuáles son** sus libros? Which are your books?

¿cuánto/-a + singular noun . . . ?	**¿cuántos/-as + plural noun . . . ?**
¿Cuánto dinero tiene? How much money do you have?	**¿Cuántas plantas** tiene? How many plants do you have?
¿Cuánta plata tiene? How much money do you have?	**¿Cuántos papeles** tiene? How many papers do you have?

¿cuál? vs. ¿qué?

¿Cuál es el problema?	What is the problem? (a selection: which one is the problem?)
¿Qué es un problema?	What is a problem? (a definition of a problem)
¿Cuál es el marxista?	Which one is the Marxist? (a selection)
¿Qué es un marxista?	What is a Marxist? (a definition)

EJERCICIOS. Fill in the blank space with the appropriate interrogative.

1. (How many) ¿ _____ documentos tienes?

2. (Which) ¿ _____ es su auto?

3. (Which ones) ¿ _____ son las máquinas de Pedro?

4. (How many) ¿ _____ computadoras tienen ellos?

5. (How many) ¿ _____ cheques tiene usted?

6. (What) ¿ _____ libro tienen Pancho y María?

7. (Which) ¿ _____ es tu oficina?

8. (Which) ¿ _____ es el juez (the judge)?

9. (How much) ¿ _____ tiempo (time) tenemos?

THE PERSONAL "a"

In Spanish, an "a" must precede the object of the verb when that object is a definite person.

> Nosotros no vemos a María. We don't see María.
>
> Ellos entienden al (a + el) Profesor Alcalá. They understand Professor Alcalá.

But: Nosotros no vemos el auto de María. We don't see María's car.

Ellos entienden los líbros técnicos. They understand the technical books.

The personal "a" is not used with the verb tener:

> Ella tiene dos amigos aquí. She has two friends here.

EJERCICIOS

1. El doctor Ramos ve _____ los pacientes todos los días.

2. Ellas entienden _____ (el) juez.

3. Tengo _____ un primo que vive allí.

4. Ella no puede visitar (to visit) _____ su familia.

5. ¿Ves tú _____ la casa blanca?

Diálogo

Supervisora	—	Buenas tardes. ¡Siéntese aquí, por favor!
Señor García	—	**Gracias.**
Supervisora	—	(Ella mira el cuestionario.) Veo que usted tiene **bastante** experiencia de radiólogo.
Señor García	—	Sí, señora. Tengo diez años de experiencia en mi **país.**
Supervisora	—	¿**Sólo** en clínicas, o en hospitales públicos también?
Señor García	—	**Bueno**, tres años en el Hospital Anglo-Chileno y siete años en un hospital militar.
Supervisora	—	Bien, muy bien. Nuestro hospital tiene una tradición de ofrecer sus servicios a **la comunidad. Ahora que el barrio** es hispano, deseamos y necesitamos gente bilingüe.
Señor García	—	Puedo hablar inglés **un poco. Claro**, tengo que estudiar más.
Supervisora	—	Bueno, por el momento su experiencia y **su manejo** del español **valen mucho** porque muy pocos del personal administrativo o profesional pueden hablar español.
Señor García	—	¿**Y los pacientes**?
Supervisora	—	Casi todos son hispanos. Bueno, señor García, ¿cuándo puede usted **comenzar**?

VOCABULARIO DEL DIALOGO

gracias	thank you	**claro**	of course
bastante	sufficient, enough	**el manejo**	ability to handle, the handling
país	country		
sólo *	only	**valen mucho**	are worth a great deal
bueno	a pause word here meaning good, OK		
		los pacientes	the patients
la comunidad	the community	**comenzar(ie)**	to begin
ahora que	now that		
el barrio	the neighborhood		
un poco	a little		

* Requires an accent as adverb. The accent is not used when *solo (alone)* is used as an adjective.

PREGUNTAS SOBRE EL DIALOGO

1. ¿Cuántos años de experiencia de radiólogo tiene el señor García?

   _____

2. ¿Qué tradición tiene el hospital?

   _____

3. ¿Qué necesita el hospital?

   _____

4. ¿Por qué valen mucho su experiencia y su manejo del español?

   _____

El señor García hablando con la supervisora

Vocabulario del capítulo

COGNATES OR NEAR COGNATES

administrativo/a

la administración

el administrador

la administradora

el auto

bilingüe

el burócrata

el café

la cafetería

el cheque

el chocolate

el cliente

la cliente

la clínica

la droga

eficiente

excelente

el grupo

el hispano

la hispana

importante

la institución

la materia

el médico

la médica

militar

el momento

municipal

negro/a

oficial

el paciente

la paciente

la persona

principal

el problema

profesional

público / a

la radiografía

el radiólogo

el servicio

la tradición

VOCABULARIO

el abogado	male lawyer	blanco/a	white
la abogada	female lawyer	bueno/a	good
el amigo	male friend	la carta	letter
la amiga	female friend	la casa	house
alguien	someone, somebody	casi	almost
alto/a	tall	claro	of course
el ambiente	atmosphere	cómodo / a	comfortable
ancho/a	wide	corto/a	short
el año	year	¿cuántos/as?	how many?
azul	blue	débil	weak
bajo/a	short	delgado/a	thin
bastante	enough	difícil	difficult
la bebida	drink	el edificio	building

el enfermero	male nurse	el pasillo	hallway, corridor
la enfermera	female nurse	peligroso/a	dangerous
la entrevista	interview	pequeño/a	small
el equipo	equipment	pobre	poor
fácil	easy	¿por qué?	why?
la facilidad	facility	porque	because
fuerte	strong	el puesto	job, position
la gente	people	que	that, which, who
gordo/a	fat	el repaso	review
grande	large, great	rico/a	rich
hábil	able, capable	rojo/a	red
la hora	hour	seguro/a	safe
incapaz	incompetent	sólo	only
el ingeniero	engineer	también	also, too
el joven	young man	la tarea	assignment
la joven	young woman	la tarjeta	card
joven	young	el técnico	technician
el juez	judge	temprano	early
largo/a	long	el tiempo	time
la leche	milk	todavía	yet, still
el libro	book	todo	everything
malo/a	bad, evil	todo/a	all
el manejo	handling	el verano	summer
el país	country	viejo/a	old

VERBOS

aprender	to learn	entender(ie)	to understand
beber	to drink	leer	to read
comenzar(ie)	to begin	ofrecer	to offer
comer	to eat	poder(ue)	to be able
comprender	to understand	querer(ie)	to wish, want
conversar	to converse, to chat	responder	to respond
creer	to believe	sentirse(ie)	to feel

FRASES

antes de la cita	before the appointment	buenas noches	good evening
		muy poco	very little
bebidas alcohólicas	alcoholic beverages	por la mañana	in the morning
buenos días	good day	por la tarde	in the afternoon
buenas tardes	good afternoon	por la noche	in the evening

Vocabulario adicional

SOME COMMONLY USED COMMANDS "MANDATOS"

¡Venga(n) acá!	Come here!	¡Quéde(n) se aquí!	Stay here!
¡No se vaya(n)!	Don't go!	¡Quéde(n) se inmóvil!	Stay still!
¡Escriba(n) aquí!	Write here!	¡Beba(n)!	Drink!
•¡Vuelva(n) mañana!	Return tomorrow!	¡Lea(n)!	Read!
¡Tenga(n) paciencia!	Be patient!	¡Coma(n)!	Eat!

---

favor de + infinitive = a command

Favor de + infinitive is often used instead of a command. For example:

Favor de hablar	=	¡Hable(n)!
Favor de comer	=	¡Coma(n)!
Favor de tener paciencia	=	¡Tenga(n) paciencia!
Favor de no ir	=	¡No se vaya!

EJERCICIOS.

Translate into Spanish using both the command form and the **favor de + infinitive** form. (Some of the commands are taken from the previous chapter.)

1. Speak! ¡ _____ usted!

   _____

2. Eat! ¡ _____ ustedes!

   _____

3. Have patience! ¡ _____ usted!

   _____

4. Read! ¡ _____ usted!

   _____

5. Drink! ¡ _____ ustedes!

   _____

6. Sign here! ¡ _____ usted!

   _____

7. Wait! ¡ _____ ustedes!

   _____

8. Fill out the questionnaire! ¡ _____ usted!

   _____

9. Return tomorrow! ¡ _____ usted!

   _____

La entrada a la sala de emergencia

El barrio de los García

Capítulo 5
La familia García

Lectura

José e* Isabel son chilenos. Ellos son de un

pueblo de la provincia de Santiago. Ellos   town

acaban de llegar a los Estados Unidos y   have just arrived

tienen muchas **esperanzas de salir adelante.**   hopes of getting ahead

José **va a comenzar** pronto su empleo de radiólogo.   is going to begin

Isabel es **maestra** y ella **espera trabajar**   teacher / hopes to work

en un programa bilingüe. Ellos tienen tres

hijos. Angel y Celia, los hijos **menores**,   younger

van a una **escuela primaria** que es bilingüe.   elementary school

César, el hijo **mayor**, va a iniciar sus   older

estudios universitarios **el semestre que viene.**   next semester

Ellos viven en un **barrio** que tiene ambiente   neighborhood

latino porque **la mayoría** de los habitantes son   majority

hispanos. Ellos viven allí porque el ambiente

les es familiar.   is familiar to them

* *y* changes to *e* when it precedes another *i* sound. Likewise *o* changes to *u* before another *o*sound: **siete *u* ocho** (seven or eight).

La gramática

LOS VERBOS: –IR

To form the present indicative of regular *-ir* verbs, remove the *-ir* from the infinitive and add the personal endings (*-o, -es, -e, -imos, -en*) to the stem of the verb.

			vivir to live	
Subject Pronoun	**Stem**	**+**	**Personal Ending**	
yo	viv	+	**o**	I live, I am living, I do live
tú	viv	+	**es**	you live, you are living (familiar), you do live
usted	viv	+	**e**	you live, you are living (polite), you do live
él	viv	+	**e**	he lives, he is living, he does live
ella	viv	+	**e**	she lives, she is living, she does live
nosotros/as	viv	+	**imos**	we live, we are living, we do live
ustedes	viv	+	**en**	you live, you are living, you do live
ellos	viv	+	**en**	they live (masculine), they are living, they do live
ellas	viv	+	**en**	they live (feminine), they are living, they do live

IRREGULAR AND STEM CHANGING -IR VERBS

ir to go				**venir** to come			
yo	**voy**	nosotros	**vamos**	yo	**vengo**	nosotros	**venimos**
tú	**vas**			tú	**vienes**		
usted		ustedes		usted		ustedes	
él	**va**	ellos	**van**	él	**viene**	ellos	**vienen**
ella		ellas		ella		ellas	

VERBS OF MOTION

Verbs of motion like **ir** and **venir** require *a* when they are followed by an infinitive or an indirect object.

Tú <u>vas</u> *a* hablar ahora.	You are going to speak now.
Yo <u>vengo</u> *a* ayudar.	I come to help.
Tomás <u>va</u> *a* mi casa.	Thomas is going to my house.
Ella <u>viene</u> *a* la oficina tarde.	She comes late to the office.

MORE IRREGULAR AND STEM CHANGING VERBS

decir	to say, tell		
yo	*digo*	nosotros	*decimos*
tú	*dices*		
usted		ustedes	
él	*dice*	ellos	*dicen*
ella		ellas	

preferir*(ie)*	to prefer		
yo	*prefiero*	nosotros	*preferimos*
tú	*prefieres*		
usted		ustedes	
él	*prefiere*	ellos	*prefieren*
ella		ellas	

pedir(i)	to ask for		
yo	*pido*	nosotros	*pedimos*
tú	*pides*		
usted		ustedes	
él	*pide*	ellos	*piden*
ella		ellas	

"ACABAR DE" CONSTRUCTIONS

In Spanish, *"acabar de* + infinitive" is used to convey the idea of an action which has *just* been completed:

Yo acabo de comer.	I have just eaten.
Tú acabas de leer el libro.	You have just read the book.
Nosotros acabamos de pagar la cuenta.	We have just paid the bill.
Ella acaba de salir.	She has just left.

EJERCICIOS. Translate into Spanish.

1. I have just read many books.

_____

2. We have just worked here.

_____

3. He has just walked a lot.

_____

4. They have just spoken Spanish.

_____

5. She has just asked for money.

_____

VERB LIST (some commonly used -*ir* **verbs**)

abrir	to open	**preferir**(*ie*)	to prefer
asistir	to attend	**recibir**	to receive
decir	to say, to tell	**reunir**	to unite, to get together
dormir(ue)	to sleep		
escribir	to write	**subir**	to go up
ir	to go	**sufrir**	to suffer
omitir	to omit	**venir**	to come
pedir(*i)*	to ask for		

EJERCICIOS ORALES. Insert the proper form of the verb.

1. Los obreros **abren** las ventanas (windows).
    (tú, ella, mis primos, yo)

_____

_____

_____

_____

2. La tía de Marta **va** al centro (downtown).
    (nosotras, Pablo, nuestro primo, yo)

_____

_____

_____

_____

3. Yo **vengo** de la escuela (school).
   (los García, tu hermano, los hijos, su suegra [mother- in-law])

   _____

   _____

   _____

   _____

4. Ustedes **dicen** que él es honesto.
   (mis padres, el esposo de María [María's spouse], yo, ellas)

   _____

   _____

   _____

   _____

5. Nosotros **recibimos** las noticias todas las noches (every night).
   (sus hermanos, tu hermana, él y yo, tú)

   _____

   _____

   _____

   _____

EJERCICIOS. Fill in the blank space with the appropriate form of both verbs:

1. ir, asistir   Tú _____ a la conferencia.

                  Juan y yo _____ a la escuela primaria.

2. pedir, decir   Usted _____ poco.

                  Ellas _____ muchas cosas (many things)

3. vivir, venir   El _____ con sus hijos.

   Los Rodríguez _____ con amigos.

4. prohibir, preferir   Nosotros _____ tal cosa (such a thing).

   Los amigos de Juan _____ muchas cosas.

5. sufrir, recibir   Mis parientes (relatives) _____ mucho.

   Tú no _____ demasiado (too much).

6. abrir, escribir   Nuestros hermanos _____ las cartas.

   Ellos nunca _____ libros técnicos.

7. venir, ir   Ustedes _____ todos los días.

   Tú y yo _____ el lunes.

8. subir, ir   Ellas _____ al coche (auto).

   Las amigas de él _____ al tren.

EJERCICIOS. Fill in the blank space with the appropriate form of the verb:

1. Nosotros siempre (sufrir) _____ los lunes.

2. Nuestros amigos (friends) no (abrir) _____ las puertas (the doors).

3. El joven quiere (asistir) _____ a la conferencia.

4. Mis primos (decir) _____ la verdad (the truth).

5. Tú (escribir) _____ en inglés y en alemán (German).

6. Yo (ir) _____ a la casa de Pedro todas las noches.

7. Juan y ella (pedir) _____ toda la información.

8. El paciente (preferir) _____ la enfermera joven.

9. Los ópticos (opticians) siempre (recibir) _____ el pago (the payment).

10. En la factura (bill) nosotros no (omitir) _____ los cálculos (the calculations).

11. El (reunir) _____ todo el dinero.

12. Ustedes nunca (subir) _____ por la escalera (by the stairway).

13. Ella (venir) _____ a protestar.

HAY there is/there are

In Spanish, **hay** translates as "there is" when followed by a singular object and as "there are" when followed by a plural subject.

Hay una casa blanca.	There is a white house.
Hay muchas casas blancas.	There are many white houses.

EJERCICIOS. Translate into Spanish.

1. There is a technical book here.

   _____

2. There are technical books here.

   _____

3. There is a tall woman here.

   _____

4. There are tall women here.

   _____

5. Is there a lot of money?

   _____

6. No, there is not a lot of money.

   _____

7. She lives in Los Angeles.

   _____

8. They open the doors (*las puertas*) every day.

_____

9. He does not tell the truth.

_____

10. I write many letters on Tuesday.

_____

11. She goes to her house every day.

_____

12. The agency omits much information.

_____

13. You (*tú*) ask for the news every night.

_____

14. You (*ustedes*) prefer the important documents.

_____

15. We receive some questionnaires.

_____

16. He gets together the documents.

_____

17. I do not go up the stairway.

_____

18. Does the patient suffer a lot?

_____

19. They come to my house on Wednesdays.

_____

20. There are many machines in the hospital.

_____

MORE POWER FOR THE SENTENCE GENERATOR

Add the new *—IR* infinitives and the new conjugated verbs that may take an infinitive (**venir a** + infinitive, **ir a** + infinitive, and **preferir** + infinitive) to our sentence generator and see how many sentences you can generate. (See sentence generator on page 60.)

1. _____
2. _____
3. _____
4. _____
5. _____
6. _____
7. _____
8. _____
9. _____
10. _____
11. _____
12. _____
13. _____
14. _____
15. _____
16. _____
17. _____
18. _____
19. _____
20. _____

EJERCICIOS. Translate into Spanish.

1. I want to tell the truth.

_____

2. Do you want to go on Monday?

    _____

3. They do not want to write letters today.

    _____

4. She needs to ask for more information.

    _____

5. We do not desire to suffer.

    _____

6. María and Juan can attend school every day.

    _____

7. The patient is able to go up the stairway.

    _____

8. She has to (must) come on Tuesday.

    _____

9. I have to ask for more money.

    _____

10. Do you have to open the windows every day?

    _____

11. John's brother hopes to receive a lot of money.

    _____

12. I do not hope to live here forever (*para siempre*).

    _____

13. He prefers to omit details (*los detalles*).

    _____

14. I am going to work every day.

_____

15. You (*tú*) are going to learn Spanish.

_____

16. He is going to live here.

_____

17. We are going to go to downtown (*al centro*).

_____

18. They are going to eat a lot on Sunday.

_____

19. The workers do not come to protest.

_____

20. I come to ask for more documentation.

_____

EL VERBO *SER*   (to be)

yo	*soy*	I am	nosotros	*somos*	we are
tú	*eres*	you are			
usted		you are	ustedes		you are
él	*es*	he is	ellos	*son*	they are
ella		she is	ellas		they are

One of the most difficult obstacles for the student of Spanish is getting over the **ser** vs. **estar** hurdle. Both **ser** and **estar** mean *to be*. But they are not interchangeable. **Ser** is used when:

1. referring to the profession, religion, nationality, or political affiliation of a person.
2. indicating origin, ownership, or the material of which something is made.
3. using impersonal expressions, such as, "it is probable," "it is necessary."
4. expressing an inherent or essential characteristic of a person or thing.
5. describing the color, shape, or size of a person or thing.
6. telling time.

The following provides details on the usage of **ser** as described in the above six categories.

1. ***Ser* is used when referring to the profession, religion, nationality, and affiliation of a person.**

Ella es **maestra.**	She is a teacher.
Nosotros no somos **católicos.**	We are not Catholics.
Ustedes son **socialistas.**	You are Socialists.
Yo soy **venezolano**	I am a Venezuelan.

When you refer to religion, nationality, profession, and political affiliation, the indefinite articles (**un, una**) are not used unless there is a qualifying adjective or you wish to make your statement emphatic.

Ella es **una** maestra **excelente** (qualifying adjective).	
Yo soy **un** venezolano. (emphatic)	I am a **real** Venezuelan.

EJERCICIOS. Fill in the blank space with the appropriate form of the verb **ser**.

1. Tú _____ supervisor.

2. Nosotros _____ obreros.

3. Ellos _____ abogados (lawyers).

4. Ella _____ enfermera.

5. Tú no _____ cubana.

6. Juanita _____ protestante.

7. El _____ judío (Jewish).

8. Ella _____ católica.

9. Usted _____ musulmán (Muslim).

10. Ellas _____ dominicanas.

11. Usted _____ republicano.

12. Ana _____ trabajadora social (social worker).

13. Pepe y Tomás _____ policías (policemen).

14. ¿ _____ tú estudiante?

15. ¿ _____ usted demócrata?

16. Ellos no _____ mexicanos.

17. El y ella _____ norteamericanos (North Americans).

18. Mis amigos _____ independientes.

19. Los González _____ ateos (atheists).

20. Tus hermanas _____ colombianas.

21. Usted _____ norteamericano.

EJERCICIOS. Answer in Spanish, using the vocabulary given in the previous exercise.

1. ¿Cuál ((What) es su partido político (political party)?

_____

2. ¿Cuál es su religión?

_____

3. ¿Cuál es su nacionalidad?

_____

4. ¿Cuál es su profesión?

_____

2. **Ser is used to indicate the origin, ownership, or material of which something is made.**

¿De dónde es usted?	Where are you from?
Soy de Puerto Rico.	I'm from Puerto Rico.
Soy puertorriqueño.	I'm Puerto Rican.
¿De quién es la máquina?	Whose machine is it?
Es de Pablo.	It is Pablo's.*
Es de aluminio.	It is aluminum.
de dónde	from where
de quién	whose

* **Note:** In Spanish *there is no apostrophe*. The preposition de must be used after the noun to express possession.

EJERCICIOS. Fill in the blank space with the appropriate form of **ser**.

1. ¿De dónde _____ ellos?

2. ¿De dónde _____ sus amigos?

3. ¿De dónde _____ tú?

4. ¿De dónde _____ tu padre?

5. Ella _____ de Nueva York.

6. Nosotras _____ de Arizona.

7. Yo _____ de Los Angeles.

8. Tú no _____ de Miami.

9. Pancho _____ de México.

10. Linda _____ de Caléxico.

11. Los cuestionarios _____ de Juan.

12. La carta _____ de María.

13. Los hijos _____ de mi amigo.

14. La escuela primaria _____ de él.

15. El programa _____ de nosotros.

16. La casa _____ de madera (wood).

17. Los motores _____ de aluminio.

18. Tus cartas _____ de papel.

19. Los libros _____ de papel grueso (thick).

3. *Ser* **is used in impersonal expressions (es + adjective)**

Es difícil subir la escalera.	It is difficult to go up the stairway.
No **es fácil** ser lógico.	It is not easy to be logical.

EJERCICIOS.

Fill in the space with the proper form of the verb **ser** and translate into English.

1. _____ esencial firmar los documentos.

   _____

2. _____ necesario ir ahora.

   _____

3. _____ imposible hablar aquí.

   _____

4. _____ importante ayudar todos los días.

   _____

5. _____ difícil comer rápidamente (rapidly).

   _____

6. _____ fácil trabajar en la oficina.

   _____

7. _____ conveniente vivir en Santa Fe.

   _____

8. _____ posible tener mucho dinero hoy.

   _____

9. _____ lógico sufrir mucho.

   _____

10. _____ urgente escribir muchas cartas.

    _____

Note: You now have a new type of construction to add to your list of verbs that take an infinitive: **desear, tener que, venir a, necesitar, querer, poder, esperar, preferir**. You may add *all impersonal constructions* to the sentence generator!

4. **Ser is used to express an
inherent or essential characteristic of someone or something.**

Tú eres **inteligente.**   You are intelligent.

La playa es **hermosa.**   The beach is beautiful.

EJERCICIOS.

Fill in the blank space with the appropriate form of **ser** and translate into English.

1. Mi amigo _____ compulsivo.

   _____

2. Ellos _____ jóvenes.

   _____

3. Nosotros _____ honestos.

   _____

4. Usted _____ alcohólico.

   _____

5. Ella no _____ fanática.

   _____

6. Yo no _____ alcohólica.

   _____

7. Tú _____ astuto.

   _____

8. Ellos no _____ irracionales.

   _____

9. Tu amigo _____ hostil.

   _____

10. Ella _____ atractiva.

_____

11. El _____ dedicado.

_____

5. Ser is used to describe the size, shape, or color of a person or thing.

Su auto es **pequeño.**   Your car is small.

La mesa es **redonda.**   The table is round.

Tus ojos son **verdes.**   Your eyes are green.

EJERCICIOS. Fill in the blank space with the appropriate form of **ser.**

1. Mi hermano _____ alto (tall).

2. Mis primas _____ medianas (medium height).

3. Nuestro auto _____ rojo.

4. ¿_____ tus ojos morenos (dark eyes)?

5. El escritorio (desk) de Juan _____ rectangular.

6. Las mesas de María _____ redondas.

7. La máquina de Pablo _____ verde.

8. Tu casa _____ grande.

9. Mis hermanos _____ altos.

10. Ella no _____ baja (short).

11. Su pelo (hair) _____ blanco (white).

12. Las figuras _____ cuadradas (square).

6. *Ser* is used to tell time.

With the expressions **¿Qué hora es?** (What time is it?) and **Es la una** (It is one o'clock.), use **es**. All other references to the hour in the present require **son las + hour:**

Son las doce.

Es la una.

Son las dos.

Son las nueve.

From the hour to the half-hour use **y + number of minutes:**

Son las dos y veinte y dos.

Son las once y diez.

The quarter hour can be expressed by using **cuarto** or **quince** and the half-hour by using **media** or **treinta**.

Son las cinco y cuarto.

After the half hour use **menos** + **number of minutes remaining**:

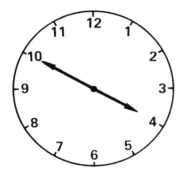

Son las cuatro menos diez.

It is ten to four./
It is four o'clock *minus* ten minutes.

Son las dos menos cuarto.

It is a quarter to two./
It is two o'clock *minus* a quarter-hour.

DE *and* POR

When reference is made to a *specific hour* of the day, use **de**:

Son las tres **de** la mañana.   It is three in the morning.

or

Son las once y media **de** la noche.   It is eleven-thirty in the evening.

Por is used when the *hour* is *not mentioned*:

Venga a la oficina **por** la tarde.   Come to the office in the afternoon.

or

Yo no trabajo **por** la mañana.   I don't work in the morning.

Since both translate as *in*, remember that you must use **de** when a specific time of day is mentioned and **por** when an hour is not given.

---
at = a + article + hour

A las cinco de la tarde tenemos clase.   At five o'clock we have class.

or

A la una y media tengo que trabajar.   At one-thirty I must work.

EJERCICIOS ORALES. La hora del día.

Answer in Spanish ¿Qué hora es?

1.
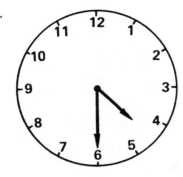

_____

2.

_____

3.
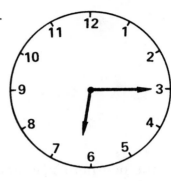

_____

4.
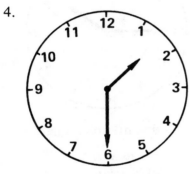

_____

5.

_____

6.

_____

7.
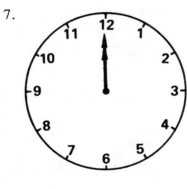

_____

8.

_____

9.
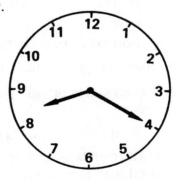

_____

REPASO (REVIEW)

Use **ser** (1) when referring to profession, religion, nationality, and political affiliation.
         (2) to describe ownership, origin, or nature of material.
         (3) in impersonal expressions.
         (4) to describe inherent or essential characteristics.
         (5) to describe size, shape, or color.
         (6) in time expressions.

EJERCICIOS.

Fill in the blank space with the appropriate form of **ser**.

Identify the rule.

1. Mis amigos _____ del Perú. _____

   Ellos _____ peruanos. _____

2. ¿De dónde _____ ustedes? _____

   Nosotros _____ de Cuba. _____

3. El _____ venezolano. _____

   El _____ de Caracas. _____

4. Ellos _____ mecánicos _____

   pero sus hermanos _____ policías. _____

5. Nosotros no _____ bomberos (firemen); _____

   _____ guardias (guards). _____

6. Tu amigo _____ alto y fuerte (strong), _____

   y _____ un estudiante excelente. _____

7. ¿De quién _____ el libro técnico? _____

   _____ de mi amigo, el ingeniero (engineer). _____

8. _____ las dos de la tarde; _____

   _____necesario estudiar ahora. _____

9. La máquina de escribir (typewriter) no _____ _____

   pequeña, pero _____ portátil (portable). _____

Translate into Spanish:

A. (véase [see] **No. 1:**

1. He is a supervisor, but you are an excellent supervisor.

   _____

2. They are Cuban, and we are North Americans.

   _____

3. You (plural) are lawyers, and she is a social worker.

   _____

4. You (*tú*) are a democrat, and I am a republican.

   _____

5. We are not Dominicans; we are Mexicans.

   _____

B. (véase No. 2):

1. Where are you from? I am from Puerto Rico. I'm Puerto Rican.

   _____

2. Whose letter is it? It is not Mary's. It is Paul's.

   _____

3. My house is made of wood. Is your house made of brick *(de ladrillo)*?

   _____

4. Marta is from Los Angeles. Her sister María is from New York.

   _____

5. The books belong to John; they are made of thick paper.

   _____

C. (véase No. 3):

1. It is easy to be logical.

   _____

2. It is impossible to eat rapidly every day.

   _____

3. It is necessary to suffer a lot.

   _____

4. It is not easy to work twelve hours a day (*al día*).

   _____

5. It is important to write letters to our friends (*a nuestros amigos*).

   _____

D. (véase No. 4):

1. We are young and we are honest.

   _____

2. They are not hostile; they are aggressive.

   _____

3. I am not an alcoholic; I am very dedicated.

   _____

4. She is attractive and she is smart (astute).

   _____

5. You (*tú*) are a fanatic and compulsive.

   _____

E. (véase No. 5):

1. Your friends are not tall; they are short.

   _____

2. María's desks are rectangular.

   _____

3. His house is white, and it is very big.

   _____

4. Our car is not red. It is green.

   _____

5. His brothers are medium-sized.

   _____

F. (véase No. 6):

1. It is two-thirty. It is necessary to go.

   _____

2. They receive a cablegram (*cablegrama*) at 4:30 every day.

   _____

3. At 5:30 in the morning, it is difficult to talk.

   _____

4. It is 1:15. At 2:05 we have to eat.

   _____

5. It is important to fill out the questionnaire at 3:00 in the afternoon.

   _____

The following exercises are designed to help you improve your sentence building power. Each sentence contains a conjugated verb or an impersonal expression that requires an infinitive:

> **desear, necesitar, querer(ie), poder(ue), esperar, tener que, preferir(ie),**
> **ir a, venir a, es posible, es necesario, es esencial, es importante**

Translate into Spanish:

1. I want to be a doctor. She wants to be a doctor also.

   _____

2. They need to write many letters. We need to sign some (*unos*) documents.

   _____

3. He is able to work every day. You (*tú*) are able to study in the afternoons.

   _____

4. My friends hope to live in New York. They hope to be engineers (*ingenieros*).

   _____

5. Do you (*usted*) prefer to have a lot of money? I prefer to suffer a lot.

   _____

6. We do not have to eat rapidly. It is 2:30 and we have to go at 3:45.

   _____

7. She is going to learn Spanish, and I am going to go to Mexico with her (*con ella*).

   _____

8. Teresa comes to receive the news, and Marta comes to protest.

   _____

9. It is necessary to tell the truth, and it is important to have a lawyer (*un abogado*).

   _____

10. It is not possible to help every day at 12:00 in the afternoon.

    _____

Diálogo

Señora García — José, son las ocho.

Señor García — Sí, sí. Ya voy,* mi **amor.**

Señora García — Hijos, es hora de comer.

Señora Williams — Bueno, señora. Yo también voy. Es fantástico ver la preparación de estos **platos** chilenos. **La comida** chilena es muy **sabrosa.**

Señora García — Por favor, Sra. Williams. Yo no soy una **gran cocinera.** Es que **las recetas** son este . . . este . . . **buenas y fáciles.**

Señor García — Ah, perdón.

Señora García — Amor, ésta es nuestra **vecina,** la señora Williams. ¿**Recuerdas**? Ella es la señora americana que quiere aprender español.

Señor García — Ah sí, es un **gran placer.** Pero usted habla español muy bien. **Gracias a Dios,** porque con mis **barbaridades** en inglés **mato perros.**

Señora García — José, por favor.

Señora Williams — Usted es muy amable, señor García, porque es evidente que el español que hablo es todavía un desastre. Pero **su señora** y la comida chilena son **grandes maestras.** Ahora hasta mis macarrones tienen **sabor** chileno.

VOCABULARIO DEL DIALOGO

amor	darling	**recordar(ue)**	to remember
los platos	the dishes, the plates	**gran placer**	great pleasure
la comida	the cooking, food, dish, meal	**gracias a Dios**	thank God
		barbaridades	atrocities
sabroso/a	delicious	**mato perros (matar perros)**	literally, to kill dogs/ excruciatingly bad
gran cocinera	great cook		
recetas	recipes	**su señora**	your wife
buenas y fáciles	good and easy	**grandes maestras**	great teachers
la vecina	neighbor (fem.)	**sabor**	flavor
¿recuerdas?	do you remember?		

* The English response "I'm coming" is translated by the Spanish *ya voy* ("I'm going.");
  este . . . este are pause words similar to "well," "ah" in English.

PREGUNTAS SOBRE EL DIALOGO

1. ¿Qué hora es?

_____

2. ¿Con quién habla la señora García?

_____

3. ¿Qué dice la señora García de sus recetas?

_____

4. ¿Habla inglés bien el señor García?

_____

5. ¿Es hispana la vecina?

_____

Una panadería

Vocabulario del capítulo

COGNATES OR NEAR COGNATES

agresivo/a

astuto/a

atractivo/a

el cablegrama

católico/a

la comprensión

compulsivo/a

la conferencia

conveniente

dedicado/a

el demócrata

la demócrata

el desastre

esencial

el estudio

familiar

fanático/a

fantástico/a

la figura

el habitante

honesto/a

hostil

importante

imposible

independiente

irracional

el latino

la latina

lógico/a

el mecánico

el motor

la nacionalidad

el norteamericano

el político

posible

la profesión

el protestante

la protestante

la provincia

rectangular

la religión

el republicano

el socialista

urgente

VOCABULARIO

el abogado	lawyer (male)	el centro	downtown
la abogada	lawyer (female)	el coche	car
el abuelo	grandfather	la cosa	thing
la abuela	grandmother	cuadrado/a	square
alemán/a	German	¿Cuál?	what/which one (when you have a choice)
el aluminio	aluminum		
el ambiente	atmosphere		
el ateo	the atheist	¿De quién?	whose (*lit.* of whom)
bajo/a	short	el dominicano	Dominican (man)
el barrio	neighborhood	la dominicana	Dominican (woman)
el bombero	fireman	la escalera	stairway
el cálculo	calculation, sum	el escritorio	desk

98

la escuela	school	la mesa	table
la esperanza	hope	moreno/a	dark
el esposo	husband	el musulmán	Moslem
la esposa	wife	el óptico	optician
los Estados Unidos	United States	el pago	payment
el estudiante	student (male)	el partido	political party
la estudiante	student female)	el pelo	hair
grande	large	el peruano	Peruvian (male)
grueso/a	thick	la peruana	Peruvian (female)
el guardia	individual guard	el policía	individual policeman
la guardia	collective body of guards	la policía	police force
		portátil	portable
el hierro	iron	primario/a	primary
el hijo	son	el pueblo	town, people
la hija	daughter	la puerta	door
los hijos	children	rápidamente	rapidly
el ingeniero	engineer	redondo	round
el judío	Jew	responsabilidad	responsibility
judío/a	Jewish	el suegro	father-in-law
el ladrillo	brick	la suegra	mother-in-law
la madera	wood	todas las noches	every night
el maestro	teacher (male)	el trabajador social	social worker
la maestra	teacher (female)		
la máquina de escribir	typewriter	universitario/a	university (adjective)
		el venezolano	Venezuelan (male)
mayor	older	la venezolana	Venezuelan (female)
mediano/a	medium height	la ventana	window
menor	younger	la verdad	truth

VERBOS

abrir	to open	memorizar	to memorize
acabar de + infinitive	to have just	pagar	to pay
		preferir(ie)	to prefer
asistir	to attend	prohibir	to prohibit
cerrar(ie)	to close	protestar	to protest
decir	to say, to tell	recibir	to receive
enseñar	to teach	reunir	to unite, to meet, to get together
escribir	to write		
explicar	to explain	recordar(ue)	to remember
ir	to go	venir	to come
iniciar	to begin, initiate	vivir	to live

Vocabulario adicional

SOME COMMONLY USED COMMANDS "MANDATOS"

¡Dé(n) melo!	Give it to me!
¡Díga(n) melo!	Tell it to me!
¡Tráiga(n) melo!	Bring it to me!
¡Hága(n) lo!	Do it!
¡No lo haga(n)!	Don't do it!
¡Vaya(n) a lavarse!	Go wash yourself (yourselves)!
¡Pida(n) _____!	Ask for _____!
¡Asista(n) _____!	Attend _____!
¡Consulte(n) con _____!	Consult with _____!
¡Sea(n) bueno(s)!	Be good!

EJERCICIOS. Translate into Spanish:

1. Go wash yourselves!   ¡ _____ ustedes!

2. Consult with my friend!   ¡ _____ usted!

3. Give it to me!   ¡ _____ ustedes!

4. Bring it to me!   ¡ _____ usted!

5. Be good!   ¡ _____ ustedes!

6. Tell it to me!   ¡ _____ usted!

7. Don't do it!   ¡ _____ ustedes!

8. Ask for the documents!   ¡ _____ usted!

WHAT'S IN THE NAME? — THE HISPANIC SURNAME

Hispanics often use their mother's surname as well as their father's. For example, Enrique Ledesma Irigoyen and Anita Molina González have chosen to use both sets of names.

Señor Enrique **Ledesma** (father's name) **Irigoyen** (mother's maiden name)

Señora Anita **Molina** (father's name) **González** (mother's maiden name)

So what do we do? We can call them by their paternal names — Mr. Ledesma and Mrs. Molina — or we can call them by their complete names — Mr. Enrique Ledesma Irigoyen and Mrs. Anita Molina González. *We should, however, not call them by their mothers' maiden names.*

A married woman does not lose or change her name. She continues to use her maiden name, except that, after she marries, she adds **de** + **her spouse's paternal name.**

Señorita Lola **Hernández** Castro

marries

Señor Osvaldo **Santaló** Pérez

and she becomes

Señora Lola **Hernández** de **Santaló**

If a woman becomes a widow, her name may reflect this change:

Señora Lola Hernández viuda de Santaló

Curiosidades

The Spanish ending *-ez* is the equivalent of the English *-son*. For example, in English Johnson is the son of John (Ericson, Peterson, etc.). In Spanish, Ramírez is the son of Ramiro, Rodríguez is the son of Rodrigo, etc. The common origin of northern European names can be seen for example in **López**, the son of Lope (Latin, lupus; English, wolf); thus the equivalent of López is Wolfson.

ESPAÑA — ¿El país de los hombres?

Use the masculine plural whenever there are masculine and feminine elements combined:

el padre (the father) + la madre (the mother) son **los padres** (the parents)

el hermano (the brother) + la hermana (the sister)
son **los hermanos** (the brother and the sister)

el hijo (the son) + la hija (the daughter) son **los hijos** (the children)

el alumno (the male student) + las alumnas (the female students) son **los alumnos**

Note: Masculine plural nouns may then refer to either a mixed group of males and females, or simply to a group of males.

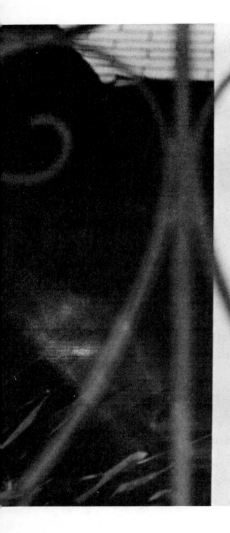

HORAS DE CONSULTA
LUNES   2 A 5 PM
MARTES
MIERCOLES   9 A 12 AM
JUEVES   2 A 5 PM
VIERNES   2 A 5 PM
SABADO   9 A 12 AM
PARA CITAS Y
EMERGENCIAS
LLAME A 428 1109

Los días de la semana

Capítulo 6
José García está trabajando

Lectura

José ya **está trabajando**. El tiene que
estar en el laboratorio de radiología
a las siete de la mañana.
Es fácil para José llegar al hospital
temprano. El **está acostumbrado** a salir
temprano de su casa y, **hasta cierto punto**,
está acostumbrado **al ajetreo** del tren
subterráneo.
El **está** muy contento con su trabajo en
el laboratorio del hospital. El **sabe manejar**
las máquinas de rayos-X y todo
el equipo técnico. Sin embargo, José
está preocupado. **Aunque** él entiende
todos los términos técnicos en inglés,
no está aprendiendo suficiente inglés para
conversar con sus amigos norteamericanos.
¡Paciencia, José!

is working

to be

at seven o'clock

is accustomed

to a certain extent

hustle and bustle

is

knows how to work

Although

is not learning

La gramática

THREE MORE "GO" VERBS

We mentioned earlier that sometimes irregular verbs have similar patterns of change that make it easier to memorize. We have seen that both **tener, venir,** and **decir** have a first person singular *go (tengo-vengo-digo)* form. The three verbs below have the same irregularity.

traer to bring			
yo	trai**go**	nosotros	traemos
tú	traes		
usted		ustedes	
él	trae	ellos	traen
ella		ellas	

hacer to do, to make			
yo	ha**go**	nosotros	hacemos
tú	haces		
usted		ustedes	
él	hace	ellos	hacen
ella		ellas	

salir to leave			
yo	sal**go**	nosotros	salimos
tú	sales		
usted		ustedes	
él	sale	ellos	salen
ella		ellas	

Add *de* after **salir** if a location is mentioned:

salgo de casa temprano   I leave home early

We have also seen that both **ser** and **ir** have a first person singular *oy* form. The verb **dar** also has this irregularity.

dar to give			
yo	d**oy**	nosotros	damos
tú	das		
usted		ustedes	
él	da	ellos	dan
ella		ellas	

EJERCICIOS. Insert the proper form of the verb.

1. Ellos **hacen** muchas cosas.
   (tú, el supervisor, usted, él y yo) _____

   _____

   _____

   _____

2. El médico de cabecera (family doctor) **da** el diagnóstico (diagnosis).
   (el urólogo, los especialistas, yo, nosotros) _____

   _____

   _____

   _____

3. La enfermera **hace** muchas cosas.
   (los miembros de la familia, tú, ellas, usted)_____

   _____

   _____

   _____

4. ¿Cuándo **sales** de la sala de operaciones (operating room)?
   (la paciente, los cirujanos [the surgeons], ustedes, ella) _____

   _____

   _____

   _____

5. La terapista (therapist) **trae** las muletas (crutches).
   (tu hermano, un miembro de la familia, yo, nosotros) _____

   _____

   _____

   _____

EJERCICIOS. Fill in the appropriate form of the verb:

1. salir   Yo _____ muy temprano.

2. dar, traer   Tú _____ toda la información.

                   Ella _____ muy poco.

                   Yo no _____ nada (anything).

3. traer, hacer   Ustedes _____ todo ahora.

                   El enfermero (male nurse) no _____ la medicina.

EJERCICIOS. Fill in the appropriate form of the verb:

1. Juan y yo (dar) _____ buenos consejos (good advice).

2. Yo (hacer) _____ mis ejercicios todos los días.

3. El doctor (dar) _____ el diagnóstico.

4. ¿Cuándo (traer) _____ usted las muletas (crutches)?

5. Nosotros no (salir) _____ hasta muy tarde (very late).

6. Tú nunca (never) (hacer) _____ mucho.

7. El doctor (dar) _____ de alta al paciente mañana (dar de alta = to release).

8. La terapista (traer) _____ los resultados (results).

9. El no (salir) _____ en una silla de ruedas (wheelchair).

10. Las enfermeras* (dar) _____ las instrucciones.

11. El especialista (traer) _____ buenas noticias.

EL VERBO *ESTAR*

estar to be				
yo	*estoy*	I am	nosotros	*estamos*	we are
tú	*estás*	you are			
usted		you are	ustedes		you are
él	*está*	he is	ellos	*están*	they are
ella		she is	ellas		they are

* **Norsa** is used in some Spanish-speaking communities in the United States. The standard form is **enfermera**.

106

Estar should be used to indicate:
1. Location
2. Temporary condition
3. An action in progress

---

1. **Location: When you think of**
   in, on, near, far, think of *estar*:

¿Dónde está usted? Estoy en El Paso, Texas.

La sala de emergencia no está lejos de aquí.

¿Está tu casa cerca? Sí, está en la calle catorce.

Where are you? I am in El Paso, Texas.

The emergency room is not far from here.

Is your house near? Yes, it is on 14th Street.

EJERCICIOS. Fill in the blank space with the appropriate form of **estar**.

1. Ella _____ en la casa de María.

2. ¿Dónde _____ ellos ahora?

3. Nosotros _____ lejos de la ciudad.

4. Pedro no _____ en la calle quince.

5. Todos mis amigos _____ cerca de la escuela (school).

6. Yo _____ aquí con usted y Marta.

7. ¿ _____ tú en clase?

8. Ellas _____ en Nueva York.

9. La colombiana _____ en California.

10. Unos cubanos _____ en Nueva Jersey.

11. El tiene que _____ en Caléxico mañana.

12. Yo no puedo _____ en los Estados Unidos hasta el martes.

13. ¿Dónde _____ usted en este (this) momento?

14. Tú _____ en mi auto.

15. Ella y yo queremos _____ en la Florida el miércoles.

16. Mi casa _____ en Las Vegas.

17. Los hermanos de Juan no _____ en la cárcel (jail).

18. Los libros técnicos _____ sobre (on) la mesa.

19. Nuestro abogado _____ en su oficina.

20. Ustedes necesitan _____ aquí todos los días.

Answer the following questions in Spanish.

1. ¿Dónde está usted en este momento?

_____

2. ¿Dónde está el congreso de los Estados Unidos?

_____

3. ¿Dónde tiene que estar usted mañana por la mañana (tomorrow morning)?

_____

4. ¿Está su casa cerca o lejos de su empleo?

_____

2. **Temporary Condition.**
   When you describe a temporary condition:

¿Cómo están ustedes? Estamos bien hoy.	How are you? We are well today.
No estamos contentos.	We are not happy.
La línea está ocupada.	The line is busy.

Exceptions: Adjectives of beauty, age, goodness, size, and color take **ser**.

Note: Adjectives that follow **ser** and **estar** agree in gender and number with the subjects.

EJERCICIOS. Fill the blank space with the appropriate form of **estar**.

1. Ella _____ muy preocupada (worried).

2. Nosotros _____ enfermos (sick).

3. Ella no _____ contenta.

4. Ellos _____ tranquilos (tranquil).

5. ¿ _____ tú nervioso (nervous)?

6. María y Pablo _____ cansados (tired).

7. Ustedes _____ muy preocupados.

8. El no _____ ocupado (busy).

9. Pablo _____ sentado (seated).

10. Ellas no _____ sentadas.

11. ¿Quién _____ acostumbrado a salir (accustomed to leaving) temprano?

12. Tú _____ bien, ¿verdad?

13. Yo no _____ ocupado en este momento.

14. ¿Cómo _____ usted?

15. Nosotras no _____ borrachas (drunk).

16. Todo el mundo (everybody) _____ contento.

17. Todos los amigos de Juan _____ furiosos.

18. Todos los hombres _____ enfermos.

19. Los abogados _____ enojados (angry) todavía.

20. Juan _____ borracho.

Answer the following questions in Spanish.

1. ¿Cómo está usted hoy?

_____

2. Cuando habla español, ¿está usted tranquilo/a o nervioso/a?

_____

3. ¿Está usted preocupado en este momento?

_____

3. **An action in progress (*estar* + *present participle*):**

In English, the present participle is the *-ing* form of the verb and is preceded by a conjugated form of the verb *to be: I am working; we are eating; she is living.*

In Spanish, to form the present participle, do the following: For **ar** verbs, remove the **ar** from the infinitive and add **ando.** For **er/ir** verbs, remove the **er/ir** from the infinitive and add **iendo.** In combination with the present tense of **estar**, the present participle forms the **present progressive** tense.

Estoy	trabaj	+ **ando.**	I am working.
Estamos	com	+ **iendo.**	We are eating.
Ella está	viv	+ **iendo.**	She is living.

EJERCICIOS. Fill in the blank space with the appropriate form of **estar.**

1. Los hombres fuertes _____ trabajando aquí.

2. Ella _____ ayudando con los pacientes.

3. Nosotros _____ firmando los documentos.

4. Usted _____ viajando sin dinero.

5. Yo _____ buscando a mis amigos.

6. Pedro _____ contestando todas las cartas.

7. ¿ _____ pagando ellos hoy?

8. Nosotras no _____ trayendo (*traer*)* las noticias.

9. Las amigas de Ana _____ comiendo platos criollos.

10. Los oficiales _____ leyendo (*leer*)* tus libros.

11. El burócrata siempre _____ durmiendo.*

12. ¿Qué _____ ofreciendo él?

13. Ellas _____ bebiendo mucho café con leche.

14. La joven _____ asistiendo a la conferencia.

15. Tú _____ diciendo (*decir*)* la verdad.

16. ¿Por qué _____ nosotros escribiendo mucho?

17. Ustedes _____ subiendo por la escalera.

18. Juan y yo _____ pidiendo (*pedir*)* más información.

19. Él _____ creyendo (*creer*)* todo.

20. Muchas mujeres _____ viniendo (*venir*)* para protestar.

21. Los González _____ haciendo mucho ahora.

* Some common **irregular present participles:**

creer . . . . **creyendo**	believing	
decir . . . . **diciendo**	saying	
dormir . . . **durmiendo**	sleeping	
ir . . . . . **yendo**	going	
leer . . . . **leyendo**	reading	
morir . . . . **muriendo**	dying	

pedir . . . **pidiendo**	asking	
poder . . . **pudiendo**	being able	
sentir . . . **sintiendo**	feeling	
traer . . . **trayendo**	bringing	
venir . . . **viniendo**	coming	

Answer the following questions in Spanish:

1. ¿Qué está haciendo usted ahora?

   _____

2. ¿Dónde está viviendo ahora?

   _____

3. ¿Qué está escribiendo en este momento?

   _____

4. En estos días (these days), ¿está usted comiendo mucho?

   _____

Translate into Spanish:

1. I am waiting here and she is signing the contract.

   _____

2. They are looking for documents.

   _____

3. He is tired, but (*pero*) he is earning a lot of money.

   _____

4. How are you? I am ill.

   _____

5. Where are we? We have to be in Miami on Tuesday.

   _____

6. The white houses are not far from the city.

   _____

7. My cousins (male) are always busy and worried.

   _____

8. He is drunk and they are furious.

   _____

9. All the men are living in Miami and they are doing a lot.

   _____

10. Who (*quién*) is asking for more information?

    _____

11. Are you accustomed to leaving early?

    _____

12. Everybody is here and everybody is drinking a lot.

    _____

13. Why are you (*ustedes*) reading many letters?

    _____

14. The young men have to be here on Friday at 7:00 in the evening.

    _____

15. She is not angry. She wants to be happy.

    _____

16. We prefer to be in the city on Sunday.

    _____

17. Where is the bathroom (*servicio, aseo, inodoro, retrete, cuarto de baño, excusado*)?

    _____

18. I am going to be here on Saturday, and I am going to be worried.

    _____

19. You (*usted*) are not here everyday and you are not working a lot.

    _____

ADJECTIVES AND THEIR MEANINGS WITH *SER* OR *ESTAR*

Often adjectives differ in meaning according to whether they are used with **ser** or **estar**. Some common examples are:

Adjective	*ser*	*estar*
aburrido/a	boring	bored
alegre	happy (by nature)	happy (at this time)
bonito/a	pretty (by nature)	pretty (at this time)
bueno/a	good, kind (by nature)	well (health); good (taste)
callado/a	taciturn (by nature)	silent (not speaking)
enfermo/a	sickly (in poor health)	ill (at this time)
feo/a	ugly (by nature)	ugly (at this time)
grande	big	big (for one's age)
joven	young (actually)	young (in appearance)
listo/a	smart, clever, alert	ready
loco/a	insane	silly, irresponsible
maduro/a	mature	ripe
malo/a	bad, evil	ill, in bad taste, broken
nervioso/a	nervous (by nature)	nervous (at this time)
nuevo/a	new (recently made)	new (in appearance)
rico/a	rich (wealthy)	rich (has become) / delicious
triste	sad (by nature)	sad (at this moment)
verde	green	green (not ripe)
viejo/a	old (actually)	old (in appearance)
vivo/a	lively	alive

estamos casados	we are married–this is our status
somos casados	we are husband and wife

REVIEW EXERCISES FOR *SER* AND *ESTAR*

Fill the blank spaces with the appropriate form of either **ser** or **estar**.

1. Mi amigo _____ de Uruguay. _____ uruguayo.

2. El enfermo (the sick man) _____ de Venezuela.

   _____ venezolano.

3. Los Martínez _____ de la República Dominicana.

   _____ dominicanos.

4. La encargada (head nurse) _____ muy enojada ahora.

5. Ellos van a _____ en su casa durante las vacaciones.

6. Ellas _____ feas hoy.

7. La comida en el hospital nunca _____ rica.

8. En general, los banqueros (the bankers) _____ ricos.

9. El _____ en el hospital; _____ mal.

10. El cura _____ acostumbrado a salir temprano.

11. ¿Qué hora es? _____ las nueve y media de la mañana.

12. _____ necesario _____ aquí a las ocho y media de la mañana.

13. Los miembros del comité _____ de Nuevo México.

14. _____ importante tomar toda la medicina.

15. Ella _____ enfermera. El hermano de ella

_____ vendedor (salesman).

16. Ella _____ comiendo poco, porque _____ enferma.

17. La paciente _____ muy nerviosa ahora.

18. En general él _____ alegre, pero en este momento él no _____ alegre.

19. El doctor no _____ en la oficina. El _____ operando.

20. ¿Dónde _____ (tú) sentado?

21. ¿Por qué _____ (ella) triste hoy?

22. _____ imposible manejar este equipo.

23. El cardiólogo va a _____ aquí hasta muy tarde.

24. ¿Dónde _____ ellos? _____ fumando (smoking) en el pasillo.

25. ¿Qué _____ (ustedes) observando (observing)?

Diálogo

Señor García	—	Mire Wallis, ¿qué hago con este paciente?
Wallis	—	Un momento, José, estoy haciendo **muchas cosas** ahora. ¡Hable con Carlos!
Señor García	—	Mire, Wallis, ¿qué hago con este paciente?
Wallis	—	Un momento, José, estoy haciendo **muchas cosas** ahora. ¡Hable con Carlos!
Señor García	—	No puedo porque él está trabajando en la sala de emergencias ahora. *(Entra el doctor Ramos)*
Doctor Ramos	—	¿**Qué tal**, señor García? ¿Tiene las radiografías de **la espalda** y del **cuello** del señor que está allí? El es mi paciente.
Señor García	—	Sí, tengo estas radiografiás. **A propósito**, estoy preparando **la serie** deplacas de la señora Whitman.
Señor García	—	Todavía están en **la máquina de revelar**.
Doctor Ramos	—	Por favor, ¡tráigame estas placas inmediatamente y también tráigame **las placas** de la espalda y del cuello en media hora! *(Sale el doctor Ramos)*
Wallis	—	¡**Qué bárbaro**! ¡Ese doctor es muy exigente!

VOCABULARIO DEL DIALOGO

muchas cosas	many things
¿Qué tal?	How is it going?
la espalda	the back
el cuello	the neck
a propósito	by the way
la serie	the series
las pruebas	the tests
la sangre	the blood
los rayos-X	the X-rays
la máquina de revelar	the developer
las placas	the X-ray plates
¡Qué bárbaro!	damn!

PREGUNTAS SOBRE EL DIALOGO

1. ¿Qué está haciendo Wallis?

   _____

2. ¿Dónde está trabajando Carlos?

   _____

3. ¿Qué quiere el doctor Ramos?

   _____

4. ¿Qué está preparando el señor García para el doctor Ramos?

   _____

5. ¿Qué están haciendo el doctor Ramos y la doctora Goodman?

   _____

Vocabulario del capítulo

COGNATES OR NEAR COGNATES

el antibiótico
el cardiólogo
la clase
el comité
contento/a
el diagnóstico
la droga
el error
el especialista
la familia
furioso/a
la instrucción
el laboratorio
la lección
la línea
la medicina
el momento
nervioso/a

ocupado/a
la operación
el ómnibus
la paciencia
preocupado/a
el pulso
los rayos X
el resultado
suficiente
la temperatura
el terapista
el término
el tipo
tranquilo/a
la transportación
el urólogo
las vacaciones

VOCABULARIO

aburrido/a	bored	la enferma	sick woman
alegre	happy	enojado/a	angry
acostumbrado/a	accustomed	el equipo	equipment
el banquero	banker	la escalera	stairway
bonito/a	pretty	feo/a	ugly
callado/a	taciturn, silent	fuerte	strong
la cárcel	jail	lejos	far
casado/a	married	listo/a	smart, ready
cuarto de baño	bathroom	maduro/a	mature, ripe
(servicio, retrete, inodoro, excusado)		el miembro	member
cerca	near	malo/a	bad, ill
el cirujano	surgeon	la(s) muleta(s)	crutch(es)
el cura*	priest	la pomada	ointment
despacio	slowly	el plato	plate
el enfermo	sick man	la propina	tip

* Note the *gender* of the article. **La cura** means *the cure.* Remember:
   El cura busca **la cura** (*The priest* looks for *the cure.*)

la quemadura	burn		
rico/a	rich, delicious	triste	sad
la sala	room	único/a	only
sentado/a	seated	el vendedor	salesman
el sótano	basement	el viaje	trip

VERBOS

dar	to give
fumar	to smoke
hacer	to do, to make
observar	to observe
salir	to leave
traer	to bring

FRASES

al día	a day
el ajetreo	hustle and bustle
el buen consejo	good advice
la buena suerte	good luck
dar de alta	to release (a patient)
hacer preguntas	to ask questions
la mala suerte	bad luck
la máquina de escribir	typewriter
el médico de cabecera	family doctor
la silla de ruedas	wheelchair
todo lo posible	all that is possible
todo el mundo	everybody

Vocabulario adicional

SOME COMMONLY USED COMMANDS: "MANDATOS"

¡Tenga(n) cuidado!	Be careful!
¡No tenga(n) miedo!	Don't be afraid!
¡Camine(n) derecho!	Walk straight!
a la derecha!	to the right!
a la izquierda!	to the left!
¡Pónga(n) lo allí/aquí!	Put it there!/here!

¡Respire(n) profundo!	Breathe deeply!
¡Tóme(n)lo!	Take it!
¡Víre(n)se!	Turn!
¡Arriba!/¡Abajo!	Up!/Down!
¡Muéva(n)se!	Move!
¡Doble (+ part of body)!	Bend!
¡Dóble(n)se!	Bend over!
¡Deténga(n)se!	Stop!
¡Manténga(n)se en esa posición!	Stay in that position!

Muestreme con el dedo donde tien dolor! tell me where you have pain

EJERCICIOS. Translate into Spanish.

1. Be careful and walk to the right!

   ¡ _____ usted!

2. Bend over. Stay in that position!

   ¡ _____ usted!

3. Don't be afraid!

   ¡ _____ ustedes!

4. Take it and put it there!

   ¡ _____ usted!

5. Turn to the left and stop!

   ¡ _____ ustedes!

6. Breathe deeply!

   ¡ _____ usted!

La clase bilingüe de Angel García

Capítulo 7
La señora García matricula a los hijos

Lectura

La señora García va hoy a la escuela
primaria del vecindario.

Ella tiene que matricular a Celia y
a Angel. El señor García **tiene ganas de ir**   is eager to go
también, pero no puede porque
él no tiene mucho tiempo libre ahora
que trabaja **el turno de día.**   the day shift
Hace muy mal tiempo hoy. **Está nevando**   It is very bad weather / It is snowing
y **hace mucho frío.**   it is very cold
La señora García tiene que esperar
mucho tiempo para matricular a sus
hijos. Ella tiene una cita **con alguien**   with someone
de la escuela a las doce. **Ya** son las   Already
doce y media y **todavía no ha visto a nadie.**   still has not seen anyone.
Ella piensa que esto es **el colmo:**   the last straw
la demora del consejero, el   the lateness
mal tiempo, el frío, **la nieve**, la   the snow
secretaria invisible de la escuela. . . .
Ella cree que José **tiene razón.**   is right

La geografía no cambia nada. En todos

los sitios es lo mismo. Nadie tiene — everywhere is the same / No one

la culpa. El burócrata, el soldado, — the blame

el funcionario. . . . Ella **siente** — feels

un gran resentimiento en contra de

ese consejero. ¡**Cuidado**, López! — Watch out

La señora García está enojada. — is angry

La clase bilingüe de Celia García

La gramática

DEMONSTRATIVE ADJECTIVES

The demonstrative adjectives agree in gender and number with the nouns they modify.

Singular			Plural		
este	lápiz	this pencil	estos	lápices	these pencils
esta	carta	this letter	estas	cartas	these letters
ese	lápiz	that pencil	esos	lápices	those pencils
esa	carta	that letter	esas	cartas	those letters
aquel	lápiz	that pencil over there	aquellos	lápices	those pencils over there
aquella	carta	that letter over there	aquellas	cartas	those letters over there

Remember:
This and *these* have the T's (es*T*e/a and es*T*os/as)

EJERCICIOS. Translate the word in parenthesis.

1. (That) _____ carta es interesante.

2. (This) _____ maestra es muy buena.

3. (That) _____ pizarra (blackboard) es negra.

4. (Those) _____ revistas son de España (Spain).

5. (That-*distant*) _____ ventana (window) está cerrada (is closed).

6. (Those-*distant*) _____ papeles tienen que estar sobre los escritorios (the desks).

7. (Those) _____ bolígrafos no son de Enrique.

8. (These) _____ cuadernos (notebooks) son de Jaime.

9. (These) _____ calificaciones o notas (grades) son altas.

DEMONSTRATIVE PRONOUNS

Demonstrative pronouns take the place of nouns. Their form is the same as the demonstrative adjective, except they are accented.

Singular		Plural	
éste ésta	this one	éstos éstas	these
ése ésa	that one	ésos ésas	those
aquél aquélla	that one over there	aquéllos aquéllas	those over there

Quiero el libro rojo; **éste** es azul.

I want the red book; this one is blue.

María no tiene la pluma de José; **ésa** es de él.

Mary does not have Joe's pen; that one is his.

There are also three neuter demonstrative pronouns: **esto, eso,** and **aquello.** They are used whenever the location or situation referred to is not specified.

Quiero **esto.**

I want this (*vague*).

Ellos quieren **eso.**

They want that (*vague*).

Aquello es bueno.

That (*vague*) is good.

EJERCICIOS. Translate the words in parenthesis.

1. Esta revista es interesante; (that one over there) _____ no es interesante.

2. Esta silla (chair) es roja (red); (that one over there) _____ es amarilla (yellow).

3. Esta pluma es de Carlos; (this one) _____ es de Juan.

4. Aquel libro de geografía es nuevo; (that one) _____ es viejo (old).

5. Aquellas ventanas están cerradas; (these) _____ están abiertas (open).

6. Estos papeles no son importantes, pero (those) _____ sí son muy importantes.

7. (These) _____ revistas son mexicanas;

   (those over there) _____ son peruanas.

8. (That) _____ periódico es viejo;

   (this one) _____ es nuevo.

9. (Those) _____ notas son muy bajas (low);

   (these) _____ son muy altas.

10. (This) _____ es un problema;

    (that) _____ es otro problema más grave.

11. (That) _____ pizarra no tiene tiza (chalk);

    (that one over there) _____ tiene mucha tiza, pero no tiene borrador (eraser).

MORE VERBS

dormir(*ue*) to sleep			
yo	d*ue*rmo	nosotros	dormimos
tú	d*ue*rmes		
usted		ustedes	
él	d*ue*rme	ellos	d*ue*rmen
ella		ellas	

deber to ought to, to owe			
yo	debo	nosotros	debemos
tú	debes		
usted		ustedes	
él	debe	ellos	deben
ella		ellas	

jugar(*ue*) to play			
yo	j*ue*go	nosotros	jugamos
tú	j*ue*gas		
usted		ustedes	
él	j*ue*ga	ellos	j*ue*gan
ella		ellas	

oír to hear			
yo	oigo	nosotros	oímos
tú	oyes		
usted		ustedes	
él	oye	ellos	oyen
ella		ellas	

pensar(*ie*) to think			
yo	p*ie*nso	nosotros	pensamos
tú	p*ie*nsas		
usted		ustedes	
él	p*ie*nsa	ellos	p*ie*nsan
ella		ellas	

coger* to get, to catch			
yo	cojo	nosotros	cogemos
tú	coges		
usted		ustedes	
él	coge	ellos	cogen
ella		ellas	

Note:

pensar + infinitive = to intend
El piensa entregar su trabajo.
He intends to hand in his work.

pensar + en + object = to think of/about
Yo pienso en Elena.
I think of Helen.

EJERCICIOS. Fill in the blank with the appropriate form of the verb.

dormir(*ue*)

1. Cuando tienes sueño (are sleepy) tú _____ .

2. El maestro _____ poco porque tiene mucho que hacer (much to do).

3. ¿ _____ ustedes toda la noche?

4. Si el niño está enfermo, a veces no puede _____ .

5. Yo _____ en esta clase, ¿verdad?

* **ger** verbs change the **g** to **j** in the **yo** form of the verb. This change occurs only in the present tense.

coger

1. Ellas _____ tres asignaturas (subjects).

2. ¿Qué cursos tú _____ este semestre?*

3. Siempre nosotros _____ catarro (cold) en invierno.

4. ¿Qué tren _____ usted para ir al Bronx?

5. Yo _____ la guagua.†

deber

1. El bebé _____ tomar solamente leche (milk).

2. Ustedes no _____ faltar (to cut, to miss)a clases.

3. ¿Cuánto _____ nosotros ahora?

4. Yo _____ entregar la tarea (homework).

5. Tú _____ llamar por teléfono por la mañana.

pensar*(ie)*

1. Los hermanos Sánchez siempre _____ antes de contestar (before answering).

2. Tenemos que (think) _____ primero (first).

3. El (intends) _____ dormir ahora.

4. Nosotros _____ ir mañana.

5. ¿Qué _____ usted de la idea?

oír

1. De aquí yo lo _____ todo.

2. ¿Puedes _____ la música?

3. Ellas no _____ los gritos (the shouts).

4. Nosotros _____ sus voces (voices).

5. ¿Qué _____ ustedes?

* In conversational Spanish the subject sometimes precedes the verb in questions. Intonation conveys the idea that it is a question and not a statement.

† "guagua" is a popular term for "bus" among Hispanics from the Caribbean region.

jugar(ue)

1. Ella _____ al béisbol (pelota) con su hermano.

2. Tú _____ a los naipes (playing cards) con tus amigos.

3. Yo _____ al fútbol después de hacer mis tareas.

4. Nosotros _____ con ellos ahora.

5. Nuestro equipo (team) _____ muy bien.

EJERCICIOS. Insert the proper form of the verb.

1. Yo **debo** comer ahora.
   (tú, ella, nosotras, Juan)

_____

_____

_____

_____

2. María no **duerme** mucho.
   (los alumnos, la maestra y yo, tú, Celia y Roberto)

_____

_____

_____

_____

3. Ellos **cogen** muchos cursos.
   (el estudiante, los padres, yo, ustedes)

_____

_____

_____

_____

4. Yo nunca (never) **pienso** así.
   (el oyente [auditor], los decanos [the deans], él y yo, usted)

   _____

   _____

   _____

   _____

5. ¿**Oye** usted ese ruido (noise)?
   (las niñas, su hijo, la joven, tú)   _____

   _____

   _____

   _____

6. Tú **juegas** al béisbol con tus amigos.
   (nosotros, ellas, los muchachos, yo)   _____

   _____

   _____

   _____

7. El conserje (janitor) **debe** limpiar el cuarto.
   (la niña, los jóvenes, yo, tú)   _____

   _____

   _____

   _____

8. Pedro y Juan **juegan** mucho. Son jugadores (gamblers) profesionales.
   (María, David y Enrique, nosotros, yo)

   _____

   _____

   _____

   _____

TENER EXPRESSIONS

Tener expressions generally relate to human emotions and physical needs.

- **Tener + noun** is often used to express the English equivalent of "to be" + adjective:

Tenemos hambre y sed y ella tiene calor y sueño.

We are hungry and thirsty and she is hot and sleepy.

Spanish Tener + noun	English "to be" + adjective
Tener + coraje	to be angry*/to be brave
+ la culpa	to be guilty/to be at fault
+ éxito	to be successful
+ frío	to be cold
+ hambre	to be hungry
+ calor	to be hot
+ miedo (de)	to be fearful (of)/afraid
+ paciencia	to be patient
+ razón	to be right/correct
+ sed	to be thirsty
+ sueño	to be sleepy
+ suerte	to be lucky

COMMON *TENER* EXPRESSIONS

- tener + _____ años — to be + _____ years old
  tener + prisa — to be in a hurry
  tener + tiempo — to have time

- The following *tener* expressions are often followed by **de + infinitive**:

  tener derecho de + infinitive — to have the right to + infinitive

  tener ganas de + infinitive — to be eager to + infinitive

Adjectives modifying **sed, suerte, hambre, razón, ganas, paciencia,** and **prisa** take feminine endings:

  Ellos tienen **mucha** hambre y no tienen **mucha** paciencia.

---

* This meaning is idiomatic and frequently used among Puerto Ricans.

MAS and MENOS combined with QUE and DE

Más and **menos** precede the noun
and are often used in combination with **que** and **de**:

Juan tiene **más** éxito **que** Pablo.   John is **more** successful **than** Paul.

Marta tiene **menos** paciencia **que** Juanita.   Martha is **less** patient **than** Joan.

Más/menos de are used only with numbers:

Juan tiene **más de** cinco libros.   John has **more than** five books.

EJERCICIOS. Translate the word in parenthesis.

1. En Las Vegas él siempre (has) _____ mucha suerte.

2. En el invierno todo el mundo (is cold) _____ .

3. La profesora y la asistente (are very successful) _____ .

4. Generalmente cuando yo duermo demasiado (I am very sleepy) _____

_____ .

5. Durante el descanso (recess) los niños juegan mucho y cuando regresan (*regresar:* to return)

a la clase (they are very hungry) _____ .

6. El (is not right) _____ siempre.

7. Nosotros (are not fearful) _____ del examen.

8. Tú siempre (are lucky) _____ cuando juegas a ese juego (game).

9. El consejero (has the right to speak) _____ con los padres.

10. (Are you in a hurry?) ¿ _____ ?

11. La madre de Juan (is not eager to bring) _____
los documentos.

EJERCICIOS: Answer in Spanish.

1. ¿Tiene usted más o menos éxito que sus colegas (colleagues)?

_____

2. En su clase de español, ¿tiene usted calor o frío?

_____

3. Cuando usted tiene mucha hambre, ¿qué come?

_____

4. En este momento, ¿tiene usted más de veinte y cinco dólares (dollars)?

_____

5. ¿Tiene usted más o menos paciencia que su profesor/a de español?

_____

HACER EXPRESSIONS

Hacer expressions are associated mainly with weather and nature.

1. In the following only the third person singular **hace** form is used:

	calor	it is hot
	frío	it is cold
	fresco	it is cool/breezy
hace	**viento**	it is windy
	buen tiempo	the weather is good
	mal tiempo	the weather is bad
	mucho tiempo	a long time ago
	poco tiempo	a short time ago

2. In the two instances below, **hacer** is conjugated:

hacer un viaje	to take/make a trip
hacer una pregunta	to ask a question*

Ellos **hacen** viajes todos los años.	They take trips every year.
Yo no **hago** preguntas los lunes.	I don't ask questions on Mondays.

EJERCICIOS. Fill in the appropriate form of **tener** or **hacer**.

1. Ellos _____ frío, cuando _____ frío.

2. Cuando (it is) _____ calor, yo siempre (am) _____ calor.

3. Nosotros (are hot) _____ cuando (it is) _____
mucho calor; es decir (that is), en el verano.

* An indirect object is usually required.

4. (It is) _____ fresco en el otoño.

5. En septiembre cuando comienzan las clases en la escuela primaria, (it is nice out—the weather is good) _____ .

6. Después de hablar (after speaking) mucho en clase, la maestra

(is very thirsty) _____ .

7. Con niños usted (have to be patient) _____ .

8. Ellos nunca (have time) _____ para estudiar.

9. A veces (sometimes) los estudiantes (ask many questions) _____ .

10. En algunos estados (some states) los alumnos bilingües (have the right) _____

_____ de aprender en su propio idioma (their own language).

11. Algunas (some) personas siempre (are in a hurry) _____ .

EJERCICIOS. Answer in Spanish.

1. ¿Cuántos años tiene usted?

_____

2. Cuando hace mucho calor, ¿tiene calor o frío?

_____

3. Cuando tiene mucha sed, ¿qué bebe/toma usted?

_____

4. Después de comer mucho, ¿tiene usted sueño?

_____

5. ¿Hace buen tiempo hoy?

_____

INDEFINITES AND NEGATIVES

	Indefinites		Negatives	
Pronouns	algo	something	nada	nothing
	alguien*	somebody	nadie*	nobody
	alguno/a	someone (of a group)	ninguno/a	no one
Adjectives	algún/alguna	some (of a group)	ningún/ninguna	none (of a group)
Adverbs	jamás	ever	jamás	never
	siempre	always	nunca	never
Conjunctions	o ___ o	either ___ or	ni ___ ni	neither ___ nor

INDEFINITES

Algo está pasando.   Something is happening.

Alguien está aquí.   Someone is here.

Algunos alumnos están perdidos.   Some students are lost.

Algunas niñas están enfermas.   Some little girls are sick.

Algún muchacho está escribiendo todavía.   Some young man is still writing.

Veo **algo** allá.   I see something there.

Vemos a* **alguien** en la biblioteca.   We see someone in the Library.

Note: **alguno** and **ninguno** drop the **o** and take an accent before masculine singular nouns. For instance:

algún muchacho and **ningún** muchacho *but* **alguna** muchacha and **ninguna** muchacha

EJERCICIOS. Translate the word in parenthesis.

1. El tiene (something) _____ .

2. María visita (some) _____ escuelas.

3. (Some) _____ muchachas reciben notas altas.

4. (Some) _____ muchachos necesitan escribir más.

5. ¿Tienen ustedes (something) _____ en el bolsillo (pocket)?

6. (Someone) _____ está estudiando para los exámenes.

7. Visitamos a (someone) _____ todos los días.

8. Vamos a dar (some) _____ libros técnicos a la biblioteca (library).

9. Ellos ven (something) _____ raro (strange).

* *Alguien/nadie* always refer to a person, of either sex, and have no plural. They are also preceded by the personal *a* when they are direct objects of the verb.

No veo a nadie (I don't see anyone).

Ellos conocen a alguien en el banco (They know someone in the bank).

More Indefinites

Ella **siempre** dice la verdad.	She always tells the truth.
Ella no dice **jamás** la verdad.	She does not ever tell the truth.
O él es muy inteligente *o* es muy presumido.	Either he is very smart or he is very presumptuous.

EJERCICIOS. Translate the word in parenthesis.

1. (Either) _____ él está comiendo (or) _____ está durmiendo.

2. María (always) _____ prepara la tarea.

3. Nosotros no tenemos frío (ever) _____

4. La profesora dice que no hace (ever) _____ mal tiempo en el mes de abril.

5. Ellos tienen (either) _____ mucho dinero (or) _____ muchos amigos.

NEGATIVES

Double Negative in Spanish

The combination of

no + verb + negative pronoun / adjective / adverb

is very often used in Spanish. It is only when the speaker wishes to be *emphatic* that he uses a negative pronoun / adjective / adverb before the verb:

No está pasando **nada**. **Nada** está pasando. *(more emphatic)*	Nothing is happening.
No veo **a nadie**. **A nadie** veo. *(more emphatic)*	I don't see anyone/anybody.
No está aquí **ninguno** de los muchachos. **Ninguno** de los muchachos está aquí.	None of (not a one of) the boys is here.
No voy **nunca/jamás** a la playa solo. **Nunca/jamás** voy a la playa solo.	I never go to the beach alone.
Ni él **ni** ella tienen paciencia.	Neither he nor she is patient.

Note: **No + verb + negative pronoun/adjective/adverb**
or

Negative pronoun/adjective/adverb + subject + verb
verb

MAS EJERCICIOS

1. El ve a (someone) _____ .

   El no ve a (anyone) _____

2. Traemos (something) _____ para Juan.

   No traemos (anything) _____ para Juan.

3. Escuchan a (someone) _____ .

   No escuchan a (anyone) _____ .

4. Yo ayudo a (someone) _____ .

   No ayudo a (anyone) _____ .

5. Vamos a tomar (something) _____ .

   No vamos a tomar (anything) _____ .

6. ¿Está pasando (something) _____ ?

   No está pasando (anything) _____ .

7. ¿Va ella con (someone) _____ ?

   Ella no va con (anyone) _____ .

8. La asistente arregla (something) _____ .

   La asistente no arregla (anything) _____ .

9. El entrenador (coach) lee (something) _____ .

   El entrenador no lee (anything) _____ .

10. ¿Oyen ustedes a (someone) _____ ?

    No oímos a (anyone) _____ .

11. El farmacéutico tiene que cobrar (to charge) (something) _____ .

    El farmacéutico no tiene que cobrar (anything) _____ .

EJERCICIOS. Reconstruct the sentences so that the negative pronoun, adjective, or adverb follows the verb.

1. Nada veo.

   _____

2. Nadie viene.

   _____

3. Nada tenemos.

   _____

4. A nadie miro.

   _____

5. Nunca va al gimnasio (gym).

   _____

6. Jamás ayudas.

   _____

7. Ninguna de las alumnas canta.

   _____

8. Nadie está estudiando hoy.

   _____

9. A nadie llamo.

   _____

MAS EJERCICIOS. Translate into Spanish.

1. Somebody wants to go now.

   _____

2. Nobody wants to help.

   _____

3. Something is happening.

_____

4. Nothing is here.

_____

5. Some female students listen.

_____

6. He always arrives late.

_____

7. Either we call someone or we go home.

_____

8. They never answer the questions.

_____

9. None of the men has money.

_____

10. I don't see anyone. Do you see someone?

_____

Diálogo

Señora García — Por favor . . . **este** . . . ¿es usted Rodríguez?

Señor López — No, señora, soy López, Rogelio López **a sus órdenes**.

Señora García — Yo **llevo media hora esperando** al señor Rodríguez. Joven, ¿no oyes? Llevo media hora aquí.

Señor López — ¡Cálmese, señora! . . . este . . . **¿cómo se llama usted?**

Señora García — Isabel Schneider de García. ¿Por qué?

Señor López — Señora García, usted no debe tener coraje. Este . . . el señor Rodríguez hace mucho aquí por nosotros los hispanos. Además, pienso que viene **ahorita**.

Señora García — Y **mientras tanto**, ¿qué hago yo? Tengo dos hijos en casa. El no debe hacerme esperar. No tiene derecho. ¿Y tú no tienes nada que ver con todo esto?

Señor López — Señora, tengo muchas ganas de ayudar, pero él siempre tiene coraje si alguien **mete las narices**. Este asunto es cosa de Rodríguez. Sólo él sabe de estas cosas.

Señora García — Entonces, ¿no hay nadie de **la Dirección** aquí ahora?

Señor López — Bueno, yo soy alguien.

Señora García — Por favor, joven. Este no es el momento para **ser bromista**.

Señor López — Espere, señora García, ahora llega. Rodríguez, **¡ven acá!**

Señora García — Muy buenas, señor Rodríguez, yo soy Isabel Schneider de García.

Señor Rodríguez — ¡Ah! ¡Cómo no, la chilena! Perdone **la demora. ¿Hace mucho que espera?**

Señora García — Bueno. **Ni mucho ni poco.**

Señor Rodríguez — Tenemos que hablar porque usted es algo especial.

Señora García — ¿Y eso?

Señor Rodríguez — Es la primera vez que una familia chilena pide la matrícula de sus hijos aquí.

Señora García — ¿Entonces?

Señor Rodríguez — Entonces tengo que hablar con la supervisora, porque esta documentación es bastante complicada.

VOCABULARIO DEL DIALOGO

...este...	a pause word
a sus órdenes	at your service
llevar + tiempo	to have been waiting + time
¿cómo se llama usted?	what is your name
ahorita	among Cubans it means "in a while"; and among Mexicans it means "right now, this very minute"
mientras tanto	meanwhile
mete las narices (meter)	stick one's nose in someone else's business
la dirección	those in charge
ser bromista	be a joker
ven acá	come here (*tú* form command)
la demora	the delay
¿Hace mucho que espera?	Have you been waiting long?
ni mucho/ni poco	neither a long nor a short time

PREGUNTAS SOBRE EL DIALOGO

1. ¿Cuánto tiempo lleva esperando la señora García?

_____

2. ¿A quién está esperando la señora García?

_____

3. ¿Por qué está preocupada la señora García?

_____

4. ¿Por qué dice el señor Rodríguez, "usted es algo especial"?

_____

5. ¿Qué tiene que hacer Rodríguez?

_____

Vocabulario del capítulo

COGNATES OR NEAR COGNATES

el adulto

el asistente

el bebé

el béisbol

el conflicto

conveniente

el dólar

especial

la fisiología

el fútbol

la geografía

el gimnasio

la idea

el idioma

el instructor

interesante

invisible

la mamá

la música

el semestre

VOCABULARIO

la alegría	happiness	enfermo/a	ill
el alumno	student	el entrenador	coach
amarillo/a	yellow	el equipo	equipment, team
la asignatura	subject		
bajo/a	short/low/under	el escritorio	desk
la biblioteca	library	el estudiante	student
el bolígrafo	pen (ballpoint)	el éxito	success
el bolsillo	pocket	España	Spain
el borrador	eraser	extraño/a	strange
la calificación	grade	la falta	absence
el colega	colleague	el farmacéutico	pharmacist
el conserje	janitor, maintenance man	la física	physics
		el funcionario	public employee
ciencias políticas	political science	grave	serious
ciencias naturales	natural science	el grito	shout, scream
ciencias sociales	social science	el historiador	historian
el cuaderno	notebook	el invierno	winter
el cuarto	room, quarter	el juego	game
el curso	course	el jugador	player, gambler
el decano	dean	la leche	milk
demasiado	too much	el niño	little boy
el descanso	recess/the break	la niña	little girl
el detalle	detail	la nota	grade

140

el naipe	playing card	la revista	magazine
el oyente	auditor	rojo/a	red
el pastel	cake	el ruido	noise
perdido/a	lost	la silla	chair
el permiso	permission	el soldado	soldier
la pizarra	blackboard	solo/a	alone
la playa	beach	la tarea	assignment, homework
la pluma	pen		
presumido/a	presumptuous	la tiza	chalk
el primero	first	la ventana	window
querido/a	dear	el vecindario	neighborhood
la química	chemistry	el verano	summer
raro/a	strange	la voz (las voces)	voice/voices
el recuerdo	memory		

VERBOS

arreglar	to arrange	inscribir	to register
beber	to drink	mandar	to send
cobrar	to charge	nevar	to snow
entregar	to hand in	pesar	to weigh
faltar	to miss	prever	to foresee
firmar	to sign	regresar	to return
indicar	to indicate	traer	to bring

FRASES

antes de contestar	before answering
asistir a la clase	to attend class
a veces	at times
estar abierto	to be open
estar bien hecho	to be well made
ni . . . ni	neither . . . nor
propio idioma	own language

Vocabulario adicional

SOME COMMONLY USED COMMANDS "MANDATOS"

¡Abra(n) el libro!	Open the book!
¡Aprénda(n) lo!	Learn it!
¡Borre(n)!	Erase!
¡Cierre(n) la ventana!	Close the window!
¡Continúe(n)!	Continue!

¡Estudie(n)!	Study!
¡Lea(n) la frase! el problema!	Read the sentence! the problem!
¡Muéstre(n)melo!	Show it to me!
¡Oiga(n) me!	Hear me or listen!
¡Pase(n) a la pizarra!	Go to the blackboard!
¡Ponga(n)!	Put!
¡Pónga(n)se...	Put on ...
el abrigo!	the coat!
la camisa!	the shirt!
los pantalones!	the pants!
la ropa!	the clothing! ✓
el sombrero!	the hat!
los zapatos!	the shoes!
el vestido!	the dress!
¡Preste(n) atención!	Pay attention!
¡Repita(n) en voz alta!	Repeat out loud!
¡Siga(n)!	Continue!
¡Tenga(n) paciencia!	Have patience!
¡No tenga(n) miedo!	Don't be afraid!
¡Vaya(n) a su sitio!	Go to your seat!
¡No se pelee(n)!	Don't fight!

(handwritten: (dont take medicin) / no toma medicine / (toma medicion) / Take medicine) / Boca ba deba) / face

(handwritten: acusto se soblal / lie down on the table)

EJERCICIOS. Translate into Spanish.

1. Pay attention!   ¡ _____ usted!

2. Repeat out loud!   ¡ _____ ustedes!

3. Continue, please!   ¡ _____ usted!

4. Go to your seats, please!   ¡ _____ ustedes!

5. Don't fight!   ¡ _____ usted!

6. Put on your coat!   ¡ _____ usted!

7. Don't be afraid!   ¡ _____ ustedes!

8. Put on your hats!   ¡ _____ ustedes!

9. Put on your shoes!   ¡ _____ ustedes!

10. Put on your shirt!   ¡ _____ usted!

Capítulo 8
El accidente de César

Lectura

Los García han sufrido **un gran disgusto**.	a great disappointment
Un coche **ha atropellado** a su hijo mayor, César.	has struck
El accidente ha producido muchos problemas:	
unos burocráticos y otros sicológicos.	
La familia García está muy **desanimada**.	disheartened
Los padres **han tenido que enfrentarse con** el	have had to confront / to face
papeleo de la burocracia y también **han**	red tape / have
tenido que aguantar preguntas y situaciones	had to tolerate
humillantes. Como es natural, **han empezado**	have begun
a lamentarse de **la mala suerte** de la familia.	the bad luck
En estos días **han pensado** mucho en su vida	they have thought
anterior, antes de emigrar a los Estados Unidos.	
A pesar de todos los problemas que **sufrieron**	Despite / suffered
en su país, Chile **se ha transformado** en un país	has been transformed
de maravillas. El accidente de César **los ha**	has
convencido que la vida en Chile **no era tan mala**.	convinced them / was not so bad
Allí ellos **nunca habían tenido** tales problemas	never had had
con los coches. A consecuencia de este accidente	
han comenzado de nuevo las inquietudes acerca	have begun
del valor de la emigración. ¿**Hemos hecho** bien	Have we done

con venir a esta ciudad y a este país?

¿Hemos mejorado realmente nuestra situación?   Have we improved

Letreros bilingües de la ciudad

La gramática

PAST PARTICIPLES OF -AR, -ER, AND -IR VERBS

To form the past participle in Spanish remove the *ar, er,* or *ir* from the infinitive and add *ado* for *ar* verbs and *ido* for *er* and *ir* verbs:

llevar	= llev	+ **ado**	= llev**ado**	carried, taken
comer	= com	+ **ido**	= com**ido**	eaten
vivir	= viv	+ **ido**	= viv**ido**	lived

The present perfect is formed by combining the present tense of the verb **haber** (to have) with the past participle of the verb:

yo	**he**	I have			nosotros	**hemos**	we have		
tú	**has**	you have	**llevado**						**llevado**
usted	**ha**	you have	+ **comido**		ustedes	**han**	you have	+	**comido**
él	**ha**	he has	**vivido**		ellos	**han**	they have		**vivido**
ella	**ha**	she has			ellas	**han**	they have		

In English the verb *to have* functions both as an indicator of possession:

> I have the book (possession).

and as an auxiliary verb:

> I have brought the book (auxiliary + past participle).

In Spanish **tener** is used to indicate possession:

> Yo tengo el libro.   I have the book.

and **haber** is used as the auxiliary verb that precedes a past participle:

> He llevado el libro.   I have brought the book.

EJERCICIOS. Give the past participle for the following infinitives.

1. hablar   _____

2. estar   _____

3. buscar   _____

4. trabajar   _____

5. tomar   _____

6. llenar   _____

7. ganar   _____

8. solicitar   _____

9. pagar   _____

10. caminar _____

11. usar _____

12. solucionar (to solve) _____

13. cruzar (to cross) _____

14. gastar (to spend) _____

15. evitar (to avoid) _____

16. sobornar (to bribe) _____

17. ofrecer _____

18. aprender _____

19. tener _____

20. querer _____

21. poder _____

22. responder _____

23. entender _____

24. vender _____

25. omitir _____

26. venir _____

27. reunir _____

28. dormir _____

29. sentir _____

30. conducir (to drive) _____

31. advertir (to warn, to advise, to point out) _____

32. huir (to flee) _____

EJERCICIOS. Translate into Spanish the words in parenthesis.

1. (They have spent) _____ todo el dinero.

2. (I have filled out) _____ la planilla.

3. (They have taken) _____ las píldoras.

4. (We have worked) _____ en esta fábrica/factoría.

5. (She has earned) _____ mucho dinero.

6. (He has looked for) _____ a su hermana.

7. (You have avoided) _____ un lío (mess).

8. Este chófer (has been) _____ en aquella oficina.

9. Los obreros (have asked for) _____ un aumento de sueldo (a raise in salary).

10. Los maestros (have left) _____ ya.

11. Los bomberos (have warned) _____ que es peligroso (dangerous).

12. (Have you gone up?) ¿ _____ ?

13. Nuestros amigos no (have slept) _____ aquí.

14. La policía (has come) _____ demasiado tarde (too late).

15. Ellos no (have responded) _____ a nuestra llamada (to our call).

16. Los niños (have understood) _____ todo.

17. Las madres (have been able to) _____ controlar todo.

18. El garaje (has offered) _____ sus servicios.

19. El muchacho (has had) _____ un choque (accident).

20. Yo (have wanted to) _____ hacer eso (that).

THE PLUPERFECT OR PAST PERFECT

The pluperfect or past perfect is formed by combining the imperfect tense of **haber** with the past participle:*

yo	**había**	I had		nosotros	**habíamos**	we had		
tú	**habías**	you had	**llevado**					**llevado**
usted	**había**	you had	+ **comido**	ustedes	**habían**	you had	+	**comido**
él	**había**	he had	**vivido**	ellos	**habían**	they had		**vivido**
ella	**había**	she had		ellas	**habían**	they had		

* Please note: The imperfect tense of all verbs is explained on page 215.

SOME IRREGULAR PAST PARTICIPLES

abrir	to open	**abierto**	opened
decir	to say	**dicho**	said
descubrir	to discover	**descubierto**	discovered
escribir	to write	**escrito**	written
hacer	to do	**hecho**	made / done
ir	to go	**ido**	gone
morir(ue)	to die	**muerto**	died
poner	to put	**puesto**	put, placed
romper	to break	**roto**	broken
ser	to be	**sido**	been
ver	to see	**visto**	seen
volver(ue)	to return	**vuelto**	returned

The participle ending *ido* requires an accent if the stem ends in a strong vowel (*a, e,* or *o*):

caer	to fall	**caído**	fallen
leer	to read	**leído**	read
oír	to hear	**oído**	heard
traer	to bring	**traído**	brought

EJERCICIOS. Translate the present/past perfect forms in parenthesis.

1. Tú no (have seen) _____ el choque.

2. ¿Qué (had said) _____ el policía?

3. Un testigo (witness) (has called) _____ _____ una ambulancia.

4. El policía (has written) _____ un reporte largo.

5. Antes de salir (before leaving), el joven (had earned) _____ el respeto de todos.

6. ¿Dónde (have been [*estar*]) _____ tú?

7. Nosotros no (have gone) _____ allí.

8. El chófer (had lost [*perder*]) _____ su licencia.

9. César (has had) _____ mala suerte (bad luck).

10. (Have you read) ¿ _____ los documentos?

11. (Had you heard) ¿ _____ las noticias ya (already)?

12. Yo (have brought) _____ toda la información.

13. El peatón (pedestrian) (had seen) _____ el accidente.

14. Ustedes (had opened) _____ la puerta del coche.

15. Nosotros (have damaged [estropear]) _____ el motor.

EJERCICIOS. Translate the past perfect forms in parenthesis.

1. (He had received) _____ mucha medicina antes de la operación.

2. Ella (had wanted) _____ una licencia de conducir (a driver's license) antes de comenzar (before beginning).

3. Nosotros (had crossed) _____ la calle muchas veces sin ver (without seeing) mucho tránsito (traffic).

4. Tú nunca (had driven) _____ en este barrio, ¿verdad?

5. El (had not seen) _____ el problema antes de su llegada (arrival) aquí.

6. ¿Cuánto (had they spent) _____ antes de llegar aquí?

EJERCICIOS. Insert the proper form of the verb.

1. Ellos **habían hablado** con Pedro.
   (nosotros, tú, yo, ustedes)

_____

_____

_____

_____

2. No **he visto** tal cosa (such a thing).
   (tú, nosotros, el testigo, los policías)

_____

_____

_____

_____

3. Ellos **han hecho** bien.
   (yo, Pepe y Juanita, usted, los ayudantes)

   _____

   _____

   _____

   _____

4. Tú **habías llevado** los documentos a la oficina.
   (los obreros, yo, ella, ellas)

   _____

   _____

   _____

   _____

5. ¿Cuándo **ha trabajado** usted allí?
   (ustedes, Pancho, tú, él)

   _____

   _____

   _____

   _____

6. **Hemos ido** al juzgado (court).
   (yo, ellos, Mercedes y yo, Elena)

   _____

   _____

   _____

   _____

7. Usted **había ofrecido** su ayuda.
   (yo, los bomberos, el camionero [truck driver], la recepcionista)

   _____

   _____

   _____

   _____

8. Ella **ha podido** arrancar [to start] su motocicleta (motorcycle).
   (nosotros, los mecánicos, tú, yo)

   _____

   _____

   _____

   _____

9. El motorista/automovilista **había conducido** muy mal.
   (el borracho [the drunk], el viejo [the old man], tus amigos, ustedes)

   _____

   _____

   _____

   _____

10. Los hermanos Gómez no **han querido** pagar la fianza (the bail).
    (la compañía de seguros [insurance company], tus padres, nosotros, yo)

    _____

    _____

    _____

    _____

11. **¿Ha solucionado** usted el problema?
    (tu abogado, tú, ellos, el cura [the priest], yo)

    _____

    _____

    _____

    _____

12. **Habíamos gastado** mucho dinero en este asunto (this matter).
    (la compañía de seguros, las hermanas Ramírez, usted, yo)

    _____

    _____

    _____

    _____

13. **¿Has cogido** el tren número cuatro?
    (los turistas, el guardia* [the guard], nosotros, usted)

    _____

    _____

    _____

    _____

14. Ella **ha roto** el parabrisas (windshield).
    (los niños, unos vándalos (vandals), un vagabundo (vagabond)

    _____

    _____

    _____

* **el guardia** is similar to **el policía**.

15. Yo no **había hablado** con él.
    (el ladrón [the thief], las muchachas, el investigador, ella)

_____

_____

_____

_____

16. ¿**Han sobornado** ellos al guardia?
    (usted, él, los criminales, tú)

_____

_____

_____

_____

SABER vs. CONOCER

	saber	to know			conocer	to know, to be acquainted with	
yo	*sé*	nosotros	*sabemos*	yo	**conozco**	nosotros	**conocemos**
tú	*sabes*			tú	**conoces**		
usted		ustedes		usted		ustedes	
él	*sabe*	ellos	*saben*	él	**conoce**	ellos	**conocen**
ella		ellas		ella		ellas	

- **Saber** means "to know" *in the sense of having knowledge or mastery of something.*
  Yo sé la historia de México.

- **Conocer** means "to know" *in the sense of being acquainted with either a person or a thing:*
  Yo conozco al señor Gómez, pero no conozco su tienda (store).

- **Saber + infinitive** means *to know how to:*
  Ellos saben conducir.   They know how to drive.

Conocer cannot take an infinitive. It can only be followed by nouns and pronouns.

EJERCICIOS. Fill in the blank space with the appropriate form of **conocer** or **saber**.

1. Yo no _____ a María, pero _____ donde ella vive.

2. María tiene veinte años, pero todavía no _____ conducir un auto.

3. El marido de Gloria _____ a la señora Blanco.

4. ¿ _____ usted la Plaza Borinqueña que está en el Bronx?

5. Todos mis colegas (colleagues) _____ hablar español.

6. ¿ _____ ustedes cuándo viene el próximo tren?

7. Nosotros no _____ si el tren ha pasado por aquí o no.

8. ¿ _____ tú el barrio donde he vivido toda mi vida?

9. El jefe de la policía no _____ todos los detalles.

10. Mis amigos _____ quien es este señor.

11. Primero tú tienes que _____ a Marta.

EJERCICIOS. Translate into Spanish.

1. They had seen the car, but they had not seen the accident.

   _____

2. The witness had called the ambulance before (*antes de*) 5:15 a.m.

   _____

3. The police had written that he had damaged the car.

   _____

4. The pedestrians had not arrived (*llegar*) on time (*a tiempo*).

   _____

5. The driver had lost control (*control*).

   _____

VERBS THAT EXPRESS DEGREES OF OBLIGATION

Maximum:	**tener que**	+ infinitive	must, have to
	hay que	+ infinitive	one must, one has to
Moral:	**deber de†**	+ infinitive	ought to, should
Minimal:	**haber de***	+ infinitive	is/are supposed to*

EXAMPLES:

Tenemos que contestar la carta.	We must answer the letter.
Hay que contestar la carta.	One must answer the letter.
Debemos de contestar la carta.	We ought to/should answer the letter.
Hemos de contestar la carta.	We are supposed to answer the letter.

EJERCICIOS. Translate into Spanish.

A. 1. One must go there.

_____

2. We are supposed to read the instructions first (*primero*).

_____

3. You ought to sign the report later (*después*).

_____

4. They have to return at 6:00.

_____

5. The policemen (*los policías*) are to (are supposed to) call his parents.

_____

6. She is supposed to help now.

_____

7. One must sign here.

_____

8. You ought to testify (*declarar*).

_____

* In popular speech among Hispanics living in the United States **estar supuesto de** is sometimes used instead of **haber de**.

† In speech the **de** is often dropped after **deber**.

B. Translate the words in parenthesis.

1. La familia (is supposed to be) _____ en California mañana.

2. El testigo (has to) _____ firmar el reporte.

3. (One must leave) _____ a la una de la tarde.

4. (We ought to) _____ comer a las cinco.

5. (One must) _____ tomar toda la medicina.

6. (You have to) _____ considerar las ventajas (the advantages).

7. El avión (is supposed to) _____ llegar a la una.

8. (They should) _____ estar allí todo el día.

OBSERVATIONS ON THE VERB *HABER*

In previous chapters we have seen that the verb **haber** has two forms:

1. **A conjugated form** which is used as an auxiliary verb with the past participle of verbs to form the perfect tenses:

   Ellos **han** solucionado el problema.
   Nosotros **habíamos** hecho todo antes de llegar.

2. **An impersonal form** (not conjugated) which like the conjugated form appears in all tenses:

HAY	there is/there are
Hay una motocicleta en el garaje y **hay** muchos autos frente de la casa.	There is a motorcycle in the garage and there are many cars in front of the house.
HABIA	there was/there were
Había solamente una luz y por eso **había** muchos problemas en esa esquina.	There was only one light and therefore there were many problems on that corner.

3. **To form the negative** place **NO** before **hay** or **había**:

   No hay peatones por aquí. There are no pedestrians around here.

EJERCICIOS. Translate into Spanish.

1. They have gone, and there are still (*todavía*) many problems.

_____

2. He had written many letters.

_____

3. There is an accident. Has she seen the accident?

_____

4. There are no witnesses.

_____

5. There was a witness there, but there were no policemen.

_____

César, víctima de un accidente de tráfico

Diálogo

César	—	Flaco, ¿has comido ya?
Flaco	—	Sí, **Indio**, pero **chico**, ¿por qué **tanto apuro**? Hemos dicho entre las siete y las ocho y has llegado a las siete **en punto**. Tú eres más yanqui que George Washington con esta **puntualidad**.
César	—	**Basta de** lecciones, profesor Flaco. No he venido **en plan de eso**. ¿Vienes o no?
Flaco	—	Ahora voy. ¿Has traído el **disco**?
César	—	**¿Qué tú crees**?
Flaco	—	Pues, ¡vámonos!
César	—	¡Oye! ¿por qué no **damos un paseo** por el barrio? Yo todavía no conozco todos **los sitios**. Casi no he salido de esta calle. Además has prometido ir **conmigo** al club ese . . . ¡caray! ¿Cómo se llama? ¿Cuál es el nombre?
Flaco	—	No sé.
César	—	Sí, hombre, sí sabes. Creo que está en **la Quinta Avenida**.
Flaco	—	Sí, **Amigos de Betances**. **Chévere**, vámonos. Pero cuidado con **los piropos**. Aquí **los títeres** no **aguantan** eso.
César	—	Mi **viejo**, yo no soy **bobo de la aldea**. Vámonos.
Flaco	—	¡Cuidado! Viene un carro . . . ¡**Cuidado**!
César	—	¿Qué? . . .

VOCABULARIO DEL DIALOGO

indio	Indian. This nickname is common in the U.S. and in Latin America. It is used affectionately towards someone who is dark and good looking like an Indian, or it can be used to insult one who is unmannerly and socially undesirable. It does not mean that one is actually of Indian extraction.
chico	kid (in popular speech it can mean "buddy")
tanto apuro	such a hurry
en punto	on the dot
puntualidad	punctuality
basta de	enough of
en plan de eso	with that in mind

disco	record
¿Qué tú crees?	colloquial form of the more formal ¿Qué crees tú? (interrogative + subject + verb), especially popular among Puerto Ricans.
¡oye!	listen (informal command)
dar un paseo	take a stroll
el sitio	the place
conmigo	with me
la Quinta Avenida	Fifth Avenue
¡caray!	wow!
¿Cómo se llama?	What is it called?
Amigos de Betances	Social club named in honor of a Puerto Rican patriot. There are many such clubs in Hispanic neighborhoods. Some are named for patriots and some take the names of hometowns.
chévere	A widely used nonstandard term meaning "fantastic," "great," or in popular parlance, "far out."
los piropos	flirtatious remarks
los títeres	the guys (literally, it means "the puppets")
aguantar	to tolerate, to stand for
bobo de la aldea	the village idiot
mi viejo	my old buddy, pal; my old man
cuidado	careful

PREGUNTAS SOBRE EL DIALOGO

1. Cuando llega César a la casa de Flaco, ¿ha comido ya Flaco?

   _____

2. ¿A qué hora ha llegado César?

   _____

3. ¿Ha venido César con el disco?

   _____

4. ¿Ha conocido ya César todos los sitios en su barrio?

   _____

5. ¿Qué ha prometido (*prometer = to promise*) Flaco?

   _____

Vocabulario del capítulo

COGNATES OR NEAR COGNATES

el accidente
la ambulancia
anterior
burocrático/a
el control
el criminal
el escándalo
espiritual
favorito/a
el garaje
el incidente
la inmigración
la insinuación

el investigador
la lesión
la licencia
el motor
la motocicleta
el motorista/automovilista
el presidente
el reporte
el respeto
la situación
el vagabundo
el vándalo
la vigilancia

VOCABULARIO

el asunto	matter	la fábrica/factoría	factory
la autopista	turnpike	fastidioso/a	annoying
el borracho	drunk	la fianza	bail
el brazo	arm	fuerte	harsh
¡caramba!	damn, wow!	el golpe	blow
el camionero	truckdriver	humillante	humiliating
el centro	downtown	el juzgado	court
cerca	near	el ladrón	thief
el chófer	driver	lastimado/a	injured, hurt
el choque	crash, accident	el lío	mess
el colega	colleague	la llamada	call
la compañía de seguros	insurance company	la llegada	arrival
		la maravilla	wonder, marvel
el cura	the priest	el marido	husband
el desánimo	discouragement	el montón	pile
la desventaja	disadvantage	el papeleo	paperwork, red tape

160

el peatón	pedestrian	tal, tales	such
peligroso/a	dangerous	el testigo	witness
la pierna	leg	la tienda	store
predilecto/a	favorite	el tránsito	traffic
profundo/a	profound	el valor	value
próximo/a	next	la ventaja	advantage
roto/a	broken		

LOS VERBOS

advertir	to warn	enfrentarse	to confront
aguantar	to endure, to tolerate (put up with)	entender(ie)	to understand
		estropear, dañar	to spoil, to damage
		evitar	to avoid
arrancar	to start	gastar	to spend
caer	to fall	huir	to flee
atropellar	to run over, to hit	lamentar	to lament
conducir	to drive	oír	to hear
coger	to get, to grab	montar	to mount (to guard)
confrontar	to confront	morir(ue)	to die
controlar	to control	prometer	to promise
considerar	to consider	romper	to break
conocer	to know	saber	to know
cruzar	to cross	sentir(ie)	to feel
dormir(ue)	to sleep	sobornar	to bribe
declarar	to declare	solucionar	to solve
descubrir	to discover	sufrir	to suffer
emigrar	to immigrate	surgir	to arise (figurative)

FRASES

a pesar de	in spite of
dar paseos	to stroll
aumento de sueldo	pay raise
en desarrollo	developing

Vocabulario adicional

SOME COMMONLY USED COMMANDS "MANDATOS"

¡Vámonos!	Let's go!
¡Mire(n)!	Look!
¡Pare(n)!	Stop!
¡Oiga(n)!	Listen!
¡Compre(n)!	Buy!
¡Muéva(n)se!	Move!
a la derecha!	to the right!
a la izquierda!	to the left!
¡No se mueva!	Don't move!
¡Tráiga(n)me + noun!	Bring + noun!
¡Incorpóre(n)se!	Sit up!
¡Hága(n)lo!	Do it!
¡Responda(n)!	Answer!

EJERCICIOS. Translate into Spanish.

1. Stop! Look! Listen!

   _____

2. Don't move!

   _____

3. Please move to the right, then to the left (*entonces* = then).

   _____

4. Please sit up and do it!

   _____

5. Buy the medicine (*medicina*) and let's go!

   _____

Capítulo 9
El accidente: la policía lo investiga

Lectura

El **golpe** del coche **ha arrojado** a César   blow / has thrown

a **la acera**, a dos o tres metros del   the sidewalk

lugar del choque. Flaco, el amigo de César,   the place

lo ayuda y **a gritos le echa la culpa**   shouting he blames

al chófer del coche. Flaco **le grita**,   shouts at him

lo insulta, **lo amenaza. Atraído** por   threatens him. / Attracted

los gritos, **un gran gentío los ha rodeado**,   a large crowd has surrounded them

pero nadie **ha logrado** calmar a Flaco.   has succeeded

Por fin llega **un patrullero**. Dos policías   a patrol car

saltan del coche. Williams, uno de los   jump out

policías, **se acerca** a César,   approaches

mientras el otro trata de calmar a Flaco.   while

Williams calma a César y **le hace algunas**   asks him some

preguntas. La conversación **entre** el policía   questions / between

y César es en español. El otro policía

no ha tenido la misma suerte.   has not had the same luck

Flaco **está enloquecido** y casi   is enraged

no puede controlarlo. Por fin Williams   cannot control him

le grita en español: "Oye muchacho,

¡ven acá! Tu amigo te quiere hablar."

La gramática

DIRECT OBJECT PRONOUNS

me	me	**nos**	us
te	you (familiar)		
lo	him / it / you	**los**	them (masculine)
la	her / it / you	**las**	them (feminine)
le*	him	**les***	them

INDIRECT OBJECT PRONOUNS

me	to me	**nos**	to us
te	to you (familiar)		
	to him	**les**	to them
le	to her		to you (plural)
	to you		

OBJECTS OF THE VERB MAY BE EITHER NOUNS OR PRONOUNS:

I see the *criminal (noun).*   I see *him/her (pronoun).*

In English, object pronouns always follow the verb.
In Spanish, when the object is a noun, it follows the verb as in English:

Yo veo al **criminal** *(noun).*

However, when the object is a pronoun, it precedes the conjugated verb:

English: **subject + verb + object pronoun**

Spanish: **subject + object pronoun + verb**

DIRECT OBJECT PRONOUNS

Ella ve al criminal. Ella **lo** ve.   She sees the criminal. She sees **him.**
Tú has visto la carta. Tú **la** has visto.   You have seen the letter. You have seen **it.**

INDIRECT OBJECT PRONOUNS

Yo **les** doy la información.   I give the information **to them.**
Yo **les** he dado la información.   I have given the information **to them.**

* In Spain and some parts of Latin America **le** and **les** are used as direct objects to refer only to persons.

164

NEGATIVE SENTENCES

The formula for negative sentences containing object pronouns is:

English: subject + negative + verb + object pronoun

Spanish: subject + no + object pronoun + verb

Pedro no escribe las cartas.	Pedro doesn't write the letters.
Pedro no **las** escribe.	Pedro doesn't write **them**.
Pedro no **les** ha dado las cartas.	Pedro has not given the letters **to them**.

EJERCICIOS.

Substitute the direct object pronoun for the direct object noun and rewrite the sentence accordingly.

1. El lee el testimonio. El _____

2. Tú has visto al testigo (witness). Tú _____

3. El alcalde (mayor) no quiere los detalles.

   El alcalde _____

4. Los abogados preparan los trámites legales (legal proceeding).

   Los abogados _____

5. El delegado (delegate) del sindicato busca la solución. El delegado del sindicato _____

   _____

6. El sargento no ve a los trabajadores. El sargento _____

7. La pasajera (the woman passenger) ha visto el incidente.

   La pasajera _____

8. El conductor abre las puertas. El conductor _____

9. El drogadicto toma la metadona. El drogadicto _____

10. La anciana (old woman) escucha a los policías.

    La anciana _____

11. Nosotros tenemos el billete de entrada (entrance ticket).

    Nosotros _____

12. Los fiadores (bailbondsmen) no conocen a María.

    Los fiadores _____

INDIRECT OBJECT PRONOUNS AND THEIR CLARIFIERS

Whenever the indirect object is a personal noun, an indirect object pronoun must be present in the sentence. Since, as we have seen, **le** and **les** refer to more than one indirect object noun, we should mention to whom the **le** and **les** refer. The following formula may be used to clarify the reference:

subject	+	indirect object pronoun	+	verb	+	object	+	personal noun
Yo	+	**le**	+	doy	+	la carta	+	al oficial.
Tú	+	**le**	+	das	+	la carta	+	a Juan.
El	+	**les**	+	da	+	la carta	+	a María y a José.

Sometimes the indirect object is a pronoun (not a personal noun). In that case use the following clarifiers.

subject	+	indirect object pronoun	+	verb	+	object	+	pronoun clarifier
Nosotros	+	**le**	+	damos	+	la carta	+	a él / a ella / a usted.
Ellos	+	**les**	+	dan	+	la carta	+	a ellos / a ellas / a ustedes.

LOCATION OF OBJECT PRONOUNS

As we have seen, object pronouns precede the conjugated verb. **If that verb is followed by an infinitive, then the object pronouns may follow and be attached to that infinitive:**

Ella va a dar el discurso ahora.	She is going to give the speech now.
Ella va a dar**lo** ahora.	She is going to give *it* now.
or	
Ella **lo** va a dar ahora.	She is going to give *it* now.
Tú **les** tienes que hablar.	You have to speak *to them*.
or	
Tú tienes que hablar**les**.	You have to speak *to them*.

Likewise they may follow and be attached to a present participle, in which case an accent mark is required to retain the original emphasis of the participle:

Estamos leyendo el testimonio.	We are reading the affidavit.
Estamos leyéndo**lo**.	We are reading *it*.
or	
Lo estamos leyendo.	We are reading *it*.

María está dándo*le* la queja a él.   Maria is giving the complaint *to him*.

or

María **le** está dando la queja a él.   Maria is giving the complaint *to him*.

Object pronouns must follow and be attached in positive commands:

¡Fírmelo!   Sign it!
¡Hágalo!   Do it!

EJERCICIOS. Fill in the blanks with the appropriate object pronoun.

1. ¿Qué (to him) _____ da la mujer policía?

   ¿Qué (to him) _____ está dando la mujer policía?

   ¿Qué está dando _____ (to him) la mujer policía?

   ¿Qué va a dar _____ (to him) la mujer policía?

2. El policía no (to them) _____ da una multa (ticket).

   El policía no (to them) _____ está dando una multa.

   El policía no está dando _____ (to them) una multa.

   El policía no (to them) _____ tiene que dar una multa.

   El policía no tiene que dar _____ (to them) una multa.

3. Yo (to her) _____ leo la queja (complaint).

   Yo (to her) _____ estoy leyendo la queja.

   Yo estoy leyendo _____ (to her) la queja.

   Yo (to her) _____ puedo leer la queja.

   Yo puedo leer _____ (to her) la queja.

4. Tú (to me) _____ enseñas la noticia de desahucio (eviction).

   Tú (to me) _____ estás enseñando la noticia de desahucio.

   Tú estás enseñando _____ (to me) la noticia de desahucio.

   Tú (to me) _____ quieres enseñar la noticia de desahucio.

   Tú quieres enseñar _____ (to me) la noticia de desahucio.

5. La víctima (to you) _____ manda el reporte.

   La víctima (to you) _____ está mandando el reporte.

   La víctima está mandando _____ (to you) el reporte.

   La víctima (to you) _____ piensa mandar el reporte.

   La víctima piensa mandar _____ (to you) el reporte.

6. Los agentes no (to us) _____ traen las planillas.

   Los agentes no (to us) _____ están trayendo las planillas.

   Los agentes no están trayendo _____ (to us) las planillas.

   Los agentes no van a traer _____ (to us) las planillas.

   Los agentes no (to us) _____ van a traer las planillas.

7. El juez (to all of you) _____ explica el pleito (lawsuit).

   El juez (to all of you) _____ está explicando el pleito.

   El juez está explicando _____ (to all of you) el pleito.

   El juez (to all of you) _____ quiere explicar el pleito.

   El juez quiere explicar _____ (to all of you) el pleito.

8. El abogado (to them) _____ pide informes confidenciales.

   El abogado (to them) _____ está pidiendo informes confidenciales.

   El abogado está pidiendo _____ (to them) informes confidenciales.

   El abogado (to them) _____ tiene que pedir informes confidenciales.

   El abogado tiene que pedir _____ (to them) informes confidenciales.

CLARIFIERS FOR *LE* AND *LES*

As you saw on the chart on the preceding page, **le** and **les** may refer to more than one person. In order to avoid ambiguity, use the following clarifiers:

le		les	
a él	to him	a ellos	to them (masculine)
a ella	to her	a ellas	to them (feminine)
a usted	to you	a ustedes	to all of you (plural)

Yo le doy a él la información.
(I give the information to him.)

Yo les doy a ustedes los documentos.
(I give the documents to you.)

Examples:

Yo **le** doy la carta **a él.**

Tú **le** das la carta **a ella.**

Juan **le** da la carta **a usted.**

I give the letter to him.

You give the letter to her.

John gives the letter to you.

EJERCICIOS.

Rewrite the sentence inserting the appropriate indirect object pronoun.

Ejemplo:

Yo escribo las cartas ___Yo le escribo las cartas_____ (a él).

1. Tú das los documentos _____ (a ella).

2. El da la información. _____ (a ellos).

3. Nosotros leemos la noticia _____ (a usted).

4. Ellos han escrito el reporte _____ (a ustedes).

5. Yo no doy la multa _____ (a él).

6. ¿Lees tú la queja? ¿_____ (a ellas)?

7. Marta y yo damos el pleito _____ (al juez).

8. Tú nunca explicas la queja _____ (a María).

9. Ustedes no dan informes confidenciales _____ (a él).

10. ¿Lee usted la carta? _____ (al policía).

EJERCICIOS. Translate into Spanish the sentence in parenthesis.

1. ¿Qué le está haciendo usted a ella? (I am giving [to] her a ticket.)

_____

2. ¿Me puedes prestar el reporte? (Yes, I can lend the report to you *[tú form]*.)

_____

3. ¿Nos van a traer la documentación? (No, they are going to bring the documentation to him.)

_____

4. ¿Qué le ha enseñado Enrique a Pancho? (Enrique has taught [to] him to fill in the report.)

_____

5. ¿Qué le está haciendo usted a él? (I am giving [to] him a ticket.)

_____

EJERCICIOS. Translate into Spanish.

1. The policewoman brings us the prisoner.

_____

2. The social worker (*trabajador social*) tells the sergeant many things.

_____

3. My lawyer writes letters to the judge (*juez*).

_____

4. The traffic policeman (*el policía de tránsito*) gives me the report.

_____

5. He explains the eviction notice (*desahucio*) to them.

_____

6. We give (*poner*) the ticket (*la multa*) to her.

_____

7. I bring the complaints (*las quejas*) to them.

_____

8. You (*plural*) explain the report to him.

_____

9. The agents are going to send the lawsuit (*el pleito*) to them (*the women*).

_____

10. He is giving the documents to you (*plural*).

_____

COMBINING DIRECT AND INDIRECT OBJECT PRONOUNS

In English the direct object precedes the indirect object:

He gives the books to me.   He gives *them* to me.

In Spanish the opposite is true. The indirect object precedes the direct object:

El me da los libros.   El me *los* da.

EJERCICIOS. Translate the object pronoun combinations in parenthesis.

1. Los fiadores me dan el anuncio.

   Los fiadores (give it to me) _____

2. El juez nos lee los detalles (details).

   El juez (reads them to us) _____

3. Las trabajadoras sociales no me dicen la verdad.

   Las trabajadoras sociales (do not tell it to me) _____

4. El abogado nos explica el caso.

   El abogado (explains it to us) _____

5. Los testigos me pueden dar testimonios (affidavits).

   Los testigos (can give them to me) _____

6. El detective nos tiene que dar los documentos confidenciales.

   El detective (has to give them to us) _____

Whenever *le* and *les* precede *lo, la, los* and *las,*
le and *les* become <u>se</u>

Indirect		*Direct*				*Direct*
le/les	+	lo/los	becomes	*se*	+	lo/los
le/les	+	la/las	becomes	*se*	+	la/las

Tú siempre les escribes cartas a tus amigos.   You always write letters to your friends.

Tú siempre *se las* escribes.   You alway write them to them.

Remember: In Spanish, the indirect object goes *before* the direct object.

EJERCICIOS. Translate the object pronoun combinations in parenthesis.

1. El no quiere darle la información.

   El (does not want to give it to her) _____

2. El delegado del sindicato prefiere darles los documentos mañana.

   El delegado del sindicato (prefers to give them to them tomorrow) _____

   _____

3. Los drogadictos les dicen la verdad.

   Los drogadictos (tell it to them) _____

4. María va a leerle las noticias.

   María (is going to read them to him) _____

5. El político le da la información.

   El político (gives it to her) _____

6. Nosotros no queremos darles la queja ahora.

   Nosotros (do not want to give it to them now) _____

GUSTAR

In Spanish, when you want to say that you like something or somebody you have to use the verb **gustar**, which translates as *to be appealing* or *to be pleasing*.

In English, when we use the verbs *to be appealing* or *to be pleasing* we include an indirect object in the sentence:

subject	+	is/are pleasing is/are appealing	+	indirect object pronoun

The book is appealing to us and the films are appealing to you.

The Spanish verb **gustar** also requires an indirect object:

indirect object pronoun	+	*gusta* + singular subject *gustan* + plural subject

Nos *gusta* el libro y **te *gustan*** las películas.

We like the book and you like the movies. [the book is pleasing **to us** and the movies are pleasing **to you**]

NEGATIVES

Negatives are expressed by placing **no** before the indirect object pronoun.

No nos *gusta* el libro y **no te** *gustan* las películas.   We don't like the book and you don't like the movies.

USE OF CLARIFIERS WITH *LE* AND *LES*

As was mentioned earlier, clarifiers are needed when using **le** and **les**. In sentences using **gustar** the clarifier may be placed in different locations, depending on the degree of emphasis desired:

*A **él le*** gusta la idea, pero ***a ella*** no ***le*** gusta el plan.

Le gusta ***a él*** la idea, pero no ***le*** gusta ***a ella*** el plan.

Le gusta la idea ***a él***, pero no ***le*** gusta el plan ***a ella*** *(usually in questions)*.

EJERCICIOS. Insert the proper form of **gustar**.

1. No me **gustan** estas soluciones.

   (este trabajo, estas ideas, sus acciones, este plan)

   _____

   _____

   _____

   _____

2. Me **gusta** este tipo de investigación.

   (sus ideas, la justicia, la clemencia, el juicio)

   _____

   _____

   _____

   _____

3. Te **gustan** los cuchillos (knives).

   (la comida criolla, este caso, las noticias, la verdad)

   _____

   _____

   _____

   _____

4. ¿A él le **gusta** esta llanta (tire)? *or* ¿Le gusta a él esta llanta?
   (las armas modernas [modern firearms], la casa de Juan, ese volante (steering wheel)

   _____

   _____

   _____

   _____

5. No nos **gusta** la muchedumbre (the crowd).
   (esta pesquisa [investigation], los arreglos, esos volantes)

   _____

   _____

   _____

   _____

6. A ellas les **gusta** mucho el trabajo.
   (los trabajos, los planes de usted, la pistola)

   _____

   _____

   _____

   _____

EJERCICIOS. Translate into Spanish.

1. I like your ideas but I don't like your plan.

   _____

2. Do you like the arrangements?

   _____

3. He does not like the crowd.

   _____

4. We don't like the complaint.

_____

5. They like the work.

_____

If the name or title of a specific person is mentioned use the following formula:

indirect object noun	+	indirect object pronoun	+	verb	+	subject
A Carlos		le		gusta		el juicio.
Al profesor no		le		gustan		los juicios
A los oficiales		les		gusta		el juicio.

When asking a question the **indirect object noun** may follow the **subject.**

¿Le gusta el juicio a Carlos?

¿Les gusta el juicio a los oficiales?

_____
gustar + infinitive
_____

When **gustar** combines with an **infinitive** use only **gusta + infinitive.**

A Juanita le **gusta juzgar** a otros.   Juanita likes to judge others.

No nos **gusta trabajar** aquí.   We don't like to work here.

EJERCICIOS. Translate into Spanish.

1. They like to read the details.

_____

2. We do not like to fill out questionnaires.

_____

3. María and Raúl like the main plan (*el plan principal*).

_____

4. Does the chief like the report?

_____

5. I like to tell the truth.

_____

6. John likes to bring the gun.

_____

7. Do you like your job?

_____

8. The bailbondsman (*el fiador*) likes the business (*el negocio*).

_____

9. Do you like to live in this city?

_____

10. We do not like your attitude (*su actitud*).

_____

OTHER VERBS THAT TAKE INDIRECT OBJECT PRONOUNS

Other verbs that function the same way as **gustar** are:

parecer	to seem, to appear
quedar	to remain, to have left
doler(ue)	to cause pain, to hurt
faltar	to be lacking
interesar	to be of interest

Remember the formula:

Indirect Object Pronoun +	*3rd person singular/plural of verb—determined by the subject* +	*Subject*
me	gusta	el pleito (the lawsuit)
	gustan	los pleitos
te	queda	un dólar
	quedan	muchos dólares
le	duele a él	el hombro (the shoulder)
	duelen a él	los hombros
nos	parece buena	la idea
	parecen buenas	las ideas
les	falta a ellos	el dinero
	faltan a ellos	cinco dólares
les	interesa a ustedes	la huella digital (fingerprint)
	interesan a ustedes	las huellas digitales

EJERCICIOS. Insert the proper form of the verb.

1. Nos **quedan** muchas planillas.
   (poco trabajo, varios testimonios, poca comida)

   _____

   _____

   _____

   _____

2. Me **queda** poco dinero.
   (muchas ideas, el plan principal, veinte dólares, mucho tiempo)

   _____

   _____

   _____

   _____

3. ¿Le **duele** a usted la espalda (your back)?
   (los ojos, la cabeza, los pies [feet], el pecho [chest])

   _____

   _____

   _____

   _____

4. ¿Te **parece** útil el libro?
   (difíciles los libros, fácil la investigación, bueno el trabajo,
   interesantes los trámites legales, difícil la acción judicial)

   _____

   _____

   _____

   _____

5. Nos **falta** tiempo (the time).
   (los comestibles, un agente de inmigración,
   un presupuesto adecuado [an adequate budget])

   _____

   _____

   _____

6. No les **interesa** a ellas el pleito.
   (los detalles, la materia, los informes confidenciales, el anuncio)

   _____

   _____

   _____

   _____

EJERCICIOS. Answer in the affirmative or negative as indicated.

1. ¿Le gusta a usted su apodo (nickname)?

   Sí, _____

2. ¿Les quedan a ustedes cigarrillos?

   No, _____

3. ¿Le gusta a usted el alcohol?

   Sí, _____

4. ¿Les queda a ustedes mucho dinero?

   No, _____

5. ¿Le parecen a usted prácticos los cinturones de seguridad (safety belts)?

   Sí, _____

6. ¿Les duelen los pies (your feet)?

   Sí, _____

7. ¿Le quedan a usted dos alternativas (alternatives)?

   No, _____

8. ¿Le interesa a usted la clemencia?

   Sí, _____

9. ¿Les falta a ustedes tiempo para terminar estos trámites legales?

   No, _____

10. ¿Le gustan a usted los anuncios públicos?

    No, _____

11. ¿Les parece a ustedes lógica (logical) la ley?

    Sí, _____

12. ¿Le duele a usted el estómago (stomach)?

    No, _____

EJERCICIOS. Translate into Spanish.

1. They have many cases left, but they do not have time.

   _____

2. My stomach and my head hurt.

   _____

3. Those laws seem adequate to us.

   _____

4. The detective is interested in the details.

   _____

5. We have only (*solamente*) two patrol cars left.

   _____

Diálogo

César — Por favor me duele mucho la cara y tengo dolores muy fuertes en el brazo derecho . . .

Williams — Do you speak English?

César — ¿Inglés? No, no hablo inglés. El muchacho ese (*él indica con el dedo*) sí, habla inglés . . . Flaco, **¡háblale en inglés!**

Williams — Está bien, está bien. Hablo español; no hay problema. Soy el policía Jim Williams del **cuartel** setenta y cinco y . . .

César — ¡Señor policía! ¡Por favor!, ¡déme algo para el dolor y por favor déme un poco de agua! Tengo mucha sed.

Williams — "Jack, bring me some water!" Joven, ¡no se mueva! Mi compañero le va a traer agua. ¡No se preocupe! ya viene la ambulancia. **Mientras** tanto necesito alguna información. ¿Su nombre, por favor?

César — Me llamo César García Schneider, pero mire señor, me parece que todavía estoy sangrando y tengo mucho dolor en la cara y en el brazo, ¿**son necesarias estas preguntas**?

Williams — Sí, no hay muchas. Quiero hacerle dos o tres más. ¿Es **ciudadano** norteamericano?

César — No señor, por favor, ahora me duelen los dedos de la mano derecha. ¡Ay, qué dolor!

Williams — Tengo solamente una pregunta más, ¿Tiene familia o parientes aquí?

César — Sí, vivo con mi familia en aquel apartamento (*él indica con la mano izquierda donde vive*) y mire, señor, mi mamá habla inglés muy bien y mi papá trabaja en el hospital Wellington.

Williams — ¿Los puedo llamar ahora?

César — No sé. Creo que sí. Sí, claro mi mamá debe estar en casa ahora.

Williams — Ya está la ambulancia . . . todo está bien. Perdone por las preguntas.

VOCABULARIO DEL DIALOGO

¡Háblale en inglés!	Speak to him/her in English! (familiar command form)
cuartel	police station
mientras tanto	meanwhile
¿Son necesarias estas preguntas?	Are these questions necessary?
ciudadano	citizen

PREGUNTAS SOBRE EL DIALOGO

1. ¿Qué le duele a César?

_____

2. ¿Dónde siente dolores fuertes?

_____

3. ¿De qué cuartel es el policía Williams?

_____

4. ¿Qué pide César?

_____

5. ¿Qué va a llegar para llevarle al hospital?

_____

Vocabulario del capítulo

COGNATES OR NEAR COGNATES

la acción
el adversario
el alcohol
la alternativa
el apartamento
el cigarrillo
la clemencia
el conductor
confidencial
el detective
el estómago
la idea

la identificación
la información
la investigación
la justicia
la materia
el oficial
la pistola
el plan
el sargento
el senador
la solución
el testimonio

VOCABULARIO

la acera	sidewalk	hacia	towards
la actitud	attitude	el informe	report
adecuado	adequate	el juez	judge
el adversario	adversary	el juicio	judgment, decision
el alcalde	mayor	la ley	law
la ampliación	enlargement	el mandamiento	warrant
la anciana	old woman	la metadona	methadone
el anuncio	announcement	el metro	meter
el apodo	nickname	la muchedumbre	crowd
el arma	firearm	la multa	fine
el arreglo	rule, arrangement	el negocio	business
el bodeguero	grocer	el oficinista	clerk
la cabeza	head	el parabrisas	windshield
el caso	case	el pasajero	passenger
los comestibles	food	el patrullero	patrol car
el cuchillo	knife	la pesquisa	investigation
el delegado	delegate	el pie	foot
el desahucio	eviction	la planilla	application, list, ticket
el discurso	speech	el pleito	law suit
el drogadicto	drug addict	el presupuesto	budget
el fiador	bailbondsman	principal	main
fuerte	strong	el prisionero	prisoner

182

la queja	complaint	útil	useful
el sindicato	labor union	la ventanilla	window (ticket office, bank teller, etc.)
la tablilla	bulletin board		
el testamento	will	el volante	steering wheel
el trámite	the carrying on of business		

VERBOS

acercarse	to approach	lograr	to succeed
acomodar	to make comfortable	mentir	to lie
agarrar	to grab	prestar	to lend
amenazar	to threaten	rodear	to surround
arrojar	to throw	saltar de + direct object	to jump out, to dash out
calmar	to calm down		
controlar	to control	sangrar	to bleed
echar la culpa	to blame	tranquilizar	to calm down
indicar	to indicate		
insultar	to insult		

FRASES

la acción judicial	legal suit
el agente de inmigración	immigration agent
el agente de seguros	insurance agent
el billete de entrada	entrance ticket
el cinturón de seguridad	safety belt
estar como enloquecido	to be beside oneself
la huella digital	fingerprint
el policía de tránsito	traffic policeman
por fin	finally
las tarifas legales	legal proceedings
la tarjeta de residencia	residency card
el testigo ocular	eyewitness

Vocabulario adicional

SOME COMMONLY USED "MANDATOS"

¡No lo/la toque(n)!	Don't touch it/him/her!
¡Empuje(n)!	Push!

ACUESTESE — *LIE DOWN*

¡Acuéste(n)lo/la	Place it/him/her
en el suelo!	on the floor (ground)!
en la cama!	on the bed!
en la camilla!	on the stretcher!
¡Déje(n)lo/la!	Let it/him/her go! Drop it/him/her!
¡Véa(n)lo/la!	See it/him/her!
¡Véa(n)los/las!	See them (*masculine*)/them (*feminine*)
¡Enséñe(n)melo/la!	Show it/him/her to me!
¡Quéde(n)se aquí!	Stay here!
¡Explíque(n)lo/la!	Explain it (*masculine/feminine*)
¡Préste(n)me . . . !	Lend me . . . !
¡Levante(n)	Raise
las manos!	your hands!
los pies!	your feet!
las piernas!	your legs!
la cabeza!	your head!

EJERCICIOS. Translate into Spanish.

1. Please, don't touch it!   ¡_____ usted!

2. Push!   ¡_____ ustedes!

3. Please place him on the bed!   ¡_____ usted!

4. Please place her on the ground!   ¡_____ ustedes!

5. Please place her on the stretcher!   ¡_____ usted!

6. Drop it!   ¡_____ usted!

7. Show it to me!   ¡_____ usted!

8. Stay here, please!   ¡_____ ustedes!

9. Please raise your hands!   ¡_____ ustedes!

10. Explain it (*feminine*)   ¡_____ usted!

11. See him tomorrow!   ¡_____ ustedes!

12. See them (*masc.*) tomorrow!   ¡_____ usted!

Capítulo 10
César ingresa en el hospital

Lectura

¡Qué lío! La policía **no ha podido** ponerse *What a mess! / has not been able*
en contacto con los padres de César. No
están en la casa. Ellos estaban casualmente *were*
muy cerca del **lugar** del accidente, **adonde** *place / where*
se han acercado atraídos por la sirena de *they have approached*
la ambulancia y por **los gritos** de la gente. *shouts*
Mientras tanto, en la ambulancia, el médico *Meanwhile*
está completamente frustrado porque no puede
comunicarse con César porque **no sabe hablar** *does not know how to speak*
español. César **se siente muy mal** porque *feels very bad*
tiene muchos **dolores** y no puede tampoco *pains*
explicarle nada al médico. César no habla
inglés. **Quiere levantarse**, pero no puede; *He wants to get up*
quiere mover **el brazo** y no puede. **Como** el *his arm / Like*
médico, César se siente frustrado por el
problema del idioma. **Por fin**, llega la *Finally*
ambulancia a **la sala de emergencia**. César *emergency room*
está muy pálido y **casi no puede moverse**. *can hardly move*
Lo sacan de la ambulancia y **lo llevan** a una *They take him out / carry him*
sala que está dividida por **cortinas amarillas**. *yellow curtains.*
El está inmovilizado.

Finalmente, él **se queda** tranquilo y **murmurando**   remains / mumbling

en español, empieza a **dormirse. Después** de unos   to fall asleep / After

minutos entra una enfermera y **le dice suavemente**:   softly says to him

Me llamo Jean Esposito. Hablo un poco de español.   my name is

Si hablas despacio, podemos **entendernos**.   If you speak slowly /
understand each other

César en la sala de emergencia

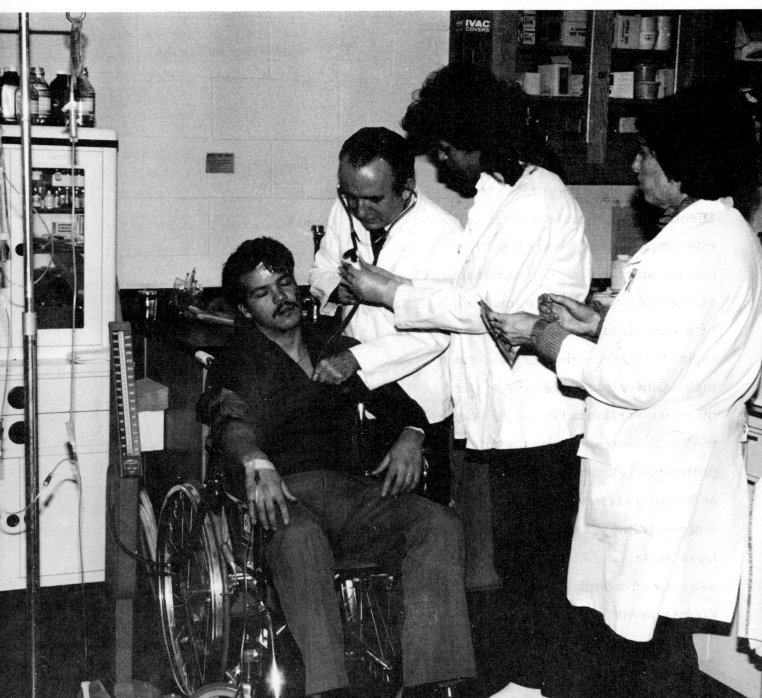

La gramática

Whenever the object pronoun of a verb refers to the same person as the subject of that verb, we have a reflexive sentence. The object pronoun is then called a reflexive pronoun.

REFLEXIVE PRONOUNS

me	myself	**nos**	ourselves
te	yourself (familiar)		
	himself		themselves (masculine)
	herself	**se**	themselves (feminine)
se	yourself		yourselves (masculine/feminine)
	itself/oneself		

REFLEXIVE VERBS

A verb whose object pronoun refers to the same person as the subject is a reflexive verb.

(yo)	**me** baño	I bathe (myself)	(nosotros)	**nos** bañamos	we bathe (ourselves)
(tú)	**te** bañas	you (fam.) bathe yourself			
usted		you bathe (yourself)	ustedes		you bathe (yourselves)
él	**se** baña	he bathes (himself)	ellos	**se** bañan	they bathe (themselves)
ella		she bathes (herself)	ellas		they bathe (themselves)

PLACEMENT OF REFLEXIVE PRONOUNS

Like the direct and indirect object pronouns, reflexive pronouns precede the conjugated verb:

Me baño.	I bathe.
Me he bañado./**Me** había bañado.	I have bathed./I had bathed.
Me voy a bañar.	I am going to bathe.
Me tengo que bañar.	I have to bathe.
Me estoy bañando.	I am bathing.

or they may follow and be attached to the dependent infinitive and the present participle.

Voy a bañar**me**.	I am going to bathe.
Tengo que bañar**me**.	I have to bathe.
Estoy bañándo**me**.	I am bathing.

They will always follow and be attached to positive commands. An accent mark is placed over the vowel in the syllable which is accented before the addition of the pronoun in order to retain the original emphasis .

¡Báñe**se**!
¡Cálmen**se**!

EJERCICIOS. Fill in the blank space with the appropriate form of the indicated verb:

preocuparse (to worry)

1. Yo no _____ mucho ahora.

2. Ella no puede _____ todos los días.

3. Algunos hipertensos _____ demasiado (too much).

4. ¿Por qué _____ ustedes?

5. Ella no va a _____ porque todo está bajo control (under control).

6. Nosotros _____ por nuestro trabajo.

7. Tú _____ cuando tienes una erupción (rash).

portarse (to behave)

1. Las niñas nunca _____ bien los domingos.

2. El inválido _____ bien contigo (with you [familiar]).

3. Aquí nadie _____ bien.

4. Ellas quieren _____ bien, pero muchas veces

   no pueden; y _____ mal (badly).

5. Nosotros _____ como santos con la fisioterapista.

casarse (to get married)*

1. Yo voy a _____ la semana que viene (next week).

2. El _____ cada cuatro años.

3. ¿ _____ ustedes?

4. ¿Cuándo _____ tú?

5. Nosotros _____ el domingo.

* See explanation of reciprocal verbs, later on in this chapter.

calmarse (to calm oneself)

1. El herido (the injured man) no _____ .

2. Usted tiene que _____ ahora; no va a pasar nada.

3. No puedo _____ porque no puedo ver.

4. Con el tranquilizante ellos van a _____ .

5. Nosotros _____ cuando vemos al guardia.

desmayarse (to faint, pass out)

1. Yo _____ al ver un cuerpo mutilado.

2. La paciente del cuarto piso _____ mucho.

3. En general los médicos no _____ al ver la sangre (blood).

4. Tú _____ a veces.

5. Si usted no come, va a _____ .

MORE REFLEXIVES

acostarse(ue)	to go to bed		
me	acuesto	nos	acostamos
te	acuestas		
se		se	
se	acuesta	se	acuestan
se		se	

sentarse(ie)	to sit (oneself) down		
me	siento	nos	sentamos
te	sientas		
se		se	
se	sienta	se	sientan
se		se	

irse	to leave		
me	voy	nos	vamos
te	vas		
se		se	
se	va	se	van
se		se	

vestirse(i)	to dress (oneself)		
me	visto	nos	vestimos
te	vistes		
se		se	
se	viste	se	visten
se		se	

sentirse(ie) to feel			
me siento	nos	sentimos	
te sientes			
se	se		
se siente	se	sienten	
se	se		

ponerse to put on, to become*			
me pongo	nos	ponemos	
te pones			
se	se		
se pone	se	ponen	
se	se		

darse cuenta de to realize			
me doy cuenta	nos	damos cuenta	
te das cuenta			
se	se		
se da cuenta	se	dan cuenta	
se	se		

acordarse de (ue) to remember			
me acuerdo	nos	acordamos	
te acuerdas			
se	se		
se acuerda	se	acuerdan	
se	se		

EJERCICIOS. Fill in the appropriate form of the verb.

acordarse(ue) de (to remember)

1. Yo no _____ nada.

2. Nosotros _____ ella.

3. Ellas _____ Paco y María.

4. El boticario (druggist) _____ nosotros.

5. El cura no puede _____ ellos.

6. Tú _____ la casa roja.

darse cuenta de (to realize)

1. El sicólogo _____ lo que (what) ha pasado.

2. Nosotros _____ que él tiene que salir mañana.

3. Yo _____ que usted es mi amigo.

4. El contador del hospital (hospital accountant) _____ que tiene que cobrar más ahora.

5. Tú y ella no _____ que hay muy poco tiempo.

* See section on "to become" later on in this chapter.

vestirse(i) (to dress)

1. Las muchachas _____ a la moda (in style).

2. Yo nunca _____ así (like that).

3. Nosotras _____ de negro (in black).

4. Ellos no saben _____

5. En las clínicas _____ de blanco.

irse (to leave)

1. Yo _____ de aquí.

2. ¿Cuándo _____ tú?

3. El cirujano (surgeon) _____ de la sala de conferencias (from the conference room).

4. Nosotros _____ pronto.

5. ¿Por qué _____ ustedes?

sentarse (to sit oneself down)

1. ¿Por qué _____ tú allí?

2. Yo no _____ en esta silla.

3. Ella _____ en el sofá.

4. Las niñas _____ en el suelo (on the ground).

5. Nosotros siempre _____ en la primera fila (the first row).

ponerse (to put on, to become [mental, emotional, or physical condition])

1. ¿Por qué _____ (tú) tan triste (sad)?

2. La mujer _____ pálida (pallid) cuando está enferma.

3. Nosotros _____ la ropa (clothing).

4. Ustedes siempre _____ contentos (happy) los fines de semana (weekends).

5. Los enfermos del hígado (those who have liver disease) _____ amarillos.

sentirse (to feel)

1. En el hospital nadie _____ cómodo (comfortable).

2. Ellos siempre _____ mal.

3. Yo no _____ bien.

4. Ella _____ incómoda.

5. Nosotros _____ responsables (responsible).

EJERCICIOS. Insert the appropriate form of the verb.

1. ¿A qué hora **te acuestas** durante la semana?
   (ustedes, nosotros, Elena, tu hermana)

   _____

   _____

   _____

   _____

2. Las terapistas no **se sientan** en aquellas sillas.
   (la ayudante, el paciente, Pablo y yo, tú)

   _____

   _____

   _____

   _____

3. ¿Cómo **se sienten** ustedes hoy?
   (tú, los pacientes, la terapista, nosotras)

   _____

   _____

   _____

   _____

4. **Me pongo** los anteojos (glasses) cuando **tengo** que leer algo.
   (los jóvenes, Ligia y Celia, tus amigos, ustedes)

   _____

   _____

   _____

   _____

5. Ellas **se van** en seguida (right away).
   (los médicos, la víctima, yo, tú)

   _____

   _____

   _____

   _____

6. **Nos vestimos** elegantemente para esta ocasión.
   (los convidados (guests), Juan Carlos, tus padres, yo)

   _____

   _____

   _____

   _____

7. Usted no **se da** cuenta de todo lo que está pasando (all that is happening).
   (los sordos [deaf people], el director, tú, nosotros)

   _____

   _____

   _____

   _____

8. El **se acuerda** de todo lo que ha pasado.
    (yo, tú, el ayudante y yo, ustedes)

    _____

    _____

    _____

    _____

9. **Me he bañado** esta mañana (this morning).
    (ustedes, tú, nosotros, el joven)

    _____

    _____

    _____

    _____

10. Los niños **van a acostarse** temprano.
    (el convidado (guest), yo, la anciana [old woman], nosotros)

    _____

    _____

    _____

    _____

As in English, many verbs in Spanish can be used either with or without a reflexive meaning:

levantar (to raise, lift)	Levanto al enfermo.	I lift the sick man.
levantarse (to get [oneself] up)	Me levanto a las cinco y media.	I get up at 5:30.
llamar (to call someone)	Ellos llaman a la policía.	They call the police.
llamarse (to be named)	El sargento se llama Roberto Ruiz.	The sergeant's name is Robert Ruiz.
lavar (to wash)	Lavamos los platos.	We wash the dishes.
lavarse (to wash [oneself])	Nos lavamos todos los días.	We wash (ourselves) every day.
despertar(ie) (to wake up, to awaken somebody)	¿Despiertas tú a Enrique todas las mañanas.	Do you wake up Enrique every morning.
despertarse(ie) (to wake up, to awaken oneself)	Tú te despiertas a las once los domingos.	You wake up at eleven on Sundays.

194

EJERCICIOS. Insert the appropriate form of the verb.

1. Pedro **se despierta** a las ocho y luego **despierta** a Juan.
   (mis primos, yo, Juan, nosotros)

   _____

   _____

   _____

   _____

2. Tú **te levantas** a las cinco de la mañana y a las cinco y media **levantas** a los otros.
   (mis padres, yo, nosotros, usted)

   _____

   _____

   _____

   _____

3. El **se llama** Alejandro Rodríguez y **llama** por teléfono todos los días.
   (yo, mi cliente, tú, su hermano mayor)

   _____

   _____

   _____

   _____

4. La enfermera **se levanta** temprano.
   (el interno, mi hermano y yo, tú, ustedes)

   _____

   _____

   _____

   _____

5. Nosotros **nos despertamos** a las ocho y a las nueve **despertamos** al niño.
(las madres, Susana, tú, yo)

_____

_____

_____

_____

Some Spanish verbs, however, change their meaning when they are used reflexively:

parar (to stop)	El tren para aquí.	The train stops here.
pararse (to stand up)	Todos **se paran** cuando entra el juez.	Everyone stands when the judge enters.
dormir(ue) (to sleep)	El duerme todo el día.	He sleeps all day.
dormirse (to fall asleep)	El **se duerme** cuando mira la televisión.	He falls asleep when he watches television.
quedar (to agree on)	En esto quedamos.	On that we agree.
quedarse (to remain)	**Nos quedamos** en casa.	We remain at home.
ver (to see)	El ve a Juan.	He sees John.
verse (to appear, to look)	Juan **se ve** bien.	John appears/looks well.

MAS EJERCICIOS. Insert the appropriate form of the verb.

1. Ellos nunca **se quedan** aquí toda la noche.
   (yo, tú, nosotros, tú y ella)

_____

_____

_____

_____

2. Yo **me paro** aquí porque el ómnibus **para** aquí.
   (los huérfanos [the orphans], usted, tú, nosotros)

_____

_____

_____

_____

3. Cuando el paralítico **se duerme** en esta silla, **duerme** todo el día.
   (yo, los gemelos [the twins], tú, nosotros)

   _____

   _____

   _____

   _____

4. Usted **se ve** bien los lunes.
   (tú, ustedes, el hipocondríaco (hypochondriac), la paciente)

   _____

   _____

   _____

   _____

5. Ellos **se quedan** en casa una semana más.
   (ella, yo, nosotras, tú)

   _____

   _____

   _____

   _____

Other verbs can only be used reflexively:

atreverse a	(to dare)	El **se atreve** a hacer todo.	He dares to do all.
alegrarse de	(to be happy)	**Nos alegramos** de estar aquí.	We are happy to be here.
suicidarse	(to commit suicide)	¿**Te** vas a **suicidar** por ella?	Are you going to commit suicide over her?
quejarse de	to complain about)	Ella **se queja** del servicio.	She complains about the service.

EJERCICIOS. Insert the appropriate form of the verb.

1. **Yo me alegro** mucho de terminar pronto.
   (los trabajadores, el radiólogo, tú, nosotras)

   _____

   _____

   _____

   _____

2. **Nos atrevemos** a discutir (to argue) el **asunto** (the matter) con el médico.
   (yo, tú, ellos, usted)

   _____

   _____

   _____

   _____

3. ¿**Se queja** usted mucho?
   (mi amigo y yo, los neuróticos, tú, nosotros)

   _____

   _____

   _____

   _____

4. Algunas personas creen que los neuróticos **se suicidan** cuando están deprimidos.
   (el sicótico, los alcohólicos, la gente anormal [the abnormal people], los drogadictos)

   _____

   _____

   _____

   _____

EJERCICIOS. Select the appropriate verb and fill in the blank space.

levantar/levantarse (to raise, lift/get up)

1. Nosotros siempre _____ a las ocho.

2. Primero yo _____ la mano (my hand), luego contesto la pregunta.

3. El _____ el pie derecho (the right foot),

   luego el pie izquierdo (the left foot); y finalmente él _____.

acostar(ue)/acostarse(ue) (to put to bed/to put oneself to bed)

1. Mi madre _____ a mi hermanita (little sister) a las siete.

2. Ellos _____ muy tarde el sábado por la noche (Saturday night).

despertar(ie)/despertarse(ie) (to wake up somebody/to wake up [oneself])

1. ¿A qué hora _____ usted a los gemelos?

2. ¿A qué hora _____ ellos?

dormir(ue)/dormirse(ue) (to sleep/to fall asleep)

1. Tú puedes _____ ocho o diez horas.

2. Tu esposo _____ fácilmente (easily).

lavar/lavarse (to wash/to wash [oneself])

1. La madre _____ la ropa del niño.

2. Ustedes _____ las manos antes de comer, ¿verdad?

llamar/llamarse (to call someone/to be named)

1. Tú _____ Pepe el gordo (Fat Joe).

2. Nosotros no podemos _____ de la oficina ahora.

parar/pararse   (to stop/to stand up)

1. Los taxis no _____ en esta esquina (corner).

2. El camillero no puede _____ en la ambulancia.

poner/ponerse   (to put, to put on, to become)

1. Yo _____ toda mi energía en mi trabajo.

2. ¿Por qué no _____ usted la chaqueta?

quedar/quedarse   (to agree/to remain)

1. Ustedes _____ en ir a ver a Juan.

2. Los inválidos van a _____ en el sanatorio.

sentar(ie)/sentarse(ie)   (to seat someone/to seat oneself)

1. La enfermera _____ al paciente en la silla de ruedas (wheelchair).

2. Como tengo la pierna rota (a broken leg), no puedo _____

ver/verse   (to see/to appear, to look)

1. Las enfermas _____ al ginecólogo cada dos meses.

2. Ellas _____ muy cansadas.

OTHER USES OF THE REFLEXIVE PRONOUN *SE*

The reflexive pronoun **se** frequently serves as a substitute for the passive voice, especially when the agent or the doer of the action is not expressed or when the subject is a thing:

Active Voice

Ellos venden la revista *Tiempo* en esta tienda.   They sell *Time* magazine in this store.

Substitute for Passive Voice – Singular Subject

La revista *Tiempo* **se vende** en esta tienda.   *Time* magazine **is sold** in this store.

Active Voice

Ellos venden periódicos en esta tienda.　　They sell newspapers in this store.

Substitute for Passive Voice – Plural Subject

Se venden periódicos en esta tienda.　　Newspapers **are sold** in this store.

Se is also used to express the impersonal *one, they,* or *you:*

Se dice que es horrible.　　They say/One says that it is horrible.

No **se** puede fumar aquí.　　One/You cannot smoke here.

EJERCICIOS. Fill in the appropriate form of the verb.

1. Aquí (is spoken) _____ español.

   En esta librería (bookstore) no (are sold) _____ estos libros.

2. Esta farmacia (pharmacy) vende maquillaje (make-up).

   En esta farmacia (is sold) _____ maquillaje.

3. El vendedor vende sillas de ruedas.

   En este negocio (are sold) _____ sillas de ruedas.

4. El cirujano tiene muchos escalpelos (scalpels).

   En este quirófano (operating room) (are seen) _____ muchos escalpelos.

5. (One needs) _____ la autorización de los padres en esta clínica.

6. El sótano (basement) es donde (are found) _____ tanques de oxígeno.

7. ¿Habla usted inglés? No, aquí (is spoken) _____ francés.

8. En los pasillos de los grandes hospitales metropolitanos

   (are spoken) _____ muchos idiomas.

9. ¿Qué hacen en el laboratorio de rayos-x? En el laboratorio

   (are made) _____ placas (plates).

10. (One sees) _____ mucho sufrimiento en una sala de emergencia.

11. (One does not make/you do not make) _____ ruido en un hospital.

EJERCICIOS. Answer in Spanish.

1. ¿A qué hora se levanta Ud. durante la semana?

_____

2. ¿A qué hora se acuesta Ud. los sábados por la noche?

_____

3. ¿Cuántas veces a la semana se baña Ud.?

_____

4. ¿Qué tipo de ropa se pone cuando hace calor?

_____

5. ¿Se acuerda Ud. de todo lo que (that) ha aprendido?

_____

6. ¿Hasta qué hora se queda usted en la clase de español?

_____

7. ¿Cuándo tiene que sentarse a la mesa?

_____

8. ¿A qué hora se viste usted?

_____

9. Antes de entrar en la clase, ¿se preocupa Ud. mucho? ¿Por qué?

_____

10. ¿Va usted a portarse bien mañana? ¿Se porta bien todos los días?

_____

11. ¿Se queja usted mucho?

_____

12. ¿A qué hora se despierta usted el domingo?

_____

13. ¿Cómo se siente usted hoy?

_____

14. ¿Cómo se llama su profesor/a de español?

_____

15. ¿Se ha desmayado usted alguna vez en su vida?

_____

RECIPROCAL ACTION

The reflexive pronouns can be used to show a reciprocal action when the subject is plural. This construction corresponds to the English "each other" or "one another":

Ellos se escriben.	They write one another/each other.
No nos hablamos todas las noches.	We don't speak to each other/one another every night.
Juan y María se casan hoy.	John and Mary are getting married (are marrying each other) today.

EJERCICIOS. Translate the words in parenthesis:

1. Carlos y Ana (look at one another) _____ con cariño (affectionately).

2. Los niños no (answer one another) _____

   porque no (hear each other) _____ .

3. Los pacientes (help each other) _____ .

4. Nosotros (hate one another: *odiar = to hate*) _____ .

TO BECOME

In Spanish, there is no single verb which is the equivalent of the English verb *to become.* That idea is expressed through different verbs, depending on the individual situation. Below you will find the most common Spanish verbs used to convey the idea of "becoming."

---

ponerse + adjective
implies a change, usually a temporary one,
in one's mental, physical, or emotional state.

Me pongo nervioso a menudo.	I become nervous often.
Ellos *se han puesto* tristes.	They have become sad.
El *se ha puesto* muy flaco.	He has become very thin.

EJERCICIOS. Fill in the appropriate form of the verb.

1. El (becomes) _____ gordo cuando come mucho.

2. Los niños (become) _____ contentos cuando les traigo juguetes (toys).

3. Nosotros (have become) _____ nerviosos al recibir las noticias.

---

hacerse + noun or adjective
*implies the realization of a long-range goal
brought about through conscious effort.*

El *se ha hecho* rico.　　　　　　　He has become rich.

Ellas *se han hecho* doctoras.　　　They (the women) have become doctors.

EJERCICIOS. Fill in the appropriate form of the verb.

1. Las mujeres (have become) _____ patólogas.

2. La enfermera quiere (to become) _____ directora del hospital.

3. Yo (have become) _____ famoso.

---

llegar a ser + noun or adjective
*implies the realization of a long-range goal
brought about as the result of a successful process.*

Tú **has llegado a ser** director de la compañía. You have become the director of the company.

Los hermanos Jiménez **han llegado a ser**　　The Jimenez brothers have become urologists.
urólogos.

EJERCICIOS. Fill in the appropriate form of the verb.

1. Tú nunca (have become) _____ cirujano plástico.

2. ¿Qué quiere usted (to become) _____ ?

3. Después de mucho trabajo, yo (have become) _____ lo que soy.

---

volverse + adjective
implies sudden or violent change.

Después de tomar unas copas,　　　After having a few drinks,
usted siempre *se vuelve* loco.　　 you become crazy.

EJERCICIOS. Fill in the appropriate form of the verb.

1. Cuando ve a su hijo sangrando, la madre (becomes) _____ histérica.

2. El (becomes) _____ áspero (gruff) cada vez que habla de sus experiencias en la guerra (war).

3. Ellos (become) _____ locos cuando ven una injusticia (injustice).

Many verbs contain within thém the idea of "becoming" when they are used reflexively:

enfermarse	to become (to get) ill
emborracharse	to become (to get) drunk
endrogarse	to become (to get) drugged
enfadarse	to become (to get) angry
enloquecerse	to become insane

Yo me enfermo cuando como comidas con mucha grasa.　　　I get ill when I eat very greasy meals.

EJERCICIOS. Fill in the appropriate form of the verb.

1. Mi tío (has become) _____ un urólogo importante.

2. Esta enfermera quiere (to become) _____ supervisora (head nurse).

3. Nosotras (get drunk) _____ a veces.

4. Cuando yo no tomo la medicina, la enfermera (gets angry) _____ .

5. Cuando los criticamos (*criticar = to criticize),* ellos (become) _____

   pálidos primero y luego ellos (become) _____ violentos.

EJERCICIOS. Fill in the appropriate form of the verb.

El sicólogo está en un manicomio (mental institution).

El señor Frías (complains) _____ mucho. El siempre dice que piensa

(commit suicide) _____ , pero nosotros creemos que él (does not dare)

_____ . Algunas veces él dice que sabe mucho más que los doctores y a

veces tiene razón, porque, como usted sabe, él es sicólogo. Otras veces él (is happy about)

_____ de no saber más que los otros pacientes.

Diálogo

Señora García	—	Ay, hijo, **imagínate** . . .
César	—	Mamá, todo está bien. No se preocupe tanto; ya me siento mucho **mejor**.
Señor García	—	No **me refiero** a tu salud, hijo. Ya sé que eres jóven y pronto **te recuperas**.
César	—	Mamá, ¿entonces de qué habla? Por favor, ha sido sólo un accidente. No **se desespere** tanto. Salgo de aquí pronto.
Señora García	—	Hijo, **no se trata sólo de** un accidente. No sé, no sé . . .
César	—	Mamá, por favor, estas son cosas que pasan aquí, en Chile, **dondequiera**.
Señora García	—	Hijo, **tesoro**. Fíjate bien en lo que te digo. Unos meses en nuestro nuevo país y papá **todavía** está sufriendo con el **bendito** inglés, los niños no tienen su documentación y ahora tú . . .
César	—	Este . . . ¿Cómo se dice, mamá? Ud. sabe, ese **refrán** del tío Julián . . . ya sé, "no hay mal que por bien no venga."
Señora García	—	Hijo, si empiezas a **citar** al tío Julián, ya sé que nosotros vamos a salir adelante pronto.
César	—	Mamá, yo sé **cuidarme** bien. Aquí todo está bien—bien chévere —como dice Flaco.
Señora García	—	Me has convencido. Si insistes, me quedo en este país un **ratito** más. Ahora tienes que mejorarte.

VOCABULARIO DEL DIALOGO

imagínate	just imagine (*tú command form*)
mejor	better
me refiero	I refer to
te recuperas	you will recover, recuperate
no se desespere	don't despair
no se trata sólo de	not just a question of
dondequiera	wherever
tesoro	treasure, dearest
todavía	still
bendito	blessed

refrán	refrain
citar	to quote
cuidarme	to take care of myself
cuidarse	to take care of oneself
un ratito	a little while
mejorarte	to get (yourself) well
mejorarse	to get oneself well

PREGUNTAS SOBRE EL DIALOGO

1. ¿Cómo está César?

   _____

2. ¿Qué piensa la señora García?

   _____

3. ¿Por qué se siente así?

   _____

4. ¿Qué le dice César a ella?

   _____

César en la cama de un hospital municipal

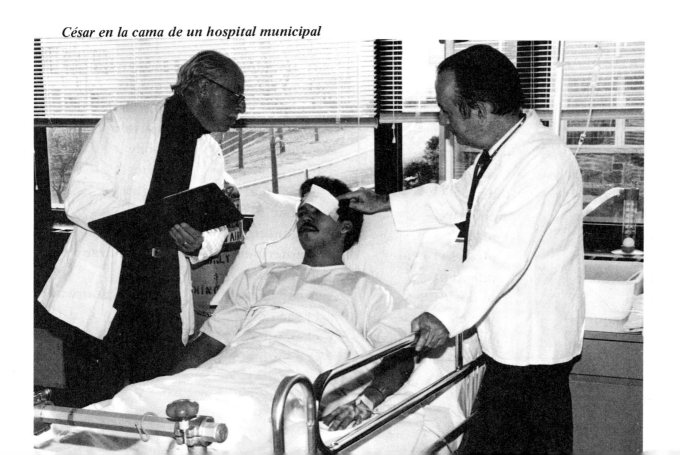

Vocabulario del capítulo

COGNATES OR NEAR COGNATES

alcohólico/a

la ambulancia

anormal

la condicıón

contento/a

el drogadicto

la emergencia

famoso/a

la farmacia

el fisioterapista

frustrado/a

el hipocondríaco

histérico/a

horrible

la injusticia

inmovilizado/a

el interno

el inválido

la lotería

metropolitano/a

el neurótico

la ocasión

el optimista

el oxígeno

pálido/a

paralítico/a

el perfume

el pesimista

plástico/a

el sicótico

responsable

el sanatorio

la sirena

el taxi

el terapista

tremendo/a

la víctima

violento/a

VOCABULARIO

los anteojos	eyeglasses	el contador	accountant
áspero/a	gruff	el convidado	guest
el ayudante	assistant	la copa	alcoholic drink
la bandera	flag	la cortina	curtain
el boticario	druggist	el cuerpo	body
el brazo	arm	el cura	priest
el calmante	sedative	derecho/a	right
la camilla	stretcher	despacio	slowly
el camillero	stretcher-bearer	elegantemente	elegantly
el cariño	affection	el enfermero	male nurse
casi	almost	la erupción	rash
la chaqueta	jacket	la escalera	ladder, stairway
el cliente	customer	el escalpelo	scalpel
completamente	completely	el esfuerzo	effort
		la esquina	corner

208

la fila	row	mutilado/a	mutilated
el gemelo	twin	el negocio	business
el ginecólogo	gynecologist	el patólogo	pathologist
gordo/a	fat	el pasillo	corridor
el grito	shout	el piso	floor
la guerra	war	la pobreza	poverty
el herido	injured man	el quirófano	operating room
el hígado	liver	la ropa	clothing
el hipertenso	hypertensive person	el ruido	noise
el huérfano	orphan	el saloncito	small room
el infierno	hell	la sangre	blood
izquierdo/a	left	el santo	saint
el juguete	toy	el sicólogo	psychologist
la librería	bookstore	el sordo	deaf person
el lío	mess	el sótano	cellar, basement
la llegada	arrival	suavemente	softly
loco / a	crazy	el suelo	ground
el manicomio	mental institution	el sufrimiento	suffering
el maquillaje	make-up	el tanque	tank
menor	younger	el tranquilizante	tranquilizer
la mesa	table	triste	sad
la moda	style	el vendedor	salesman

VERBOS

acercarse	to approach	despertar(ie)	to awaken someone
acostar(ue)	to put to bed	desesperarse	to despair
acostarse(ue)	to go to bed	despertarse(ie)	to wake oneself up
afeitarse	to shave	desvestirse(i)	to undress oneself
aflojar	relax, loosen	dirigirse a	to address
alegrarse de	to be happy about	discutir	to argue
atreverse a	to dare	dormirse(ue)	to fall asleep
averiguar	to find out	emborracharse	to become drunk
bañar	to bathe someone	encontrarse(ue)	to find oneself
bañarse	to bathe oneself	endrogarse	to become drugged
casarse	to get married	enfadarse	to become angry
comunicarse	to communicate with	enfermarse	to become ill
criticar	to criticize	enloquecerse	to become insane
cuidarse	to care for oneself	ganar	to win
desayunarse	to eat breakfast	incorporarse	to sit up
descorazonarse	to get discouraged	irse	to leave
desmayarse	to faint	lavarse	to wash oneself

levantar	to get up, to lift	preocuparse	to worry
levantarse	to get oneself up	quedar	to agree
limpiar	to clean	quedarse	to remain
llamar	to call someone	quejarse	to complain
llamarse	to be named	recuperarse	to recuperate
llevar	to carry	sacar	to take out
moverse(ue)	to move	sacudir	to shake
murmurar	to mumble	sentarse(ie)	to sit down
odiar	to hate	sentirse(ie)	to feel
parar	to stop	suicidarse	to commit suicide
pararse	to stand	verse	to appear, to seem to be
ponerse	to become		
portarse	to behave	vestirse(i)	to dress oneself

FRASES

a la moda	in style
acordarse(ue) de	to remember
al igual	the same as
bajo control	to be under control
con cariño	affectionately
darse cuenta de	to realize
en seguida	at once
lo que	that which
llegar a ser (+ noun or adjective)	to become (after a long term)
mientras tanto	meanwhile
ponerse en contacto	to get in touch with
silla de ruedas	wheelchair
el tanque de oxígeno	oxygen tank
todo lo que está pasando	all that is happening
volverse(ue) (+ adjective)	to become (suddenly)

Vocabulario adicional

SOME COMMONLY USED "MANDATOS"

¡Haga(n) un puño!	Make a fist!
¡Dé frente al aparato!	Face the machine!
¡Acuéste(n)se	Lie down
sobre la mesa!	on the table!
boca arriba!	head up!
boca abajo!	head down!

¡Afloje(n) el cuerpo!	Relax your body!
¡Cuíde(n)se!	Take care of yourself!
¡Desvísta(n)se hasta la cintura!	Undress to the waist!
¡Láve(n)se!	Wash yourself!
¡Láve(n)se la mano herida!	Wash your injured hand!
¡Láve(n)se los dedos del pie!	Wash your toes!
¡Limpie(n) la herida con alcohol!	Clean the wound with alcohol!
¡Lláme(n)me!	Call me!
¡Estire(n)	Stretch
el brazo derecho/izquierdo!	your right/left arm!
la pierna derecha/izquierda!	your right/left leg!
el pie derecho/izquierdo!	your right/left foot!
la mano derecha/izquierda!	your right/left hand!
¡No se desespere(n)!	Don't despair!
¡Apriete(n) el timbre!	Press! Squeeze the buzzer!
¡Voltée(n)se!	Turn
a la derecha!	to the right!
a la izquierda!	to the left!

EJERCICIOS. Translate into Spanish.

1. Please make a fist!   ¡ _____ usted!

2. Turn to the left!   ¡ _____ usted!

3. Please, press the buzzer!   ¡ _____ usted!

4. Don't despair!   ¡ _____ ustedes!

5. Please, call me!   ¡ _____ ustedes!

6. Clean the wound with alcohol!   ¡ _____ usted!

7. Take care of yourself!   ¡ _____ usted!

8. Please, face the machine!   ¡ _____ usted!

9. Please, undress to the waist!   ¡ _____ usted!

10. Stretch your left arm!   ¡ _____ usted!

11. Wash your injured hand!   ¡ _____ usted!

12. Relax your body!   ¡ _____ usted!

13. Lie down on the table!   ¡ _____ usted!

14. Please, wash your toes!   ¡ _____ usted!

15. Stretch your left leg!   ¡ _____ usted!

Capítulo 11
La trabajadora social

Lectura

La señorita Robinson era trabajadora social.
Su posición era muy importante en el hospital
porque—**además**—**sabía** hablar español. La   besides / knew how
señorita Robinson **estaba trabajando** en la   was working
sala de emergencias cuando **trajeron** a César.   they brought in
Hace unos años no había nadie como ella   A few years ago there was no one
empleada en el hospital. **Es decir**, nadie   employed / That is to say
podía hablar español para ayudar y orientar
a **la gran cantidad** de pacientes hispanos que   the large number
empezaban a venir al hospital. Sin embargo,   were beginning to come
hace cinco años, una serie de manifestaciones five years ago
organizadas por los residentes del barrio,
cambió la situación. Uno de los resultados de changed
las manifestaciones **fue emplear** como trabajadora was to employ
social a una persona bilingüe. **Así fue como**   And that was how
la señorita Robinson **obtuvo** su empleo.   obtained
Antes de comenzar su trabajo en el hospital,   Before beginning
la señorita Robinson **había vivido** en México y had lived
había trabajado en Puerto Rico como trabajadora had worked.
social.

César **creía** que ella **desempeñaba** — believed / was playing

un papel importante en el hospital, — an important role

porque ella **se esforzaba** mucho — was making a great effort

en ayudar a los hispanos que no sabían inglés.

Siempre **les resolvía** sus problemas burocráticos y — would resolve for them

siempre **les ayudaba** con el fastidioso **papeleo**. — would help them / red tape

César, como tantos otros **extranjeros**, no sabía — foreigners

nada de los diferentes seguros médicos y de los

mil papeles que **hay que rellenar al ingresar en** — one must fill out on checking in

un hospital. Gracias a la ayuda de la señorita

Robinson, César **estaba aprendiendo lo necesario** — was learning what was necessary

para sobrevivir en un mundo burocrático. — in order to survive

¡Felicidades, César! — Congratulations.

César conversando con la trabajadora social

La gramática

THE IMPERFECT TENSE

In an earlier chapter we discussed the compound past tenses. In this chapter we will introduce the **imperfect** tense, one of two simple past tenses. To form the imperfect of regular *ar* verbs, drop the *ar* from the infinitive and add the following personal endings: *–aba, –abas, –aba, –ábamos, –aban.*

ayudar to help			
yo	ayud*aba*	nosotros	ayud*ábamos*
tú	ayud*abas*		
usted		ustedes	
él	ayud*aba*	ellos	ayud*aban*
ella		ellas	

To form the imperfect of regular *er* and *ir* verbs, drop the *er* and *ir* from the infinitive and add the following personal endings: *-ía, -ías, -ía, -íamos, -ían.*

comer to eat			
yo	com*ía*	nosotros	com*íamos*
tú	com*ías*		
usted		ustedes	
él	com*ía*	ellos	com*ían*
ella		ellas	

vivir to live			
yo	viv*ía*	nosotros	viv*íamos*
tú	viv*ías*		
usted		ustedes	
él	viv*ía*	ellos	viv*ían*
ella		ellas	

The imperfect tense is used when you are referring to an action that **was going on, used to go on,** or **would go on habitually.** For example: **tú ayudabas** can mean: you were helping, you used to help, or you would help (habitually)

Since the first and third person singular forms are identical, subject pronouns are used to identify the subject of the verb.

There are only three irregular verbs in the imperfect tense:

ser	to be			ver	to see		
yo	*era*	nosotros	*éramos*	yo	*veía*	nosotros	*veíamos*
tú	*eras*			tú	*veías*		
usted		ustedes		usted		ustedes	
él	*era*	ellos	*eran*	él	*veía*	ellos	*veían*
ella		ellas		ella		ellas	

ir	to go		
yo	*iba*	nosotros	*íbamos*
tú	*ibas*		
usted		ustedes	
él	*iba*	ellos	*iban*
ella		ellas	

THE PRINCIPAL USES OF THE IMPERFECT TENSE

1. **Use of the imperfect tense to express a habitual, customary, or repeated activity in the past**

   Ellos se levant*aban* a las cinco los martes.

   They used to get up at 5:00 on Tuesdays.

   Ella me escrib*ía* todas las semanas.

   She would write me every week.

2. **Use of the imperfect tense to express an action that had been going on in the past**

   Nosotros com*íamos* mientras ellos le*ían* el periódico.

   We were eating while they were reading the newspaper.

   Yo los mir*aba*, pero ellos no me mir*aban*. a mí.

   I was looking at them, but they were not looking at me.

3. **Use of the imperfect tense to express a mental action, an emotion, or a physical condition in the past with such verbs as pensar, creer, saber, amar, esperar, and querer**

   El no sab*ía* nada de eso.

   He didn't know anything about that.

   Tú no quer*ías* salir de la casa, porque est*abas* muy cansado.

   You did not want to leave home, because you were very tired.

216

4. Use of the imperfect tense to describe the background of an action and to tell the time of day in the past

Era un día caluroso del verano.

It was a hot summer's day.

Eran las cinco cuando él venía al trabajo.

It was 5:00 when he came/would/used to come to work.

EJERCICIOS. Insert the proper form of the verb.

1. Los burócratas no **querían** darme la información.
   (la trabajadora social, mis amigos, tú, ellas)

   _____

   _____

   _____

   _____

   _____

2. Yo **tenía** mucho dinero en los años cincuenta (the fifties).
   (mis padres, el gobierno federal, nosotros, las instituciones privadas)

   _____

   _____

   _____

   _____

3. Usted **se acostaba** muy temprano cuando **era** joven.
   (mis hermanos, él y yo, tu niña, tú)

   _____

   _____

   _____

   _____

4. Nosotros nunca le **hacíamos** daño (harm) al niño.
   (tú, el perro [dog], ellos, yo)

   _____

   _____

   _____

   _____

5. Tú **decías** a menudo que no **tenías** ganas de **quejarte** (complain) más.
   (tus amigas, las víctimas, yo, nosotros)

   _____

   _____

   _____

   _____

6. Ellos siempre **prometían** (*prometer = to promise*) muchas cosas, pero nunca nos **daban** nada.
   (usted, tú y él, el casero [landlord], tú)

   _____

   _____

   _____

   _____

EJERCICIOS. Fill in the appropriate form of the verb in the imperfect tense.

poder, querer, necesitar	Yo _____	firmar la carta.
guardar, traer, hacer	Tú _____	todo.
servir, decir, beber	Usted _____	mucho.
vivir, practicar, estar	El _____	en Miami.
levantarse, acostarse, salir	Ella _____	tarde siempre.
venir, ir, comenzar	Nosotros _____	a escribir.
perder, usar, ponerse	Ustedes _____	los guantes.
pedir, quejarse, dormir	Ellos _____	poco.
ver, tomar, esperar	Ellas _____	un ómnibus.

EJERCICIOS.

Translate the word in parenthesis with the appropriate form of the verb in the imperfect.

1. El empleado en el Departamento de Servicios Sociales

   (knew) _____ los detalles.

2. El fisioterapista (would help — *ayudar*) _____ a los incapacitados.

3. Muchos de los obreros (were dying — *morir*) _____ de la epidemia.

4. Los epilépticos (used to come — *venir*) _____ a este especialista.

5. El Departamento de Desempleo (Unemployment) used to give — *dar*) _____

   _____ cheques cada dos semanas.

6. Los desempleados (unemployed) (would wait — *esperar*) _____
   horas en las colas (lines).

7. Nosotros nunca (would receive — *recibir*) _____
   ascensos (promotions) automáticamente.

8. Los miembros de mi familia siempre (used to do — *hacer*) _____
   trabajo voluntario para la comunidad.

9. Nuestro hijo (used to need — *necesitar*) _____ cuidado especial.

10. Por muchos años después del accidente la pierna derecha me (used to hurt — *doler*)

    _____

11. La mayoría de la población (believed — *creer*) _____ en Dios (God).

12. Por muchos años los basureros (sanitation men) no (would not collect — *recoger*)

    _____ la basura (garbage) los martes y los jueves.

13. El fotógrafo (was taking — *sacar*) _____ muchas fotos.

14. Cuando éramos jóvenes (we would sleep — *dormir*) _____ todos
    en el mismo cuarto.

PAST ACTION IN PROGRESS

To explain past action in progress, you may use the imperfect of the verb or you may use **estaba, estabas, estaba, estábamos**, and **estaban** + **the present participle:**

> **Ellos estaban hablando** con él,
> y él **estaba leyendo** el periódico.

> They *were talking* to him,
> and he *was reading* the newspaper.

EJERCICIOS. Translate into Spanish.

1. I used to worry a lot.

   _____

2. They would usually pick up (*recoger* = *to pick up*) the check on Tuesdays.

   _____

3. We played baseball every day in the playground (*campo de juego*).

   _____

4. When she was young, she would always work ten hours a day.

   _____

5. When you were in grammar school, did you always have problems with the counselors?

   _____

   _____

6. It was 9:30 in the morning and I was waiting for the social worker.

   _____

7. We used to fight (*pelear* = *to fight*) a lot.

   _____

8. It was necessary to call the parents.

   _____

9. The manager rejected (*rechazar*) our offer (*oferta*) every week.

   _____

10. Nobody would worry about her.

   _____

EJERCICIOS. Answer in Spanish.

1. ¿Dónde vivía usted durante los años sesenta (the sixties)?

   _____

2. ¿Hasta qué hora trabajaba usted cuando tenía quince años?

   _____

3. Cuando era joven, ¿a dónde iba los domingos?

   _____

4. Cuando era joven, ¿se preocupaba por su salud (about your health)?

   _____

5. ¿Qué hacía cuando tenía que ir al dentista?

   _____

6. ¿A quién le escribía cuando era niño?

   _____

7. Cuando estaba en la escuela secundaria, ¿a qué hora se acostaba los sábados por la

   noche?   _____

   _____

8. ¿A dónde iba usted los veranos cuando tenía diez años?

   _____

MORE ON ADJECTIVES: COMPARATIVE FORMS AND COMBINATIONS

Subject + Verb + **más** (more) / **menos** (less) + **que** (than) + object/person compared	

Tú tienes **más que** ellos y ellos tienen **menos que** tú.	You have more than they, and they have less than you.

EJERCICIOS.

1. El tiene (more) _____ que ella y

   ella tiene (more than) _____ Juan.

2. Nosotros ganamos (less) _____ que Luis,

   pero él gana (less than) _____ tú.

3. Pedro ve (more) _____ que yo,

   y yo veo mucho (more) _____ que usted.

4. Tu hijo está perdiendo (more) _____ que Panchito

   pero (less) _____ que yo.

5. El jefe protesta (more than) _____ los empleados;

   ellos protestan (less than) _____ él.

Subject + Verb + **más** (more) / **menos** (less) + adjective + **que** (than) + object/person compared

---

EJERCICIOS.

1. Mis documentos son (more) _____ complicados.

   (than) _____ los documentos de Juan.

2. Su hijo parece (less) _____ inteligente

   (than) _____ mi hijo.

3. Su formulario es (more) _____ complicado

   (than) _____ mi formulario.

4. Nosotros somos (less) _____ pobres

   (than) _____ la hermana Teresa.

5. Ella es (much more) _____ habladora (talkative)

   (than) _____ tú.

Subject + Verb + **más** (more) / **menos** (less) + noun + **que** (than) + object/person compared

---

EJERCICIOS.

1. El argentino tiene (fewer) _____ problemas que yo, porque tengo

   (much more)_____responsabilidad que él.

2. Usted necesita (less) _____ medicina que su esposo; él tiene que

   tomar (more) _____ píldoras que usted.

3. Su caso tiene (fewer) _____ posibilidades que el caso de ella.

4. Tu enfermedad es (more) _____ peligrosa

   (than) _____ la enfermedad de Juan.

5. Ellos reciben (much more) _____ dinero, pero trabajan (much less)

   _____ que nosotros.

Subject + Verb + **más** (more) / **menos** (less) + **de** (than) + number

---

EJERCICIOS.

1. En este momento tengo (more than) _____ veinte puntos (stitches)
   en el dedo.

2. Hay (more than) _____ cinco personas esperándome (waiting for me).

3. No hay (less than) _____ diez niños retrasados (retarded children) aquí.

4. Tenemos que cobrar (more than) _____ mil dólares todos los años.

5. Tú nunca pagas (less than) _____ dos dólares por hora.

EJERCICIOS. Translate into Spanish.

1. They (*feminine*) are more intelligent than their brothers.

   _____

2. We have less patience than you have.

   _____

3. He has to wait more than ten minutes here.

   _____

4. You (*plural*) can buy more than I, because you have more money than I.

   _____

5. She is happier than we are because she has fewer problems than we do.

   _____

THE SUPERLATIVE

By placing the appropriate form of the definite article (**el/la . . . los/las**)
before **más** or **menos**, and by substituting *de* for *que*, the superlative can be formed:

Positive:
Mi trabajo es difícil.   My job is difficult.

Comparative:
Mi trabajo es **más** difícil **que** tu trabajo.   My job is more difficult than your job.
Mi trabajo es **menos** difícil **que** tu trabajo.   My job is less difficult than your job.

Superlative:
Mi trabajo es **el más** difícil **de** todos.   My job is the most difficult of all.
Mi trabajo es **el menos** difícil **de** todos.   My job is the least difficult of all.

* The definite article agrees in gender and number with the adjective.

224

EJERCICIOS. Translate into Spanish.

1. El auto de Jorge es (the oldest) _____ en nuestro barrio.

2. Estas pólizas son (the most) _____ completas de todas.

3. Su ropa es (the most) _____ cara de toda la ropa aquí.

4. Esta casa es (the oldest) _____ de todas.

5. Este apartamento es (the dirtiest — *sucio*) _____ de todos.

6. Estos informes son (the most important) _____ de todos.

7. Esta infección es (the most) _____ peligrosa de todas.

8. Esta escuela para niños retrasados mentales es (the most expensive) _____
_____ de todas.

9. Este rumbo (route) es (the longest) _____ de todos.

10. Estos camiones (trucks) son (the cheapest) _____ baratos de todos.

11. Ese tipo de incendio (fire) es (the most common) _____
común de todos que hemos tenido en el edificio.

IRREGULAR ADJECTIVE COMPARISONS

Some adjectives have both irregular and regular forms.

| Adjective | COMPARATIVE | | SUPERLATIVE | |
	Regular Form	Irregular Form	Regular Form	Irregular Form
viejo (old)	más viejo	mayor	el más viejo	el mayor
grande (big)	más grande	mayor	el más grande	el mayor
pequeño (small)	más pequeño (objects)	menor	el más pequeño	el menor
joven (young)	más joven (only persons)	menor	el más joven	el menor
bueno (good)	más bueno	mejor	el más bueno	el mejor
malo (bad)	más malo	malo	el más malo	el peor

● The regular form **más joven(es)** generally refers only to persons:
  1. Arturo es **más joven que** Rosa. El es **el más joven** de todos.
  2. Ellas son **las más jóvenes** de todas las mujeres aquí.

- The irregular forms **mayor(es)** and **menor(es)** are used when referring to a person's age:

    1. ¿Es usted **mayor** o **menor** que ella? Ella es **mayor** que yo.
    2. Ellas son **las mayores** de todos los clientes.

- The regular forms **más grande(s)** and **más pequeño/a(s)** refer to the size of objects and persons:

    1. Su apartamento es **más grande** que el del señor Romero.
    2. ¿Quién es **el más pequeño** de la clase?

- The regular forms of **más bueno/a(s)** and **más malo/a(s)** underscore the moral nature of a person and are usually used when a person's character is referred to. Otherwise, the irregular and regular forms are interchangeable:

    1. Ese cura es **el más bueno** de todos. Es un santo (saint).
    2. Estos violadores son **más malos** que los ladrones (crooks).

EJERCICIOS. Translate the word in parenthesis.

1. ¿Quién es (the oldest) _____ de los tres hermanos?

2. La abuelita del señor Chávez es (older) _____ que mi abuelo.

3. El sacerdote es (the best) _____ maestro de todos en nuestro barrio.

4. Estos regalos son (the smallest) _____ de todos.

5. Si Juana tiene veinte y cinco años y Laura tiene veinte y dos, ¿quién es (older)?

   _____ ¿Quién es (younger) _____

6. Ellas son (the oldest) _____ residentes del sanatorio.

7. Estos señores vienen con muchas trampas (tricks). Ellos son (the worst men) _____

   _____ de la comunidad.

8. Este tipo de seguro (insurance) es (the best)_____de todos.

9. No estoy de acuerdo (I don't agree). Creo que es (the worst)* _____.

   Es (worse) _____ que una póliza de veinte años.

10. Esta licencia es (older) _____ que la de mi hermano, pero la de Pepe

    es (the oldest) _____ de todas.

11. La tarjeta postal es (the cheapest) la manera _____ de
    comunicarnos.

*insurance

226

TAN vs. TANTO

---
tan (as) + **adjective/adverb** + **como** (as)

Ella es **tan** inteligente **como** su madre.   She is *as* intelligent *as* her mother.

El corre **tan** rápido **como** Juanita.   He runs *as* rapidly *as* Juanita.

---
tanto(a) (as much/many) + **noun** . . . + **como** (as)

Tú tienes **tanto** dinero **como** yo.   You have *as much* money *as* I.

Ellos compran **tantas** cosas **como** nosotros.   They buy *as many* things *as* we do.

EJERCICIOS. Insert the appropriate form.

1. El ha perdido (as much) _____ peso (weight) (as) _____ yo.

2. Ellos tienen (as many) _____ dependientes

   (as) _____ él _____.

3. El guardia tiene (as much) _____ miedo

   (as) _____ ustedes.

4. Ellos son (as) _____ trabajadores (as) _____ nosotras.

5. Yo soy (as) _____ pobre (as) _____ ellos.

6. Esta demanda legal es (as) _____ seria (as)_____ aquélla.

7. La nacionalidad de sus padres es (as) _____ importante

   (as) _____ su nacionalidad.

8. La trabajadora social tenía que llenar (as many) _____ papeles

   (as) _____ tú.

9. Las destrezas (skills) son (as) _____ necesarias

   (as) _____ conocimiento (knowledge).

10. La información sobre la planificación familiar es (as) _____

    esencial (as) _____ la consulta con el médico.

11. Nosotros no nos preocupábamos (as much) _____

    (as) _____ nuestros padres.

Diálogo

Señorita Robinson	—	Escucha, César, **mientras** tú dormías yo me encargaba de unos **trámites burocráticos** pero todavía quedan estas planillas por llenar.
César	—	¡Escucha tú, si no hablo inglés . . . !
Señorita Robinson	—	¡No te preocupes! ¡No te preocupes!
César	—	No es que me preocupo, este . . . quería decirte que . . .
Señorita Robinson	—	¿Qué te pasa? **Desconfías** porque soy mujer, ¿Es eso lo que te fastidiaba?
César	—	Qué va. ¿Qué tú crees? ¿Qué es lo que tú piensas? Tú crees que yo hago todo **a lo macho.** ¡Olvídate de eso!
Señorita Robinson	—	Bueno, menos mal. Yo sólo quería decirte . . . **vaya,** no importa.
César	—	Está bien, está bien, **adelante** con el papeleo.
Señorita Robinson	—	Entonces, íbamos a completar estas planillas aquí. Dime tu nombre completo, tú sabes, nombre de pila y apellidos.
César	—	César Antonio García Schneider. ¿Bonito, eh? ¿Qué más querías?
Señorita Robinson	—	Un poema. Ahora, ¡pon tu firma aquí en esta hoja!
César	—	¿Vale?
Señorita Robinson	—	No seas bruto. Escríbela de nuevo y esta vez con la mano derecha. Ahora saca del cajoncito tu **carnet de residencia.**
César	—	Ay, señorita, ahora la historia se pone complicada. Lo tenía en mi **billetera,** pero cuando el accidente . . . No sé, **a lo mejor** Flaco lo tiene.
Señorita Robinson	—	Bueno luego podemos hacerle una **llamada. Acércate** a mí para **comprobar** si me he equivocado en cuanto a estos datos biográficos.

César	— Vaya, tú eres muy **mandona**, señorita Robinson. ¿Por qué no te acercas tú a mí?
Señorita Robinson	— César, por favor, **déjate de tonterías.** Acércate, **suave, suave.**

VOCABULARIO DEL DIALOGO

mientras	while
trámites burocráticos	bureaucratic red tape
desconfías	do you have doubts
a lo macho	(really) like a man
vaya	go on
adelante	onward
carnet de residencia	residence card or identification
billetera	wallet
a lo mejor	probably
llamada	call
acércate a mí (acercarse)	to come over to me, to approach
comprobar	to prove, to corroborate
mandona	pushy women (domineering)
déjate de tonterías	stop the nonsense
suave	easy now

PREGUNTAS SOBRE EL DIALOGO

1. ¿Qué hacía César mientras que la señorita Robinson se encargaba de los problemas?

   _____

2. ¿Cuál es el apellido materno de César?

   _____

3. ¿Dónde tenía César su carnet de residencia antes del accidente?

   _____

4. ¿Según César como era la señorita Robinson?

   _____

5. Por fin, ¿qué le dice la señora Robinson a César?

   _____

Vocabulario del capítulo

COGNATES OR NEAR COGNATES

automáticamente
biográfico / a
el combate
competente
completo/a
complicado/a
el dentista

el departamento
divorciado/a
esencial
el fisioterapista
la infección
la licencia
la manifestación

la posibilidad
el residente
la responsabilidad
el resultado
separado/a
el sexo
el voluntario

VOCABULARIO

la abuelita	little grandma	el dicho	saying
además	besides	difunto/a	deceased
la altura	height	Dios	God
el apellido	last name	el edificio	building
el ascenso	promotion	la enfermedad	illness
barato/a	inexpensive	la epidemia	epidemic
la basura	garbage	el epiléptico	epileptic
el basurero	garbage collector	el foco	focus
el cajón	the drawer	el fotógrafo	photographer
el cajoncito	the little drawer	el gobierno	government
caloroso/a	hot	los guantes	gloves
el camión	truck	el incapacitado	handicapped person
la carpeta	portfolio	el incendio	fire
casado/a	married	el ladrón	thief
el casero	landlord	mensualmente	monthly
la cola	line	la oferta	offer
común	common	el perro	dog
consciente	conscious	el peso	weight
la consulta	consultation	la población	population
el coraje	courage	el refrán	saying
la costumbre	custom	el retrasado mental	retarded person
los datos	data	la ropa	clothing
el dependiente	dependent, clerk	el rumbo	route
el desempleo	unemployment	el sacerdote	priest
el desempleado	unemployed person	la salud	health
la destreza	skill	el santo	saint
		sucio/a	dirty

ORDINAL NUMERALS

primero/a	first	**sexto/a**	sixth
segundo/a	second	**séptimo/a**	seventh
tercero/a	third	**octavo/a**	eighth
cuarto/a	fourth	**noveno/a**	ninth
quinto/a	fifth	**décimo/a**	tenth

Ordinals agree in gender and number with the nouns they describe. *Primero* and *tercero* drop the *o* before masculine singular nouns:

primer (tercer) edificio	the first (third) building
but	
los primeros edificios	the first buildings
la primera vez	the first time

VERBOS

acreditar	to authorize	**parecer**	to appear, to seem
amar	to love	**pelear**	to fight
comenzar	to begin	**practicar**	to practice
completar	to fill out	**quitar(se)**	to remove
comunicar	to communicate	**recoger**	to pick up
desconfiar	to lack confidence in	**rechazar**	to reject
esforzarse	to make an effort	**rellenar**	to fill out again
llenar	to fill	**resolver**	to resolve
morir(ue)	to die	**sobrevivir**	to survive
obtener	to get, to obtain	**subir**	to ascend
olvidarse	to forget		
orientar	to guide, to familiarize		

FRASES

campo de juego	playground
la demanda legal (el pleito)	legal claim
desempeñar el papel	to play the role
la escuela secundaria	high school
el fastidioso papeleo	detailed paperwork
nombre de pila	first name
la planificación familiar	family planning
tal vez	perhaps
la tarjeta postal	postcard
hace unos años	some years back
trámites burocráticos	red tape

¿Cuántas veces?	How many times?
mil veces	a thousand times
muchas veces	many times
pocas veces	a few times

Vocabulario adicional

SOME COMMONLY USED "MANDATOS"

¡Escúche(n)lo/la!	Listen to it/him/her!
¡Hable(n) despacio!	Speak slowly!
¡Lláme(n)nos por teléfono!	Call us on the telephone!
¡Pída(n) les ayuda!	Ask them for help!
¡No se meta(n)!	Don't get involved!
¡Léa(n)lo/la con cuidado!	Read it carefully!
¡Explíque(n)melo!	Explain it to me!
¡Pruébe(n)los/las!	Try them!
¡Díga(n)melo!	Say/Tell it to me!
¡Recója(n)lo/la!	Pick it up!
¡Consérve(n)los/las!	Keep them!
¡Empuje(n)!	Push!
¡Refúte(n)lo!	Argue it!/Dispute it!
¡Guárde(n)lo/la!	Keep it!

EJERCICIOS. Translate into Spanish.

1. Listen to him!   ¡ _____ ustedes!

2. Speak slowly!   ¡ _____ usted!

3. Call us on the telephone!   ¡ _____ ustedes!

4. Pick it up (masculine object)!   ¡ _____ usted!

5. Keep it (feminine object)!   ¡ _____ ustedes!

6. Read it carefully(*la receta*)!   ¡ _____ usted!

7. Try them!   ¡ _____ ustedes!

8. Push!   ¡ _____ usted!

9. Keep them!   ¡ _____ ustedes!

10. Ask them for help!   ¡ _____ usted!

11. Don't get involved!   ¡ _____ ustedes!

Capítulo 12
En el juzgado

Lectura

El señor y la señora García llegaron **juntos**	together
al juzgado. El señor García **pudo** acompañar	Court / could
a su esposa porque él ahora trabaja	
el turno de noche en el hospital,	the night shift
así que en vez de ir a casa a dormir,	thus instead of going
fue directamente al juzgado, para estar	he went
cerca de su hijo mayor.	close to
La señora García está muy preocupada,	
porque **no ha podido conseguir** del Consulado	has not been able to get
chileno **la fe de bautismo** y los otros	Baptismal Certificate
documentos de identidad. A las nueve	
menos cuarto, los García **se reunieron con**	got together with
la señorita Jordan, la abogada del caso.	
Todos **se saludaron** y **se abrazaron** y en los	greeted each other / embraced each other
pocos minutos que **quedaban** antes del juicio,	were remaining
la abogada les explicó a los García los	
planes que tenía para **el proceso.**	the trial

La gramática

THE PRETERITE TENSE

In the last chapter you were introduced to the **imperfect tense**, one of the two simple past tenses. In this chapter, you will become familiar with the **preterite**, the other simple past tense.

To form the preterite of regular *ar* verbs, drop the *ar* from the infinitive and add the following personal endings: *-é, -aste, -ó, -amos, -aron.*

	firmar	to sign			
yo	firm**é**	I signed	nosotros	firm**amos**	we signed
tú	firm**aste**	you signed			
usted		you signed	ustedes		you signed
él	firm**ó**	he signed	ellos	firm**aron**	they signed
ella		she signed	ellas		they signed

To form the preterite of regular *er* and *ir* verbs, drop the *er* and *ir* from the infinitive and add the following personal endings: *-í, -iste, -ió, -imos, -ieron.*

	aprender	to learn			
yo	aprend**í**	I learned	nosotros	aprend**imos**	we learned
tú	aprend**iste**	you learned			
usted		you learned	ustedes		
él	aprend**ió**	he learned	ellos	aprend**ieron**	they learned
ella		she learned	ellas		they learned

	recibir	to receive			
yo	recib**í**	I received	nosotros	recib**imos**	we received
tú	recib**iste**	you received			
usted		you received	ustedes		you received
él	recib**ió**	he received	ellos	recib**ieron**	they received
ella		she received	ellas		they received

THE PRETERITE vs. THE IMPERFECT

The **preterite tense** is used to report or narrate actions or events that are seen as fully completed or definitely terminated, regardless of how long these actions or events lasted.

El abogado **denunció** el juicio.	The lawyer denounced the judgment.
¿**Viste** el accidente?	Did you see the accident?

The **imperfect tense** describes what *was going on* without indicating an end to the action. The **preterite tense** indicates what *went on* or *did go on:* that is, it tells us that the action was completed. The English equivalent to the preterite in Spanish is usually the simple past: *I came. I saw. I conquered.*

Ella **conversaba** con el casero cuando yo la *vi.*	She **was talking** to the landlord when I **saw** her.

In emphatic and negative statements and questions, *did* is used in English but not in Spanish. *Never use the preterite of* hacer *with a second verb in such constructions.* The word "did" is not translated in Spanish.

Sí, ellos **nos llamaron.**	Yes, they did call us.

EJERCICIOS. Fill in the appropriate form of the verb.

1. Yo **firmé** todos los documentos.
   (el juez [judge], ellas, tú, nosotras)

   _____

   _____

   _____

   _____

2. Ellos **recibieron** la declaración jurada (affidavit).
   (usted, los jueces [judges], el abogado [the lawyer], yo)

   _____

   _____

   _____

   _____

3. Tú **ganaste** (*ganar* = to earn) poco el año pasado.
   (yo, el bracero, nuestros amigos, nosotros)

   _____

   _____

   _____

   _____

4. Nosotros **esperamos** aplazar [to adjourn] la sesión.
   (la abogada, yo, tú, los acusados [the accused ones])

   _____

   _____

   _____

   _____

5. Los jueces **aprendieron** todo lo necesario (all that was necessary).
   (tu amigo, yo, tú, el policía)

   _____

   _____

   _____

   _____

EJERCICIOS. Fill in the appropriate form of the verb in the preterite tense.

quejarse, trabajar	yo _____ aquí.
aprender, caminar, subir	tú _____ rápidamente.
ofrecer, preguntar	usted _____ mucho.
buscar, pedir	él _____ su huella digital (fingerprint).
vivir, estudiar	ella _____ aquí.
pelear (to fight), admitir, investigar	nosotros _____ poco.
firmar, necesitar	ustedes _____ los papeles.
apelar (to appeal), denunciar (to denounce)	ellos _____ a la corte (the court).

VERBOS IRREGULARES Y EL VERBO "VER" EN EL PRETERITO

		tener to have				
yo	*tuve*	I had	nosotros	*tuvimos*	we had
tú	*tuviste*	you had			
usted		you had	ustedes		you had
él	*tuvo*	he had	ellos	*tuvieron*	they had
ella		she had	ellas		they had

		hacer to do, to make				
yo	*hice*	I did	nosotros	*hicimos*	we did
tú	*hiciste*	you did			
usted		you did	ustedes		you did
él	*hizo*	he did	ellos	*hicieron*	they did
ella		she did	ellas		they did

		saber to find out				
yo	*supe*	I found out	nosotros	*supimos*	we found out
tú	*supiste*	you found out			
usted		you found out	ustedes		you found out
él	*supo*	he found out	ellos	*supieron*	they found out
ella		she found out	ellas		they found out

		querer to want				
yo	*quise*	I wanted	nosotros	*quisimos*	we wanted
tú	*quisiste*	you wanted			
usted		you wanted	ustedes		you wanted
él	*quiso*	he wanted	ellos	*quisieron*	they wanted
ella		she wanted	ellas		they wanted

<table>
<tr><td colspan="6" align="center">poder to be able</td></tr>
<tr><td>yo</td><td>pude</td><td>I was able</td><td>nosotros</td><td>pudimos</td><td>we were able</td></tr>
<tr><td>tú</td><td>pudiste</td><td>you were able</td><td></td><td></td><td></td></tr>
<tr><td>usted</td><td></td><td>you were able</td><td>ustedes</td><td></td><td>you were able</td></tr>
<tr><td>él</td><td>pudo</td><td>he did</td><td>ellos</td><td>pudieron</td><td>they were able</td></tr>
<tr><td>ella</td><td></td><td>she was able</td><td>ellas</td><td></td><td>they were able</td></tr>
</table>

<table>
<tr><td colspan="6" align="center">pedir to ask for, request</td></tr>
<tr><td>yo</td><td>pedí</td><td>I asked for</td><td>nosotros</td><td>pedimos</td><td>we asked for</td></tr>
<tr><td>tú</td><td>pediste</td><td>you asked for</td><td></td><td></td><td></td></tr>
<tr><td>usted</td><td></td><td>you asked for</td><td>ustedes</td><td></td><td>you asked for</td></tr>
<tr><td>él</td><td>pidió</td><td>he asked for</td><td>ellos</td><td>pidieron</td><td>they asked for</td></tr>
<tr><td>ella</td><td></td><td>she asked for</td><td>ellas</td><td></td><td>they asked for</td></tr>
</table>

<table>
<tr><td colspan="6" align="center">ver to see</td></tr>
<tr><td>yo</td><td>vi</td><td>I saw</td><td>nosotros</td><td>vimos</td><td>we saw</td></tr>
<tr><td>tú</td><td>viste</td><td>you saw</td><td></td><td></td><td></td></tr>
<tr><td>usted</td><td></td><td>you saw</td><td>ustedes</td><td></td><td>you saw</td></tr>
<tr><td>él</td><td>vio</td><td>he saw</td><td>ellos</td><td>vieron</td><td>they saw</td></tr>
<tr><td>ella</td><td></td><td>she saw</td><td>ellas</td><td></td><td>they saw</td></tr>
</table>

EJERCICIOS.

Fill in the blank space with the appropriate form of the verb in the preterite.

pedir   1. ¿ _____ tú los documentos de identidad?

2. La abogada _____ la declaración jurada.

3. Nosotros no _____ nada.

4. Ellos _____ todo lo necesario.

ver

1. Yo no _____ nada.

2. ¿ _____ tú a los acusados?

3. Ellos _____ la declaración jurada.

4. Alguien _____ el documento.

5. Nosotros _____ al juez ayer.

hacer

1. Sus amigos no _____ nada por la causa.

2. Ella _____ muchos errores, pero ahora dice que va a cambiar su actitud.

3. Nosotros _____ todo lo posible (everything possible) para protegerlo.

4. Tú _____ más que yo, pero yo _____ mucho más que los demás (the rest).

5. Ellos no _____ más que estorbar (disturb) todo.

tener

1. Yo _____ miedo al entrar en la corte.

2. Ella _____ que volver a la cárcel.

3. Nosotros _____ menos problemas que ella.

4. Tú _____ que arreglar la fianza ayer.

5. Vds. _____ que hacerlo rápidamente.

querer

1. Tú _____ violar el estatuto (statute).

2. ¿Quién _____ ir a la corte?

3. El juez de testamentarías (surrogate judge) _____ juzgar el caso hoy.

4. Ellos no _____ levantarse.

5. Nosotros nunca _____ hacer daño (to do harm) a nadie.

poder

1. Yo no _____ cruzar (to cross) la calle porque había tráfico (*tránsito*).

2. Ella no _____ contestar las preguntas.

3. Ningún testigo _____ ver al ladrón en la oscuridad (darkness).

4. Nosotros _____ llegar a tiempo.

5. Tú _____ sentarte tranquilo, ¿verdad?

saber   1. El juez _____ la verdad.

2. Nosotros nunca lo _____ todo.

3. Yo _____ todo lo necesario.

4. ¿Quién lo _____ ?

5. Ellos no _____ hasta ayer.

EJERCICIOS. Translate into Spanish

1. They did everything possible to protect him.

   _____

2. We saw the documents; then we saw the judge.

   _____

3. She found out the truth yesterday.

   _____

4. They did not want to break (violate) the law.

   _____

5. I spoke to Mr. Rodríguez in the court.

   _____

6. They had to return to jail.

   _____

7. You were not able to answer the questions.

   _____

8. I made an error; I requested the documents.

_____

VERBOS QUE CAMBIAN SU ORTOGRAFIA

llegar*	to arrive				
yo	lle**gué**	I arrived	nosotros	lleg**amos**	we arrived
tú	lleg**aste**	you arrived			
usted		you arrived	ustedes		you arrived
él	lleg**ó**	he arrived	ellos	lleg**aron**	they arrived
ella		she arrived	ellas		they arrived

buscar†	to look for				
yo	bus**qué**	I looked for	nosotros	busc**amos**	we looked for
tú	busc**aste**	you looked for			
usted		you looked for	ustedes		you looked for
él	busc**ó**	he looked for	ellos	busc**aron**	they looked for
ella		she looked for	ellas		they looked for

MAS VERBOS IRREGULARES

decir	to say, to tell				
yo	*dije*	I said	nosotros	*dijimos*	we said
tú	*dijiste*	you said			
usted		you said	ustedes		you said
él	*dijo*	he said	ellos	*dijeron*	they said
ella		she said	ellas		they said

* Verbs whose infinitives end in *gar* change the *g* to *gu* before *e.*
† Verbs whose infinitives end in *car* change the *c* to *qu* before *e.*

		estar	to be			
yo	*estuve*	I was	nosotros	*estuvimos*	we were
tú	*estuviste*	you were			
usted		you were	ustedes		you were
él	*estuvo*	he was	ellos	*estuvieron*	they were
ella		she was	ellas		they were

EJERCICIOS.

Fill in the blank space with the appropriate form of the verb in the preterite.

llegar

1. ¿Cuándo _____ los reportes?

2. Los braceros (day workers) _____ la semana pasada.

3. Yo nunca _____ tarde.

4. Nosotros _____ sin las declaraciones juradas.

5. La periodista (woman reporter) _____ con los trámites legales (legal red tape) en la mano (in her hand).

buscar

1. ¿Por qué _____ usted esa información?

2. Ellos no _____ medidas drásticas (drastic measures).

3. Yo _____ la orden de registro (search warrant) en todas partes (everywhere).

4. Tú lo _____ ayer, ¿verdad?

5. Nosotros no _____ nada en aquel entonces (at that time).

estar

1. ¿Dónde _____ tú anteayer (day before yesterday)?

2. Yo _____ en la cárcel (jail) por más de dos años.

3. Los testigos (witnesses) _____ en el avión mucho tiempo.

4. El abogado defensor _____ con ellos.

5. Su esposo y yo _____ en el tribunal con la fianza (bail).

decir   1. Yo _____ esto en público.

           2. El nos lo _____ en privado.

           3. Vds. _____ que iban a darnos más informes.

           4. Nosotros le _____ lo que pasó.

           5. Tú me _____ una mentira (lie). Ella me

              _____ la verdad.

EJERCICIOS. Translate into Spanish

1. When did the witness (*el testigo*) arrive?

    _____

2. They said it in public.

    _____

3. We looked for the information everywhere.

    _____

4. We were in court with bail.

    _____

5. I was there for more than three hours.

    _____

6. I saw the document the day before yesterday.

    _____

7. You told them a lie. They told me the truth.

    _____

8. He said that they arrived without money.

    _____

9. She looked for a lawyer.

    _____

AUN MAS VERBOS IRREGULARES

---

dar   to give

---

yo	*di*	I gave	nosotros	*dimos*	we gave
tú	*diste*	you gave			
usted		you gave	ustedes		you gave
él	*dio*	he gave	ellos	*dieron*	they gave
ella		she gave	ellas		they gave

---

ser / **ir**   to go/to be

---

yo	*fui*	I was, I went	nosotros	*fuimos*	we were, we went
tú	*fuiste*	you were, you went			
usted		you were, you went	ustedes		you were, you went
él	*fue*	he was, he went	ellos	*fueron*	they were, they went
ella		she was, she went	ellas		they were, they went

---

dormir*   to sleep

---

yo	*dormí*	I slept	nosotros	*dormimos*	we slept
tú	*dormiste*	you slept			
usted		you slept	ustedes		you slept
él	*durmió*	he slept	ellos	*durmieron*	they slept
ella		she slept	ellas		they slept

---

sentir   to feel

---

yo	*sentí*	I felt	nosotros	*sentimos*	we felt
tú	*sentiste*	you felt			
usted		you felt	ustedes		you felt
él	*sintió*	he felt	ellos	*sintieron*	they felt
ella		she felt	ellas		they felt

---

* **Morir** (to die) is conjugated in the same way.

venir	to come				
yo	*vine*	I came	nosotros	*vinimos*	we came
tú	*viniste*	you came			
usted		you came	ustedes		you came
él	*vino*	he came	ellos	*vinieron*	they came
ella		she came	ellas		they came

EJERCICIOS.

Fill in the blank space with the appropriate form of the verb in the preterite.

dar

1. El testigo no _____ una descripción completa.

2. Las víctimas les _____ a ellos una descripción incompleta del violador (rapist).

3. Los asaltantes (assailants) le _____ muchos golpes (punches) al viejo.

4. Nosotros le _____ el reporte oficial.

5. Tú te _____ cuenta del soborno (the bribe).

ser / ir

1. Ustedes no _____ a la corte.

2. El _____ ladrón (thief); ahora es trabajador social.

3. Yo _____ con mi abogada.

4. El presidiario (prisoner) _____ a la cárcel inmediatamente.

5. ¿ _____ ellos con alguien?

dormir

1. El declaró bajo juramento (swore) que nunca _____ en esta casa.

2. Vds. _____ casi todo el día.

3. Nosotros _____ en el parque contra la ordenanza municipal.

4. Yo no _____ cuando estuve detenido (arrested).

5. ¿ _____ ellos después de ocurrir el crimen?

sentir

1. La ladrona (woman thief) se _____ muy avergonzada (embarrassed).

2. Yo _____ lástima por ella (pity).

3. Nosotros lo _____ mucho cuando oímos la noticia de su muerte (death).

4. Ellos no _____ nada.

venir

1. Yo _____ a defender al señor Morales.

2. Tú _____ a declararte en favor de la señorita Matuche.

3. Ellos no _____ a entregarse (turn themselves in).

4. Nosotros _____ sin esperanza (without hope).

5. Ella _____ con un pasaporte falso.

EJERCICIOS. Fill in the appropriate form of the preterite.

1. Ayer yo (**levantarse**) _____ muy tarde.

2. Los ciudadanos norteamericanos no (**tener**) _____ mucha esperanza.

3. El delincuente (**ir**) _____ a hablar con el abogado.

4. El juez (**decir**) _____ que no podemos continuar así.

5. Estas conclusiones no me (**parecer**) _____ justas.

6. ¿Cuántas veces (**venir**) _____ usted a este sitio (location)?

7. Nunca (**llegar**) _____ ella antes de las siete.

8. Yo no (**dormir**) _____ en toda la noche.

9. Nosotros (**hablar**) _____ ayer de su situación.

10. Tú (**quejarse**) _____ del juicio (judgment).

11. Ella me (**dar**) _____ toda la información.

12. ¿Por qué (**terminar**) _____ ellos tan tarde?

13. La abogada nunca (**alegar** [to allege]) _____ esto en público.

14. El chófer no (**frenar** [to brake]) _____ hasta el último momento.

15. El (**venir**) _____ con el vino (the wine).

16. Su madre por fin (finally) (**saber**) _____ la verdad.

THE PRETERITE vs. THE IMPERFECT

The meaning of some verbs changes significantly as those verbs are translated into English from the preterite and the imperfect.

	Imperfect	*Preterite*
conocer	Tú conocías al acusado en Miami. (You knew the defendant in Miami.)	Tú conociste al acusado en Miami. (You met the defendant in Miami.)
poder	Yo no podía interrogar al acusado. (I was not able to question the defendant.)	Yo no pude interrogar al acusado. (I tried but failed to question the defendant.)
querer	Nosotros no queríamos aceptar la oferta. (We did not want to accept the offer.)	Nosotros no quisimos aceptar la oferta. (We refused to accept the offer.)
saber	El testigo lo sabía todo. (The witness knew everything.)	El testigo lo supo todo. (The witness found out everything.)
tener	Ella tenía un contrato con él. (She had [possessed] a contract with him.)	Ella tuvo un contrato con él. (She had—but no longer has—a contract with him.

EJERCICIOS. Translate into Spanish

1. They knew the witness. They met her in Los Angeles.

   _____

2. He was not able to see the defendant. He tried but failed to see the defendant.

   _____

3. I did not want to speak to the defendant. I refused to speak to the defendant.

   _____

4. You know everything, but I found out yesterday.

   _____

5. We used to have a witness. They had a witness.

   _____

TIME CONSTRUCTIONS

1. **hace + period of time   + que + presente   =   have been . . . ing for . . . period of time**

Hace + dos horas	+ que + yo hablo	= I have been speaking for two hours.
Hace + tres días	+ que + escribimos	= We have been writing for three days.

2. **hacía + period of time   + que + imperfecto   =   had been . . . ing for . . . period of time.**

Hacía + dos horas	+ que + yo hablaba	= I had been speaking for two hours.
Hacía + tres días	+ que + escribíamos	= We had been writing for three days.

3. **hace + period of time   + que + pretérito   =   ago**

Hace + dos horas	+ que + yo hablé	= Two hours ago I spoke./ I spoke two hours ago.
Hace + tres días	+ que + escribimos	= Three days ago we wrote./ We wrote three days ago.

EJERCICIOS. Fill in the blank spaces with the appropriate form of the verb.

1. Hace dos horas que tú lo _____ (said).

2. Hacía varios días que el abogado _____ (had been writing) el reporte.

3. Hace varias semanas que yo lo _____ (have been looking for it).

4. Hacía dos años que ellos _____ (had been working here).

5. Hace mucho tiempo que Vds. _____ (did it).

6. Hace pocos días que él los _____ (saw).

7. Hace más de un año que nosotros _____ (went) allí.

8. Hace veinte días que la policía _____ (have been investigating) el crimen.

9. Hacía un mes que yo no le _____ (had been speaking) a él.

10. Hace sesenta días que ella _____ (received) el aviso final (final notice).

11. Hace menos de una semana que los vecinos _____
    (have been complaining [*quejarse = to complain*]).

EJERCICIOS. Translate into Spanish

1. They have been writing for three hours

   _____

   _____

2. She had been sleeping for several minutes when he entered.

   _____

   _____

3. Two years ago we went to that city.

   _____

   _____

4. Four months ago I gave the information to the judge.

   _____

   _____

5. We have been speaking for more than sixty minutes.

   _____

   _____

6. Tomás had been receiving our letters for four months.

   _____

   _____

7. You have been living in the house for twenty years.

   _____

   _____

8. She has been looking for evidence (*evidencia*) for six months.

   _____

   _____

9. We signed the contract five years ago.

_____

_____

10. They had been walking (*caminar*) for several hours when they found (*encontrar*) the man.

_____

_____

El juzgado municipal

Diálogo

Abogado	—	Usted alegó, señor García, que mi cliente no **frenó** en el **semáforo,** ¿verdad?
César	—	No dije exactamente eso . . . dije pues . . .
Abogado	—	Está bien. Luego añadió usted en **la declaración jurada** que mi cliente iba a una **velocidad** muy **alta,** ¿verdad?
César	—	Sí, señor, según mis **cálculos,**sí, pienso que sí, porque cuando lo ví . . .
Abogado	—	Por favor, conteste solamente la pregunta con un sí o no.
César	—	Bueno.
Abogado	—	¡Dejemos esto por el momento! Si **el juez** me permite, tengo una serie de **preguntas biográficas** que le quiero hacer al **demandante.**
Juez	—	¿Con qué **propósito?**
Abogado	—	Estas preguntas **pondrán de manifiesto** el carácter del demandante.
Juez	—	Bien, pero tienen que tener algo que ver con **el pleito**; no quiero perder tiempo aquí.
Abogado	—	Sí, señor. Ahora bien, señor García, ¿dijo Ud. que es residente?
César	—	No, señor. No lo dije porque no tengo mi carnet de residencia.
Abogado	—	¿Está trabajando?
César	—	No, señor, porque no soy residente todavía; soy estudiante.
Abogado	—	¿Cuándo consiguió usted permiso para matricularse en la escuela en este país?

César	—	Pues, todavía no lo tengo. Pero es **injusto** lo que usted está haciendo con estas preguntas . . .
Abogado	—	Por favor, conteste sí o no.
César	—	Señor juez, es verdad que no soy ciudadano ni residente y que no tengo permiso para matricularme en la escuela pero esto no indica que soy un **indocumentado.**
Abogado	—	Joven, cuidado con estas conclusiones porque me parecen acusaciones . . .
Juez	—	*Basta.* No podemos seguir así. Hagamos un receso. ¡Vengan los abogados a mi oficina!

VOCABULARIO DEL DIALOGO

frenó	stopped (Vd., él, ella)
frenar	to brake, to stop
semáforo	traffic light
la declaración jurada	the sworn statement
velocidad alta	high speed
los cálculos	the figures, the calculations
el juez	the judge
preguntas biográficas	biographical questions
propósito	the purpose, reason
pondrán de manifiesto	will demonstrate (make manifest)
el demandante	the plaintiff
el pleito	the lawsuit, litigation, suit
injusto/a	unjust
indocumentado/a	a person lacking documents for identification (illegal alien)
basta	enough

PREGUNTAS SOBRE EL DIALOGO

1. ¿Según el abogado, ¿qué alegó César?

_____

2. ¿Qué tipo de preguntas le quiere hacer el abogado a César?

_____

3. ¿Según el abogado, ¿qué pondrán de manifiesto estas preguntas?

_____

4. ¿Qué le dijo al juez el abogado?

_____

5. ¿Qué le explicó César al juez?

_____

La abogada defensora de César en la Corte

Vocabulario del capítulo

COGNATES OR NEAR COGNATES

la acusación

el convicto

la causa

el crimen

drástico/a

el error

la evidencia

falso/a

final

grave

la identidad

el impacto

el proceso

en privado

en público

el reporte

el residente

el status

el tráfico

VOCABULARIO

el acusado	defendant	el juicio	judgment
anteayer	day before yesterday	la lástima	pity
el asaltante	assailant	la medida	measure
avergonzado/a	embarrassed	la mentira	lie
el aviso	announcement	la muerte	death
la ayuda	help	la orden	order
el bracero	contract laborer from Mexico	el pasaporte	passport
el bufete	lawyer's office	el periodista	journalist
la cárcel	jail	el presidiario	convict
la charla	chat, talk	el proceso	trial
el delincuente	delinquent	el receso	recess
los demás	the rest	el reclamante	claimant
detenido/a	arrested, detained	el sitio	place, location
la esperanza	hope	el soborno	bribe
el estatuto	statute	el testigo	witness
exactamente	exactly	el tribunal	court
la fianza	bail	último/a	last
el golpe	punch, blow	la verdad	truth
el hecho	deed, fact	el vino	wine
el indocumentado	illegal alien	el violador	rapist

VERBOS

admitir	to admit	estorbar	to disturb
abrazar	to embrace	fijar	to set, to fix
añadir	to add	frenar	to stop
apelar	to appeal	ganar	to earn
aplazar	to adjourn, to delay	interrogar	to interrogate
arreglar	to arrange	investigar	to investigate
citar	to summon	juzgar	to judge
conseguir	to obtain	participar	to participate
culpar	to blame	pelear	to fight
declarar	to declare	prender	to grasp
defender	to defend	proteger	to protect
deliberar	to deliberate	recibir	to receive
detener	to detain	reclamar	to sue
denunciar	to denounce	saludar	to greet
durar	to last	verificar	to verify
entregarse	to turn oneself in	violar	to violate

FRASES

el abogado defensor	defense attorney
bajo juramento	under oath
la declaración jurada	deposition, sworn statement
en privado	in private
en torno a	in relation to
en vez de	instead of
estar detenido	to be detained, arrested
el gran jurado	grand jury
hacer daño	to do harm
el juez de testamentarías	surrogate judge
medidas drásticas	drastic measures
la ordenanza municipal	municipal ordinance, law
la orden de registro	search warrant
poner de manifiesto	to point out
poner al día	to bring up to date
todo lo posible	everything possible

Vocabulario adicional

SOME COMMONLY USED "MANDATOS"

¡Frene(n)!	Put the brakes on! Stop!
¡Acelere(n)!	Speed up!
¡Páre(n)se!	Stop! Stand still!
¡Déje(n)lo!	Leave it! Drop it!
¡Termine(n)!	Finish!
¡Continúe(n)!	Continue!
¡Resuélva(n)lo!	Solve it
¡Declare(n)!	Declare!
¡Permíta(n)me!	Allow me! Permit me!
¡Entrégue(n)se!	Turn yourself in!
¡Confórme(n)se con eso!	Let it go at that!

EJERCICIOS. Translate the following commands into Spanish.

1. Please put the brakes on!   ¡ _____usted!

2. Please continue!   ¡ _____ustedes!

3. Turn yourself in!   ¡ _____usted!

4. Finish!   ¡ _____ustedes!

5. Allow me!   ¡ _____usted

6. Solve it!   ¡ _____ustedes!

7. Leave it!   ! _____usted!

8. Let it go at that!   ¡ _____ustedes!

9. Stop!   ¡ _____usted!!

10. Speed up!   ¡ _____ustedes!

Capítulo 13
El timo*

Lectura

Cuando José comenzó a trabajar, la supervisora
le dijo que **a pesar** de su mucha experiencia él   despite
iba a perder su nuevo empleo si no aprendía   was going to lose
inglés. **Como a José le interesa conservar**   As José was interested in saving
su trabajo, **él se ha matriculado** en una clase   has registered
de noche que ofrece **la escuela secundaria** de su   high school
barrio. José está muy contento en la clase, pero
cuando menos lo esperaba surgió un problema. En   when he was least expecting it / developed
el hospital **le han cambiado su turno de trabajo.**   they have changed his work schedule
José tiene que trabajar **de noche**, y no puede   at night
continuar con su clase de "**inglés para extranjeros.**"   English for Foreigners
José está muy desorientado y no sabe qué hacer.
Afortunadamente, **un vecino le enseña** un anuncio   a neighbor shows him
que ha salido en los periódicos **de estos días.**   recently
Es una clase de inglés por correspondencia, pero
cuesta mucho dinero. José no tiene **otra salida**   costs / another alternative
y **envía** el dinero para el curso a **la dirección**   sends / address
indicada.

* timo = fraud

José espera **ansiosamente**, pero **no recibe nada**.	eagerly / doesn't receive anything
Escribe una carta y no le contestan. Vuelve	
a escribir, pero **todo es en vano**. José está	all is in vain
furioso. **No tiene ni su dinero, no los libros**	he has neither his money nor books
y su trabajo **peligra**.	is in danger
Un día José habla con **el cartero** y le explica	mailman
su problema. El cartero le dice que usar el	
correo **para timar** a la gente es un **delito**	to deceive / crime
federal y **le recomienda** hablar con un	recommends (to him)
supervisor en **la oficina de correos**	post office
lo antes posible.	as soon as possible
José se siente más tranquilo, porque	
piensa que algo se podrá hacer.	

En Correos, venta de sellos

La gramática

OBJECT PRONOUN COMBINATIONS

As we saw in an earlier chapter, when a verb takes both a direct and indirect object pronoun, the indirect object pronoun precedes the direct object pronoun:

Subject		Indirect		Direct		Verb	
Usted	You	me	to me	lo	it	da.	give.
Usted	You	nos	to us	lo	it	ha dado.	have given.

If a reflexive pronoun is used with an object pronoun (direct or indirect), the reflexive pronoun will precede the direct or indirect object pronoun:

Subject		Reflexive		Object Pronoun		Verb	
Yo	I	me	myself	lo	it	pongo.	put on.
Tú	You	te	yourself	las	them	has puesto.	have put on.

The object pronoun combinations will precede the conjugated verb unless there is a dependent infinitive or a present participle in which case the combination may follow and be attached to the infinitive or the present participle.

Juan no **me las** quiere dar.

or   John doesn't want to give them to me.

Juan no quiere dár**melas***.

Tú **nos lo** estás enseñando.

or   You are showing it to us.

Tú estás enseñándo**noslo**.*

A Reminder About *LE* or *LES* before *LO, LA, LOS,* and *LAS*

Indirect		Direct			
le		lo			lo
		la			la
	+		=	SE +	
les		los			los
		las			las

* Note: When two object pronouns are attached to the dependent infinitive, an accent mark is placed over the vowel of the infinitive ending (*ar, er, ir*). An accent mark is also placed on the next to the last syllable of a present participle when either one or two pronouns are added and attached.

EJEMPLOS

(Yo) **le** doy el producto **a él.**	I give the product to him.
(Yo) **SE LO** doy **a él.**	I give it to him.
(Yo) **le** doy la ropa **a ella.**	I give the clothing to her.
(Yo) **SE LA** doy **a ella.**	I give it to her.
(Yo) **les** doy los paquetes **a ellos.**	I give the packages to them.
(Yo) **SE LOS** doy **a ellos.**	I give it to them.
(Yo) **les** doy las lámparas **a ellos.**	I give the lamps to them.
(Yo) **SE LAS** doy **a ellos.**	I give them to them.
(Yo) voy a dar**le** el televisor **a él.**	I am going to give him the television.
(Yo) voy a dár**SELO a él.**	I am going to give it to him.

OR

(Yo) **le** voy a dar el televisor **a él.**	I am going to give him the television.
(Yo) **SE LO** voy a dar **a él.**	I am going to give it to him.
(Yo) estoy dándo**les** las compras **a ellos.**	I am giving the purchases to them.
(Yo) estoy dándo**SELAS** a ellos.	I am giving them to them.

OR

(Yo) **les** estoy dando las compras **a ellos.**	I am giving the purchases to them.
(Yo) **SE LAS** estoy dando **a ellos.**	I am giving them to them.

EJERCICIOS. Replace the direct object noun with its direct object pronoun and make the corresponding changes.

1. El le da el dinero a Pablo. _____

   El _____

2. María les escribe una carta a ellos. _____

   María _____

3. Pepe no quiere darme los libros. _____

   Pepe _____

4. Estoy dándoles las compras a ellas. _____

   Estoy _____

5. Ellos le enseñan la libreta de depósitos (deposit book) al niño.

   Ellos _____

6. El prendero (pawnbroker) no puede darle el anillo (the ring) a María.

   El prendero _____

7. El almacén (the department store) les ha mandado (*mandar = to send*) el cheque a ellos.

   El almacén _____

8. Los vendedores de libros van a decirnos la verdad. Los vendedores de libros.

   _____

9. El lavandero (the laundry man) no quiere devolverme la ropa.

   El lavandero _____

10. El tramposo (the cheater) no le da el cambio (change).

    El tramposo _____

11. Ustedes se ponen los abrigos.

    Ustedes _____

12. El consumidor (consumer) le da la blusa de seda (silk blouse) al dependiente (clerk).

    El consumidor _____

13. Nosotros le traemos la mercancía (the merchandise).

    Nosotros _____

14. Las hermanas Guzmán tienen que mandarles el paquete a ellas.

    Las hermanas Guzmán _____

EJERCICIOS. Translate into Spanish.

1. The sales clerk sells them (*las cortinas*) to her.

   _____

2. He shows it (*el contrato*) to them (*los clientes*).

   _____

3. We send it (*la cartera* = *the wallet*) to him.

   _____

4. She is going to sell them (*los discos* = *the records*) to them (*las mujeres*).

_____

5. The merchants (*los mercaderes*) have sold them (*los instrumentos científicos*) to them (*los biólogos*). _____

_____

6. We are giving it (*el impermeable* = *the raincoat*) to her.

_____

7. I put it on (*el suéter*).

_____

8. Do you give them (*los zapatos* = *the shoes*) to us for nothing (*gratis*)?

_____

9. The peddler (*el mercachifle*) wants to show them (*los cubiertos* = *the silverware*) to us.

_____

10. I am going to send them (*los cheques*) to you (*familiar singular*).

_____

11. He has sold it (*la alfombra* = *the rug*) to you (*polite plural*).

_____

12. We close it (*la ventana*) for her.

_____

13. She opens them (*los regalos* = *the gifts*) for him.

_____

14. You (*Tú*) have to bring him to us.

_____

15. The landlord (*el casero*) does not want to show them (*los apartamentos*) to me.

_____

FORMAL COMMANDS: USTED (Vd.) and USTEDES (Vds.)

In Spanish, to form formal commands, take the "yo" form of the present tense of the verb, drop the *o*, and for *ar* verbs add add *e* for the *usted* form and *en* for the *ustedes* form.

Infinitive	*"yo" form*	*Vd. command*	*Vds. command*
pensar(ie)	piens*ø*	piens*e*	piens*en*
trabajar	trabaj*ø*	trabaj*e*	trabaj*en*

For *er* and *ir* verbs add *a* for the *usted* form and *an* for the *ustedes* form:

decir	dig*ø*	dig*a*	dig*an*
tener	teng*ø*	teng*a*	teng*an*
coger	coj*ø*	coj*a*	coj*an*
dormir(ue)	duerm*ø*	duerm*a*	duerm*an*
sentir(ie)	sient*ø*	sient*a*	sient*an*
pedir(i)	pid*ø*	pid*a*	pid*an*

The pronouns *usted* and *ustedes* need only be added for emphasis. To make a command negative, place *no* before the command:

Positive		*Negative*	
¡Haga esto!	Do this!	¡No haga esto!	Don't do this!

EJERCICIOS. Put the following infinitives in the appropriate command form:

	usted command	ustedes command
1. (leer)	¡ _____ las instrucciones!	¡ _____ las instrucciones!
2. (traer)	¡No _____ la lámpara!	¡No _____ la lámpara!
3. (trabajar)	¡No _____ aquí!	¡No _____ aquí!
4. (comer)	¡No _____ todo!	¡No _____ todo!
5. (ayudar)	¡ _____ al consumidor!	¡ _____ al consumidor!
6. (escribir)	¡No _____ mucho!	¡No _____ mucho!
7. (decir)	¡ _____ la verdad!	¡ _____ la verdad!
8. (traer)	¡ _____ el contrato!	¡ _____ el contrato!
9. (creer)	¡No _____ eso!	¡No _____ eso!
10. (mirar)	¡ _____ arriba (up)!	¡ _____ arriba!
11. (pedir[i])	¡No _____ más!	¡No _____ más !

12. (tener)   ¡ _____ cuidado! ¡ _____ cuidado!

13. (calentar[ie])   ¡ _____ la comida! ¡ _____ la comida!
     (to heat)

14. (estacionar)   ¡No _____ allí! ¡No _____ allí!
     (to park)

15. (contar[ue])   ¡ _____ el cambio! ¡ _____ el cambio!

16. (comprar)   ¡No _____ esto! ¡No _____ esto!

17. (esperar)   ¡ _____ un minuto! ¡ _____ un minuto!

VERBS WHOSE SPELLING CHANGES IN THE PRETERITE AND IN FORMAL COMMANDS

- Verbs ending in *car* change the *c* to *qu* before *e*. This change occurs in the formal commands and in the preterite.

	Preterite	*Formal Commands*	
buscar	yo busqué	¡Busque usted!	¡Busquen ustedes!

- Verbs ending in *gar* change the *g* to *gu* before *e*.

agregar (to add, to attach)	yo agregué	¡Agregue usted!	¡Agreguen ustedes!

- Verbs ending in *zar* change the *z* to *c* before *e*.

gozar (to enjoy)	yo gocé	¡Goce usted!	¡Gocen ustedes!

- Verbs ending in *guar* change the *gu* to *gü* before *e*.

averiguar (to find out)	yo averigüé	¡Averigüe usted!	¡Averigüen ustedes!

IRREGULAR FORMAL COMMANDS

	usted	*ustedes*
dar	dé	den
ir	vaya	vayan
ser	sea	sean
estar	esté	estén

In affirmative commands object pronouns and reflexive pronouns follow and are attached to the verb:

Command Form of Verb + Indirect + Direct Object

---

usted	*ustedes*	
¡Fírmelo!	¡Fírmenlo!	Sign it!

Command Form of Verb + Indirect + Direct Object

---

usted	*ustedes*	
¡Escríbale a él una carta!	¡Escríbanle a él una carta!	Write him a letter!
¡Escríbasela a él!	¡Escríbansela a él!	Write it to him!

Command Form of Verb + Reflexive + Object Pronoun

---

usted	*ustedes*	
¡Póngase los guantes!	¡Pónganse los guantes!	Put on the gloves!
¡Póngaselos!	¡Pónganselos!	Put them on!

In negative commands the object pronouns and reflexive pronouns precede the verb:

No + object pronoun/reflexive + command form of verb

---

usted	*ustedes*	
¡No lo firme!	¡No lo firmen!	Don't sign it!
¡No se ponga el abrigo!	¡No se pongan el abrigo!	Don't put on the coat!
¡No se lo ponga!	¡No se lo pongan!	Don't put it on!
¡No le escriba a él una carta!	¡No le escriban a él una carta!	Don't write him a letter!
¡No se la escriba a él!	¡No se la escriban a él!	Don't write it to him!

In positive commands a written accent is required over the stressed vowel of the verb, except in the case of **den + single object pronouns.**

EJERCICIOS. Replace the direct object noun with its direct object pronoun and make the corresponding changes.

1. ¡Tráigame el anuncio!

   _____

2. ¡Pídales a ellos los detalles!

   _____

3. ¡Déme los instrumentos!

_____

4. ¡Cómprele a él la mercancía!

_____

5. No nos manden los archivos!

_____

6. ¡Póngase la bufanda (the scarf)!

_____

7. ¡No les mande la copia (the copy) a los investigadores!

_____

8. ¡Escríbanles a ellos los hechos (the facts)!

_____

9. ¡Denle a ella los detalles!

_____

10. ¡No se pongan las camisas (the shirts)!

_____

11. ¡No le diga a ella la sugerencia (suggestion)!

_____

12. ¡Tráiganos el correo!

_____

EJERCICIOS. Translate into Spanish.

1. Bring it (*el automóvil*) to them (*los mecánicos*)!

¡ _____ usted!

2. Give it (*la información*) to them (*los inspectores*)!

   ¡ _____ ustedes!

3. Don't send him to her!

   ¡ _____ ustedes!

4. Don't put them (*los pantalones*) on!

   ¡ _____ ustedes!

5. Open them (*las puertas del refrigerador*) for her!

   ¡ _____ usted!

6. Ask it of them (*el favor*)!

   ¡ _____ ustedes!

7. Don't bring it (*la oferta*) to her!

   ¡ _____ ustedes!

8. Put it (*el vestido*) on!

   ¡ _____ usted!

9. Don't tell it (*la mentira*) to us!

   ¡ _____ ustedes!

10. Show it (*el precio = the price*) to them (*los consumidores*)!

   ¡ _____ usted!

PARA vs. POR

Even though "para" and "por" both mean "for" at times, they are not interchangeable. Each is used in different contexts.

Use **para**: 1. to express purpose
2. to express destination
3. to express the use for which something is intended
4. to express "by" or "for" a certain time
5. to express "for" in comparisons
6. to express the idea "about to"
7. to express the idea "to become"
8. to express the idea "according to"

1. To express purpose:

Apelamos **para** recobrar el dinero.

We appealed in order to recover the money/ for the purpose of recovering the money.

2. To express destination:

Estos contratos son **para** ella.

These contracts are for her.

Ahora mismo él sale **para** el Departamento de Agricultura.

Right now he is leaving for the Department of Agriculture.

3. To express the use for which something is intended:

La consumidora compra comidas **para** su familia.

The consumer buys foods for her family.

4. To express "by" or "for" a certain time:

Usted tiene que estar aquí **para** las dos.

You have to be here by two o'clock.

Para mañana haga ustedes todas las diligencias.

For tomorrow do all the errands.

5. To express "for" in comparisons:

Para ser extranjero (foreigner), él sabe mucho de las leyes.

For a foreigner, he knows a lot about the laws.

6. To express the idea "about to":

Estamos **para** salir.

We are about to leave.

7. To express the idea "to become":

Ella estudia **para** abogada.

She studies/is studying to become a lawyer.

8. To express the idea "according to":

Para Juan, esta investigación es importante.

According to John, this investigation is important.

Use **por**: 1. to express "for the sake of," "on account of," "in exchange for"
2. to express indefiniteness and duration of time
3. to express the place through, around, on or along which motion takes place
4. to express manner, means, or cause
5. to express "for" when it means "in quest of" after certain verbs
6. to express an unfinished action
7. to form many idiomatic expressions

1. To express "for the sake of," "on account of," "in exchange for"

El lo hace **por** codicia.	He does it on account of greed/out of greed.
Nosotros te podemos dar dos dólares **por** el bolígrafo.	We can give you two dollars for the ballpoint pen.

2. To express indefiniteness and duration of time:

Vengan ustedes a la oficina del agente de viajes **por** la mañana.	Come to the office of the travel agent in the morning.
¿**Por** cuánto tiempo vas a estar aquí?	For how long are you going to be here?

3. To express the place through, around, on, or along which motion takes place:

La pareja camina **por** el centro comercial.	The couple walks through the commercial center.
Los domingos no hay nadie **por** aquí.	On Sundays there is no one around here.
Por este lado no se ve nada.	On/Along this side nothing is seen.

4. To express manner, means, or cause:

No viajamos **por** avión.	We do not travel by plane.
Todo está arreglado **por** orden alfabético.	All is arranged in alphabetical order.
Por usted nos quedamos aquí esta noche.	Because of you we remain here tonight.

5. To express "for" when it means "in quest of" after certain verbs: **ir, enviar, venir, preguntar**

(Yo) he preguntado **por** el tenedor de libros varias veces.	I have asked for the bookkeeper various times.
Ellos han venido **por** su niño.	They have come for their child/little boy.

6. To express an unfinished action (por + infinitive):

Los cálculos están **por** hacer.	The calculations are still to be done.

7. To form many idiomatic expressions:

por favor	please	**por supuesto**	of course	**por desgracia**	unfortunately
por ejemplo	for example	**por lo visto**	apparently	**por lo menos**	at least
por fin	finally	**por poco**	almost	**por cierto**	indeed

EJERCICIOS.

Insert *por* or *para* as required in the blank space.

1. La abogada lo hace (for) _____ bondad (kindness)

   no (for) _____ la recompensa (compensation).

2. El tiene dos trabajos (in order to) _____ mejorar (to improve)
   su situación económica.

3. ¿Cuando vas a partir (to leave) (for) _____ el Departamento
   de Viviendas (Housing Authority)?

4. ¡Estén ustedes en el Departamento de Viviendas (in) _____ la
   mañana porque los caseros (landlords) están en el centro (in) _____ la tarde!

5. El cartero pasa (by) _____ tu casa muy temprano.

6. Ella lo trae (for) _____ ellos.

7. Lo hacemos (in order to) _____ ayudar a los consumidores.

8. (Unfortunately) _____ tenemos tres investigaciones (still to be

   done) _____ .

9. Ella lo hace (for) _____ la causa.

10. Ustedes deben de dejar este asunto (for) _____ el próximo año (next year).

11. Silencio, por favor. Ella está (about to) _____ hablar.

12. Los atletas (the athletes) corren (*correr* = *to run*) (through) _____
    las calles.

13. ¿Ha enviado usted (for) _____ mí?

14. El comerciante no necesita la pistola/el revólver (in order to) _____
    protegerse (to protect himself).

15. (For) _____ ser extranjero, usted sabe mucho de los
    negocios (business) de este país.

16. ¿Como van ustedes a Washington? Vamos (by) _____ tren o

   (by) _____ automóvil.

17. Ella no quiere pagar cuarenta y cinco dólares (for) _____ las sandalias (the sandals).

18. Tenemos que tener todo listo (everything ready) (by) _____ las dos de la mañana.

19. Estas vitaminas son (for) _____ tu niña.

20. (At least) _____ he hecho estos ejercicios.

EJERCICIOS. Answer in Spanish.

1. ¿Por qué llama la gente a la oficina de Protección del Consumidor?

   _____

2. ¿Por cuánto tiempo ha vivido usted en esta ciudad?

   _____

3. ¿Le gusta a usted ir de compras (go shopping) por la mañana o por la noche?

   _____

4. Cuando usted va a un almacén, por lo general, ¿cuándo dinero paga por la mercancía que compra?

   _____

5. ¿Trabaja usted por el dinero o por amor al trabajo?

   _____

EJERCICIOS. Read in Spanish, inserting *por* or *para* as required:

_____ desgracia, Juanito y Panchito son enemigos. Un día _____

_____ la mañana, Juanito pasa _____ el parque. No hay

nadie _____ allí. Juanito está _____ sentarse en

un banco (bench) cuando ve a Panchito. _____ no hablar con su

enemigo, Juanito corre _____ todo el parque hasta llegar a la entrada

(the entrance). Allí él se sienta _____ unos segundos (seconds) porque está

cansado. De repente aparece (**aparecer** = *to appear*) Panchito y al mismo tiempo (at the same

time) los dos muchachitos dicen, "tenemos que estar en la escuela _____

las ocho." Los dos salen juntos (together)_____la escuela.

EJERCICIOS. Translate into Spanish.

1. When are you going to leave for Puerto Rico?

   _____

2. I must work a lot in order to survive (*sobrevivir*).

   _____

3. These records (*datos*) are for your lawyer.

   _____

4. I don't want to pay three hundred dollars for this stove (*la estufa*).

   _____

5. Give me all of the information by tomorrow.

   _____

6. They do it for him (for his sake).

   _____

7. My mother has lived alone (*sola*) for fifteen years.

   _____

8. These packages are for you.

   _____

9. For a beginner (*principiante*), you understand a lot.

   _____

10. We don't walk along these streets in the evening.

   _____

José García en Correos

Diálogo

Señor Thantos	—	Por favor, ¡pase usted!
José García	—	Ah, usted habla español. Perdone **la molestia**. Este . . . soy José García. El cartero, Remedios Garmendía, que es mi vecino, me ha dicho que usted puede ayudarme.
Señor Thantos	—	Sí ¡cómo no! Para no **equivocarnos** y **malgastar** el tiempo, dígame, ¿es este asunto algo relacionado con un **truco** para defraudarle?
José García	—	Sí, señor, por eso estoy aquí. He perdido mucho dinero y creo que tengo derecho a **reclamarlo**. Por favor, señor Thantos, déme un buen consejo.
Señor Thantos	—	Escúcheme bien, señor García. Por desgracia el Servicio Postal no tiene autoridad para devolverle su dinero. Sólo un tribunal puede hacer esto.
José García	—	No entiendo. ¿No puede usted recobrar el dinero?
Señor Thantos	—	Un momento, señor García. No digo que no puedo ayudarle; es que el Servicio Postal no le puede devolver su dinero. Podemos ayudarle **en cuanto a** preparar **una queja**. Se la puedo enviar al Servicio de Inspección Postal.
José García	—	Está bien. Ahora comprendo la situación. Mire, tengo **todito** aquí — recibos, sobres, y hasta la hoja de propaganda que la compañía esa me ha enviado.
Señor Thantos	—	Muy bien. Démelo todo . . . y así **yo mismo** puedo comenzar a preparar los documentos necesarios.

VOCABULARIO DEL DIALOGO

la molestia	the annoyance, the trouble, the bother
equivocarse	to make a mistake, to be mistaken
malgastar	to waste
truco	trick
reclamar	to demand
en cuanto a	with respect to
una queja	a complaint
todito	every little thing
yo mismo	I myself

PREGUNTAS SOBRE EL DIALOGO

1. ¿Con quién habla José?

_____

2. ¿Puede el Servicio Postal devolverle el dinero?

_____

3. ¿Qué va a hacer el señor Thantos para ayudarle a José?

_____

4. ¿Le ha traído José algo para darle al señor Thantos?

_____

5. ¿Quién va a comenzar a preparar los documentos necesarios?

_____

José García abriendo su apartado postal

Vocabulario del capítulo

COGNATES OR NEAR COGNATES

la agricultura
comercial
conveniente
la copia
económico/a
el favor
la inspección

el inspector
el instrumento
la licencia
el mecánico
nocturno/a
la pistola
postal

el producto
la protección
el revólver
el refrigerador
el silencio
la situación
la vitamina

VOCABULARIO

el abrigo	coat	la entrada	entrance
afortunadamente	fortunately	la estufa	stove
el almacén	department store	el extranjero	foreigner
el amor	love	el hecho	fact
el anillo	ring	junto/a	together, united
el árbol	tree	el lavandero	laundry man
el archivo	file	listo/a	ready
el atleta	athlete	el mercachifle	peddler
el banco	bench	la mercancía	merchandise
la bondad	kindness	mismo/a	same
la bufanda	scarf	el negocio	business
la camisa	shirt	la oferta	offer
el cartero	mailman	los pantalones	pants
el casero	landlord/ housing agent	el paquete	package
		la pareja	couple
científico/a	scientific	el precio	price
la cocina	kitchen	el prendero	pawnbroker
la codicia	greed	la prensa	press (newspaper)
el comerciante	businessman	previo/a	prior, previous
las compras	purchases	el principiante	beginner
el consumidor	consumer	el propietario	landlord
las cortinas	the curtains	recién	recently
el crimen	crime	la recompensa	compensation
la diligencia	errand	la respuesta	response, answer
la encrucijada	trap, bind	la ropa	clothing
el enemigo	enemy	la sandalia	sandal

la suerte	luck	el truco	trick
la sugerencia	suggestion	el vecino	neighbor
el televisor	T.V. set	los zapatos	shoes
el tramposo	cheater		

VERBOS

aconsejar	to advise	jurar	to swear
agregar	to add	malgastar	to waste
apelar	to appeal	mandar	to send, to command
averiguar	to find out	matricularse	to enroll
calentar	to heat	mejorar	to better
cambiar	to change	ofrecer	to offer
comprar	to buy	olvidarse	to forget
conservar	to save	peligrar	to be in danger
defraudar	to defraud	permitir	to permit
desarrollar	to develop	probar	to try, prove
desorientar	to disorient	protegerse	to protect oneself
devolver	to return an object	recobrar	to get back
enviar	to send	sobrevivir	to survive
equivocarse	to be wrong	surgir	to appear, to develop
estacionar	to park	timar	to defraud, to deceive
gozar (de)	to enjoy	tratarse	to deal with, be about
imponer	to impose (a fine)		
iniciar	to begin, initiate		

FRASES

agente de viajes	travel agent
al mismo tiempo	at the same time
el apartado postal	post office box
a pesar de	in spite of
correr un mayor riesgo	to run a greater risk
el Departamento de Salud, Educación y Bienestar	Department of Health, Education and Welfare
El Departamento de Vivienda	Housing Authority
de repente	suddenly
ir de compras	to go shopping
la escuela secundaria	high school
en cuanto a	with respect to
la libreta de depósitos	bank deposit book
lo más pronto posible	as soon as possible
poner al tanto	to inform

por cierto	indeed, by the way
por desgracia	unfortunately
por lo menos	at least
por lo visto	apparently
por poco	almost
por supuesto	of course
programa de correo	correspondence course
el próximo año	next year
el tenedor de libros	bookkeeper
turno de trabajo	work schedule/shift

Vocabulario adicional

SOME COMMONLY USED "MANDATOS"

¡Agárre(n)lo(s)!	Grasp it (them)/Grab it (them)!
¡Devuélva(n)lo(s)!	Return it (them)!
¡No se olvide(n)!	Don't forget!
¡Recuérde(n)lo(s)!	Remember it (them)!
¡Entrégue(n)lo(s)!	Hand it (them) over!
¡Ofrézca(n)lo(s)!	Offer it (them)!
¡Júre(n)lo/la!	Swear to it!
¡Envíe(n)lo(s)!	Send it (them)!
¡Exámine(n)lo(s)!	Examine it (them)!
¡Pruébe(n)lo(s)!	Try it (them)!
¡Investígue(n)lo(s)!	Investigate it (them)!
¡Pase(n)!	Come in!

EJERCICIOS. Translate into Spanish.

1. Return them! ¡ _____ ustedes!

2. Investigate them! ¡ _____ usted!

3. Remember it, please! ¡ _____ ustedes!

4. Don't forget! ¡ _____ usted!

5. Hand them over! ¡ _____ ustedes!

6. Please send them! ¡ _____ usted!

7. Try it! ¡ _____ ustedes!

8. Examine them! ¡ _____ usted!

9. Please come in! ¡ _____ ustedes!

Capítulo 14
La contribución sobre ingresos

Lectura

La semana que viene los García irán a la   next week

oficina del licenciado Rivera.* No será

por lo del accidente de su hijo, **sino**   because of / but rather

por algo menos serio, pero tal vez más

complicado: **la contribución sobre ingresos**.   income tax

Los García, aunque no son **ciudadanos**,   citizens

tendrán que hacer una declaración de

ingresos para ver si **deben** dinero o si   they owe

recibirán un **reembolso** del gobierno.   refund

Felizmente, este año no tendrán que   Happily

romperse tanto la cabeza con las   rack their brains

planillas porque hay **un folleto**   pamphlet

bilingüe que lo explica todo.

Además, el licenciado Rivera sabrá

aconsejarles bien sobre las complicadas

leyes de las contribuciones. El   laws

licenciado Rivera fue parte de un

proyecto federal que estudió la forma

*Licenciado = a person with a baccalaureate degree, usually title is used with lawyers.

de **aclarar** estas leyes de las   better explain
contribuciones a los hispanos.
El **les cobrará** cuarenta dólares por   will charge them
sus servicios, pero los García piensan
que **valdrá la pena** porque es muy difícil   will be worthwhile
estar al día de tantas leyes. Ellos le   to be up to date on
llevarán al licenciado Rivera todos
los cheques, **recibos** y **facturas** que   receipts / bills
probarán sus gastos e ingresos. Muy   will prove
pronto, los García serán unos **expertos**   expert
contadores.   accountants

La oficina del contador

La gramática

THE FUTURE TENSE

The future tense is formed by adding the following endings to the infinitive of most verbs:
-é, -ás, -á, -emos, án:

	ayudar	*entender*	*recibir*
yo	ayudar**é** I will help	entender**é** I will understand	recibir**é** I will receive
tú	ayudar**ás** you will help	entender**ás** you will understand	recibir**ás** you will receive
usted él ella	ayudar**á** you/he/she will help	entender**á** you/he/she will understand	recibir**á** you/he/she will receive
nosotros	ayudar**emos** we will help	entender**emos** we will understand	recibir**emos** we will receive
ustedes ellos ellas	ayudar**án** you/they/they will help	entender**án** you/they/they will understand	recibir**án** you/they/they will receive

The future tense corresponds to the English "shall" or "will" and is used to express future actions or conditions.

EJERCICIOS. Insert the proper form of the verb.

1. El contador público certificado (C.P.A.) **cobrará** mucho por sus servicios.
   (los bancos, él, ustedes, ellas)

   _____

   _____

   _____

   _____

2. Yo le **mandaré** a usted el recibo.
   (el agente de seguros, ellos, yo, tú)

   _____

   _____

   _____

   _____

3. La compañía no **comerciará** (to trade) con esos países.
   (el contribuyente, yo, nosotros, ustedes)

   _____

   _____

   _____

   _____

4. Nosotros lo **investigaremos** temprano mañana.
   (yo, tú, tú y tus hermanos, ella)

   _____

   _____

   _____

   _____

5. ¿Dónde **necesitarás** tú la próxima extensión telefónica?
   (el inquilino [the tenant], ellos, nosotras, yo)

   _____

   _____

   _____

   _____

EJERCICIOS. Fill in the appropriate future form of the verb.

1. recibir, mandar, ver   Yo lo _____ esta tarde.

2. trabajar, estar, comer   Tú _____ aquí a las cinco.

3. acostarse, levantarse   Usted _____ muy temprano.

4. pelear, asistir, seleccionar Ella _____ otra vez.

5. coger, tomar, hallar   Nosotros _____ el subterráneo.

6. dormir, quedarse, vestirse   Ustedes _____ en mi casa.

7. lavarse, jugar, beber   Ellos _____ todas las noches.

8. oír, escuchar, estudiar   Ellas _____ el consejo del abogado.

THE CONDITIONAL TENSE

The conditional tense is formed by adding the following endings to the infinitive of most verbs: *-ía, -ías, -ía, -íamos, ían*:

	ayudar	*entender(ie)*	*recibir*
yo	ayudar*ía* I would help	entender*ía* I would understand	recibir*ía* I would receive
tú	ayudar*ías* you would help	entender*ías* you would understand	recibir*ías* you would receive
usted él ella	ayudar*ía* you/she/he would help	entender*ía* you/she/he would understand	recibir*ía* you/she/he would receive
nosotros	ayudar*íamos* we would help	entender*íamos* we would understand	recibir*íamos* we would receive
ustedes ellos ellas	ayudar*ían* you/they/they would help	entender*ían* you/they/they would understand	recibir*ían* you/they/they would receive

El dijo que me *ayudaría*.	He said that he would help me.
Yo creía que tú *recibirías* todo el dinero.	I thought that you would receive all the money.

The conditional tense corresponds to the English "should" or "would." When "should" implies a moral obligation **deber + infinitive** must be used.

Usted **debe** decirnos la verdad.	You should tell us the truth.

When "would" refers to a repeated action in the past, then the imperfect must be used:

Ellas siempre **salían** temprano.	They would/used to always leave early.

EJERCICIOS. Insert the proper form of the verb in the conditional.

1. ¿Cuál de los libros sobre impuestos federales **preferirían** ellas?
   (su contador, tú, usted, tu abogado)

   _____

   _____

   _____

   _____

2. El dijo que **ayudaría** con todo.
   (yo, tú, ellos, el beneficiario)

   _____

   _____

   _____

   _____

3. Yo no dije que **me levantaría** temprano.
   (los directores, el burócrata, tus amigos, nosotros)

   _____

   _____

   _____

   _____

4. El no sabía si yo lo **entendería**.
   (tú, él, ustedes, nosotras)

   _____

   _____

   _____

   _____

IRREGULAR VERBS IN THE FUTURE AND CONDITIONAL TENSES

Infinitive	*Irregular Stem*	*Future*	*Conditional*
decir	*dir*	diré, dirás, etc.	diría, dirías, etc.
haber	*habr*	habré, habrás, etc.	habría, habrías, etc.
hacer	*har*	haré, harás, etc.	haría, harías, etc.
poder	*podr*	podré, podrás, etc.	podría, podrías, etc.
poner	*pondr*	pondré, pondrás, etc.	pondría, pondrías, etc.
querer	*querr*	querré, querrás, etc.	querría, querrías, etc.
saber	*sabr*	sabré, sabrás, etc.	sabría, sabrías, etc.
salir	*saldr*	saldré, saldrás, etc.	saldría, saldrías, etc.
tener	*tendr*	tendré, tendrás, etc.	tendría, tendrías, etc.
venir	*vendr*	vendré, vendrás, etc.	vendría, vendrías, etc.

EJERCICIOS. Put the verbs in parenthesis in the future tense.

1. Yo (decir) _____ la verdad mañana.

2. El representante dice que (haber) _____ una reunión en su oficina.

3. Los acreedores (creditors) (necesitar) _____ calcular los ingresos brutos (gross income).

4. Los casados (married couple) (querer) _____ mandar una declaración conjunta (joint declaration).

5. Los señores García (poder) _____ reclamar a sus sobrinos como dependientes.

6. Ahora algunos burócratas (poner) _____ toda la información en una computadora.

7. ¿A qué hora (salir) _____ usted mañana por la mañana para el Tribunal del Distrito?

8. El contribuyente (tax payer) (tener) _____ preparado su cheque el jueves.

9. ¿(Venir) _____ él sólo?

10. Ustedes (llegar) _____ temprano para el certificado.

The verb *poder* in the conditional

In the conditional the verb **poder** translates as "could":

¿**Podría** usted hacerme el favor?   Could you do me the favor?

EJERCICIOS. Insert the proper form of the verb.

1. Tú **comenzarás** temprano, ¿verdad?
   (ellos, Pancho, María y Roberto, nosotras)

_____

_____

_____

_____

2. Yo no **haré** nada mañana.
   (tú, ellos, nosotros, usted)

   _____

   _____

   _____

3. Ellos dicen que **saldrán** a eso de las cinco (about five o'clock).
   (tú, ustedes, nosotras, yo)

   _____

   _____

   _____

4. Nosotros nunca **llegaríamos** tan tarde.
   (ellos, yo, tú, usted)

   _____

   _____

   _____

5. El director dijo que **tendría** más cuidado.
   (los niños, yo, nosotros, tú)

   _____

   _____

   _____

"I WONDER"

One way to convey the idea of "I wonder" in Spanish is as follows:

English	Spanish
Wonder + interrogative pronoun + verb in the present tense	Interrogative pronoun + verb in the future tense

I wonder who he is?	¿Quién será él?
I wonder where we are?	¿Dónde estaremos?
I wonder why they have good luck?	¿Por qué tendrán ellos buena suerte?
I wonder what she does?	¿Qué hará ella?

EJERCICIOS. Translate into Spanish.

1. I wonder where our tax return (*la declaración de salario e impuestos*) is?

   _____

2. I wonder how old they are?

   _____

3. I wonder who knows the laws?

   _____

4. I wonder when we will receive the receipts?

   _____

5. I wonder what they are doing here?

   _____

6. I wonder how they can charge forty dollars (*dólares*)?

   _____

7. I wonder who will do the work?

   _____

8. I wonder who has the standard deduction (*deducción normal*)?

   _____

PROBABILITY

The future and conditional tenses can be used to express probability.

- **Probability in the present may be conveyed with:**

    1. probablemente + verb in present tense

        ¿Quién es ese señor?   Probablemente es el juez.

    2. future tense of the verb

        ¿Quién es ese señor?   Será el juez.

- **Probability in the past may be conveyed with:**

    1. probablemente + verb in past tense

        ¿Quién era ese señor?   Probablemente era el juez.

    2. conditional tense of the verb

        ¿Quién era ese señor?   Sería el juez.

When "will" indicates "willingness," use the present tense of **querer** and not the future tense:

Ella quiere salir ahora.	She wants (is willing) to leave now.	
Ella saldrá ahora.	She will leave now.	*(future time indicated)*
¿Quiere usted salir ahora?	Will you leave now?	*(polite request implied)*

EJERCICIOS. Indicate the two ways in which probability can be expressed:

1. ¿Quién es esta señorita?   _____ la hermana de Juan.

    _____ la hermana de Juan.

2. ¿Quién era su
    ayudante (helper)?   _____ el señor Martínez.

    _____el señor Martínez

3. ¿Quiénes son ellos?   _____ los beneficiarios.

    _____ los beneficiarios.

4. ¿Qué impuestos paga ella?   _____ los impuestos del Estado.

    _____ los impuestos del Estado.

5. ¿Quién era este señor?   _____ el tenedor de libros (bookkeeper).

    _____ el tenedor de libros .

6. ¿Qué hora era?   _____ las tres de la tarde.

    _____ las tres de la tarde.

THE PASSIVE VOICE

The formula for the passive voice construction is the same in both Spanish and English:

Subject	+	"to be" (ser)	+	Past Participle	+	by (por)	+	Agent
Los libros	+	son	+	leídos	+	por	+	los abogados.
The books	+	are	+	read	+	by	+	the lawyers.
La ley	+	fue	+	escrita	+	por	+	los contadores.
The law	+	was	+	written	+	by	+	the accountants.
El préstamo	+	será	+	pagado	+	por	+	el banco.
The loan	+	will be	+	paid	+	by	+	the bank.

The past participle in Spanish functions as an adjective and therefore agrees with the subject in number and gender.

REFLEXIVE SUBSTITUTE FOR THE PASSIVE VOICE

The passive voice construction which we just outlined is used almost exclusively in the written language. A more common form of the passive voice is expressed by using the reflexive object *se* before the third person of the verb, which will be singular or plural, depending on the subject:*

			singular	+	singular subject
se	+	3rd person	plural	+	plural subject

Se investiga este tipo de problema aquí.　　This type of problem is investigated here.

Se investigan los asaltos
en otro departamento.　　The assaults are investigated in another department.

In both of these examples no agent was expressed. If the agent is expressed, then the passive construction which uses **ser** + **past participle** must be used.

EJERCICIOS. Insert the appropriate form of the passive voice in the blank spaces.

1. No (is used) _____ este tipo de contrato ahora.

2. La ley (was changed) _____ por el congreso.

3. Aquí (is needed [*necesitar*]) _____ mucho dinero.

4. Estos beneficios (were given) _____ por el gobierno federal.

5. Su crédito (is examined) _____ por ellos cada año.

*For more information on the reflexive pronoun used as a substitute for the passive voice, see Capítulo 9.

6. La tabla (the schedule) (was prepared) _____ por la Asociación de Contadores Certificados.

7. Su petición (request) (was rejected [*rechazar*]) _____ el mes pasado.

8. Los contratos (will be broken [*romper*]) _____ si la administración no cumple la palabra (keep its word).

9. Los impuestos (were imposed [*imponer*]) _____ por el municipio.

10. La ley (will be revised [*revisar*]) _____ este año.

11. Sus deducciones (are calculated [*calcular*]) _____ cuatro veces al año.

12. Su nombre (was put) _____ en la lista por su jefe (boss).

SINGULAR FAMILIAR OR *TU* COMMANDS

With a few exceptions the affirmative "tú" command has the same form as the third person singular of the present tense:

Infinitive	3rd Person Singular of Present Indicative	"Tú" command
ayudar	ayuda	¡Ayuda (tú)!
traer	trae	¡Trae (tú)!
dormir	duerme	¡Duerme (tú)!

The pronoun "tú" need only be used for emphasis.
The negative "tú" command is formed by adding **s** to the "usted" command form:

Usted command	Negative "tú" command
¡Ayude!	¡No ayudes!
¡Traiga eso!	¡No traigas eso!
¡Duerma!	¡No duermas!

EJERCICIOS.
Change the usted command to a tú command and then give the negative.

1. ¡Coma usted!   ¡ _____ tú! ¡No _____ !

2. ¡Trabaje usted!   ¡ _____ tú! ¡No _____ !

3. ¡Aconseje Vd!   ¡ _____ tú! ¡No _____ !

4. ¡Consulte Vd!   ¡ _____ tú! ¡No _____ !

5. ¡Advierta Vd!   ¡ _____ tú! ¡No _____ !

6. ¡Envíe Vd!   ¡ _____ tú! ¡No _____ !

7. ¡Cambie Vd!   ¡ _____ tú! ¡No _____ !

8. ¡Vuelva Vd!   ¡ _____ tú! ¡No _____ !

9. ¡Recuerde Vd!   ¡ _____ tú! ¡No _____ !

10. ¡Pase Vd!   ¡ _____ tú! ¡No _____ !

11. ¡Ofrezca Vd!   ¡ _____ tú! ¡No _____ !

12. ¡Examine Vd!   ¡ _____ tú! ¡No _____ !

Use the "ustedes" command form for both the affirmative and negative plural familiar commands.

SOME IRREGULAR *TU* COMMANDS

Infinitive	Affirmative	Negative
decir	¡Di!	¡No digas!
hacer	¡Haz!	¡No hagas!
ir	¡Ve!	¡No vayas!
poner	¡Pon!	¡No pongas!
salir	¡Sal!	¡No salgas!
ser	¡Sé!	¡No seas!
tener	¡Ten!	¡No tengas!
venir	¡Ven!	¡No vengas!

PLACEMENT OF OBJECT PRONOUNS AND REFLEXIVE PRONOUNS IN COMMANDS

In affirmative commands object pronouns and reflexives follow and are attached to the verb. In affirmative commands, also, an accent mark is placed over the stressed syllable of the verb when there are more than two syllables.

¡Ayúdame!	Help me!
¡Tráemelos!	Bring them to me!
¡Ponte el sombrero!	Put on the hat!
¡Póntelo!	Put it on!

Note: The reflexive familiar "te" is used with familiar reflexive commands.

In **negative commands** the object pronouns and the reflexive pronouns precede the verb:

¡No me ayudes!	Don't help me!
¡No me los traigas!	Don't bring them to me!
¡No te pongas el sombrero!	Don't put on the hat!
¡No te lo pongas!	Don't put it on!

EJERCICIOS. **Insert the appropriate command and substitute an object or reflexive pronoun for the noun.**

1. ¡Dame la carta! _____

   (Neg.) _____

2. ¡Ponte los guantes (gloves)! _____

   (Neg.) _____

3. ¡Léenos el párrafo (paragraph)! _____

   (Neg.) _____

4. ¡Tráeles a ellos las carpetas (folders)! _____

   (Neg.) _____

5. ¡Prepárame la cama (the bed)! _____

   (Neg.) _____

6. ¡Dile a él la verdad! _____

   (Neg.) _____

7. ¡Límpiale a ella el brazo (arm)! _____

   (Neg.) _____

8. ¡Dales a ellas los papeles! _____

   (Neg.) _____

9. ¡Cómpranos las comidas! _____

   (Neg.) _____

10. ¡Dime las noticias! _____

    (Neg.) _____

11. ¡Ponte la ropa! _____

    (Neg.) _____

12. ¡Enséñale a él el recibo! _____

    (Neg.) _____

EJERCICIOS. Change the "usted" command to the "tú" command.

1. ¡Váyase de aquí!   _____

2. ¡No se levante tarde!   _____

3. ¡Márchese (*marcharse = to leave*)
    de aquí!   _____

4. ¡No cambie esto!   _____

5. ¡Trabaje hasta las ocho!   _____

6. ¡Use esta máquina!   _____

7. ¡Acuéstese temprano!   _____

8. ¡Quítese (*quitarse = to remove*)
    la ropa sucia! (dirty clothes)   _____

9. ¡Suba la escalera!   _____

10. ¡Váyase!   _____

11. ¡No se preocupe!   _____

12. ¡Cálmese!   _____

EJERCICIOS. Translate into Spanish using both the "usted" and "tú" command forms:

	Usted	Tú
1. Don't speak!	¡ _____ !	¡ _____ !

2. Don't go!　¡ _____ !　¡ _____ !

3. Look!　¡ _____ !　¡ _____ !

4. Come here!　¡ _____ !　¡ _____ !

5. Don't get up late!　¡ _____ !　¡ _____ !

6. Don't drink!　¡ _____ !　¡ _____ !

7. Don't run!　¡ _____ !　¡ _____ !

8. Be careful!　¡ _____ !　¡ _____ !

9. Sit down!　¡ _____ !　¡ _____ !

10. Don't be impatient! (ser + *impaciente*)

¡ _____ !　¡ _____ !

11. Read it (*la información*)! ¡ _____ !　¡ _____ !

12. Write them (*las cartas*)! ¡ _____ !　¡ _____ !

13. Do the work! ¡ _____ !　¡ _____ !

Diálogo

Señor García	—	Oye Rivera, ¿no podremos buscar ayuda aquí?
Señor Rivera	—	Sí, se puede, pero **habrá** problemas con los agentes federales, habrá problemas.
Señor García	—	Caramba, Rivera, nos sacarán hasta los dientes.
Señora García	—	Mira Rivera, lo que queremos reclamar es **legítimo.**
Señor Rivera	—	A mí no me tendrás que convencer. Es a ellos y **te garantizo,** cien por cien, que te investigarán. Estoy convencido de que este año cada planilla que llegue con esta deducción será **rechazada** por la computadora.
Señor García	—	Vale, vale, por los cien dólares que nos **ahorraremos** no **vale la pena.**
Señora García	—	Pero de todas formas irán con nosotros **por si acaso.**
Señor Rivera	—	No te preocupes, no habrá problemas. Mira, Pepe, ¿tendrás algún recibo de la Asociación Chilena-Americana?
Señor García	—	Sí, lo tengo en casa.
Señor Rivera	—	Bueno, guárdalo bien.

VOCABULARIO DEL DIALOGO

habrá	there will be
legítimo/a	legitimate
te garantizo	guarantee you
rechazada	rejected
ahorraremos	we will save
no vale la pena	is not worth it
por si acaso	just in case

PREGUNTAS SOBRE EL DIALOGO

1. ¿Con quiénes van a tener problemas los García?

2. ¿De qué está seguro Rivera?

_____

3. ¿Qué cantidad de dinero pueden ahorrar los García si incluyen esta deducción?

_____

4. Si hay problemas, ¿qué hará Rivera?

_____

5. ¿Dónde tiene el señor García el recibo de la Asociación Chilena-Americana?

_____

El contador de los García

Vocabulario del capítulo

COGNATES OR NEAR COGNATES

el asalto
la administración
la asociación
el beneficio
el beneficiario
bilingüe
el burócrata
el certificado
el congreso
el contrato
el crédito

la deducción
el dependiente
el distrito
el dólar
el experto
la extensión
federal
normal
la reunión
telefónico / a

VOCABULARIO

el acreedor	creditor	el folleto	booklet
la apelación	appeal	el guante	glove
el aumento	increase	el impuesto	tax
el beneficio	benefit	el inquilino	tenant
la cama	bed	legítimo /a	legitimate
la cantidad	amount	el párrafo	paragraph
la carpeta	folder, porfolio	la petición	request, petition
el contribuyente	taxpayer	el próximo proyecto	next project
la devolución	refund	la tabla	schedule
la factura, el recibo	bill		

VERBOS

ahorrar	to save	imponer	to impose
aconsejar	to advise	marcharse	to go
asistir	to attend	quitarse	take off, remove
coger	to catch, seize, grab	reclamar	to claim
comerciar	to trade	revisar	to revise, to review
convertirse	to become	romper	to break
garantizar	to guarantee		
hallar	to find		

FRASES

a eso de	about (response to time)
agente de seguros	insurance agent
comprobar las declaraciones	to substantiate claims
cumplir la palabra	to keep one's word
la declaración conjunta	joint declaration
la declaración de salario e impuestos	wage and tax return
la deducción normal	standard deduction
estar endeudado	to be indebted
la excepción por ceguera	exemption for blindness
los ingresos brutos	gross income
mantenerse al tanto	to keep up to date
por si acaso	just in case
romperse la cabeza	to rack one's brains
el Servicio de Impuestos Internos	Internal Revenue Service
el Tribunal de Reclamaciones	Small Claims Court
valer la pena	to be worthwhile

Vocabulario adicional

SOME COMMONLY USED "MANDATOS"

¡Juzgue(n)!	Judge!
¡Cuénte(n)lo!	Count it!
¡Seleccione(n)!	Select!
¡Compruebe(n)!	Validate! Prove!
¡Devuelva(n)!	Return (an object)!
¡Calcule(n)!	Calculate!
¡Notifique(n)!	Notify!
¡Suspenda(n)!	Stop! Suspend!
¡Súme(n)lo!	Add it up!
¡Agrégue(n)lo!	Add it up!
¡Pague(n)!	Pay!

Capítulo 15
La póliza de seguros*

Lectura

Hace **un par** de días, José García
recibió una carta certificada del
gerente de una **compañía de seguros**.
En la carta, el gerente le pedía
a José que **fuera** a las oficinas de
la compañía. El gerente quería que
José **le llevara** algunos documentos
a su **sucursal**.
José **se preocupó**: ¿Qué querría el
gerente?
Éste quería que José **explicara**
algunas de las **cantidades** que él
había declarado en la planilla
original. **Al traducir** la carta al
español, José no pudo comprender por
qué tenía que sufrir **de nuevo** todo
el proceso burocrático. José le dio
la carta a su esposa y le pidió que
revisara su traducción. Pronto todo
estuvo aclarado. El gerente dudaba

a couple

manager / insurance company

go

to bring him
branch office
worried

The latter / to explain
amounts

Upon translating

again

review
was cleared up

*póliza = policy

que José **ganara** la cantidad que había   earned

escrito en la planilla.

El matrimonio **se indignó mucho** de que   became very indignant

el gerente **pensara** de esta forma.   would think

José decidió cambiar su compañía de

seguros.

El señor José García hablando con el agente de seguros

La gramática

The Subjunctive

THE INDICATIVE MOOD vs. THE SUBJUNCTIVE MOOD

The **indicative mood** reflects knowledge or certainty. It is based on **what is**, and is used in principal or main clauses that express positive certainties or ask direct questions. Until now all of the verb forms presented have been in the indicative mood.

The **subjunctive mood** is based on **what may, might, or could be**, and is used in subordinate or dependent clauses when those clauses imply a *command* or reflect an *emotion, a wish, a request, an order, a doubt, a denial, indefiniteness, uncertainty, inconclusiveness, or a statement contrary to fact*. Before we examine the kinds of clauses that require a subjunctive verb form, let us look at how to form the present and imperfect or past subjunctive.

PRESENT SUBJUNCTIVE

To form the present subjunctive, take the first person singular (*yo* form) of the present indicative, drop the *o* and add the below endings:

ar verbs		*er/ir* verbs	
-e	-emos	-a	-amos
-es		-as	
-e	-en	-a	-an

	pensar(ie) piensø	**hacer** hagø	**conocer** conozcø
yo	pi*e*ns*e*	hag*a*	conoz*ca*
tú	pi*e*ns*es*	hag*as*	conozc*as*
usted			
él	pi*e*ns*e*	hag*a*	conozc*a*
ella			
nosotros	p*e*ns*emos*	hag*amos*	conozc*amos*
ustedes			
ellos	pi*e*ns*en*	hag*an*	conozc*an*
ellas			

301

	acordarse(ue) me ac*uerd*ø	**pedir(i)** pid*ø*	**dormir(ue)** d*uerm*ø
yo	me acuerd*e*	pid*a*	duerm*a*
tú	te acuerd*es*	pid*as*	duerm*as*
usted			
él	se acuerd*e*	pid*a*	duerm*a*
ella			
nosotros	nos acord*emos*	pid*amos*	durm*amos*
ustedes			
ellos	se acuerd*en*	pid*an*	duerm*an*
ellas			

REMEMBER THE RULES . . .

- Regular verbs ending in *-car* change the *-c-* to *-qu-* before *e*:

indicar to indicate				**sacar** to get			
yo	indi*que*	nosotros	indi*quemos*	yo	sa*que*	nosotros	sa*quemos*
tú	indi*ques*			tú	sa*ques*		
usted		ustedes		usted		ustedes	
él	indi*que*	ellos	indi*quen*	él	sa*que*	ellos	sa*quen*
ella		ellas		ella		ellas	

- Regular verbs ending in *-gar* change the *-g-* to *-gu-* before *e*:

pagar to pay			
yo	pa*gue*	nosotros	pa*guemos*
tú	pa*gues*		
usted		ustedes	
él	pa*gue*	ellos	pa*guen*
ella		ellas	

- Regular verbs ending in *-ger, -gir* change the *-g-* to *-j-* before **o** or **a**:

	escoger to choose		
yo	esco*ja*	nosotros	esco*jamos*
tú	esco*jas*		
usted		ustedes	
él	esco*ja*	ellos	esco*jan*
ella		ellas	

- Regular verbs ending in *-zar* change the *-z-* to *-c-* before **e**:

	gozar to enjoy		
yo	go*ce*	nosotros	go*cemos*
tú	go*ces*		
usted		ustedes	
él	go*ce*	ellos	go*cen*
ella		ellas	

EJERCICIOS. Put the infinitive in parenthesis in the appropriate form of the present subjunctive:

1. que nosotros (preparar) _____

2. que él y ella (sentarse)(ie) _____

3. que yo (decir) _____

4. que tú (comer) _____

5. que Pancho (levantarse) _____

6. que la máquina (funcionar) _____

7. que ustedes (tener) _____

8. que Juan y Marta (salir) _____

9. que los políticos (retirarse [to withdraw]) _____

10. que Jaime y yo (descubrir [to discover]) _____

11. que los hombres (ver) _____

12. que ella (conversar) _____

13. que nadie (conocer) _____

14. que mis amigas (investigar) _____

15. que tú y yo (eliminar) _____

16. que usted (poner) _____

17. que los niños (crecer [to grow]) _____

18. que alguien (pagar) _____

19. que ellas (venir) _____

20. que la comunidad (escoger) _____

21. que pocas personas (terminar) _____

22. que muchas personas (comenzar)(ie) _____

23. que ella y yo (pasar) _____

24. que el capitán (escuchar [to listen to]) _____

25. el secretario (recordar[ue] [to remember]) _____

26. que ustedes (hallar [to find]) _____

27. que tú (introducir) _____

28. que el proyecto (tener) _____

29. que tus planes (valer [to be worth]) _____

30. que yo (hablar) _____

31. que nosotras (ayudar) _____

32. que él (recoger) _____

33. que los voluntarios (hacer) _____

34. que tú y él (pensar)(ie) _____

35. que ellos (dormir)(ue) _____

SOME IRREGULAR PRESENT SUBJUNCTIVES

Verbs that do not end in *o* in the first person indicative have irregular present subjunctives:

	ser	ir	dar
yo	sea	vaya	dé
tú	seas	vayas	des
usted			
él	sea	vaya	dé
ella			
nosotros	seamos	vayamos	demos
ustedes			
ellos	sean	vayan	den
ellas			

	estar	saber
yo	esté	sepa
tú	estés	sepas
usted		
él	esté	sepa
ella		
nosotros	estemos	sepamos
ustedes		
ellos	estén	sepan
ellas		

EJERCICIOS.

Put the infinitive in parenthesis in the appropriate form of the present subjunctive:

1. que ella (ser)   _____

2. que los agentes (estar)   _____

3. que nosotros (dar)   _____

4. que ustedes (saber)   _____

5. que el reportero (ir) _____

6. que yo (estar) _____

7. que tú (dormir) _____

8. que José y nosotros (hacer) _____

9. que los gerentes (dedicarse) _____

10. que los caballeros (gentlemen) (alegrarse) _____

11. que el periódico (vender) _____

12. que nadie (vivir) _____

13. que nosotras (trabajar) _____

14. que ella (golpear) _____

15. que yo (impedir) _____

16. que tú (pronunciar) _____

17. que Panchito (venir) _____

18. que el público (acordarse [to remember]) _____

19. que los representantes (cuidar) _____

20. que el ladrón (matar [to kill]) _____

21. que ustedes y ella (traficar [to deal in]) _____

22. que tú y yo (creer [to believe]) _____

23. que la gente (aguantar [to tolerate]) _____

24. que el gobernador (contestar) _____

25. que ella (preferir[ie] [to prefer]) _____

THE IMPERFECT SUBJUNCTIVE

To form the past or imperfect subjunctive, take the third person plural (*ellos* form) of the preterite, drop the *ron* and add the following endings for *-AR*, *-ER*, and *-IR* verbs:

-ra (se)*	-ramos (semos)
-ras (ses)	
-ra (se)	-ran (sen)

EJEMPLOS.

	pensar (pensaron)	hacer (hicieron)	coger (cogieron)
yo	pensara (pensase)	hiciera (hiciese)	cogiera (cogiese)
tú	pensaras (pensases)	hicieras (hiciese)	cogieras (cogieses)
usted él ella	pensara (pensase)	hiciera (hiciese)	cogiera (*cogiese*)
nosotros	pensáramos (pensasemos)	hiciéramos (hiciesemos)	cogiéramos (cogiesemos)
ustedes ellos ellas	pensaran (pensasen)	hicieran (hiciesen)	cogieran (cogiesen)

MAS EJEMPLOS.

	pedir (pidieron)	dormir (durmieron)	lavarse (se lavaron)
yo	pidiera	durmiera	me lavara
tú	pidieras	durmieras	te lavaras
usted él ella	pidiera	durmiera	se lavara
nosotros	pidiéramos	durmiéramos	nos laváramos
ustedes ellos ellas	pidieran	durmieran	se lavaran

* The *se* form, which simply replaces the *ra* form, may be used interchangeably, except in one or two instances.

	conocer (conocie~~ron~~)	volver (volvie~~ron~~)	ir, ser (fue~~ron~~)
yo	conocie*ra*	volvie*ra*	fue*ra*
tú	conocie*ras*	volvie*ras*	tú fue*ras*
usted			
él	conocie*ra*	volvie*ra*	fue*ra*
ella			
nosotros	conocié*ramos*	volvié*ramos*	nos fué*ramos*
ustedes			
ellos	concie*ran*	volvie*ran*	fue*ran*
ellas			

---

	leer	leye~~ron~~	to read		
yo	leye*ra*		nosotros	leyé*ramos*	
tú	leye*ras*				
usted			ustedes		
él	leye*ra*		ellos	leye*ran*	
ella			ellas		

EJERCICIOS. Put the infinitive in parenthesis in the appropriate form of the imperfect or past subjunctive:

1. que ellos (ir) _____

2. que yo (dar) _____

3. que tú (tener) _____

4. que José y ellas (estar) _____

5. que tus enemigos (salir) _____

6. que yo (ser) _____

7. que nosotras (decir) _____

8. que ustedes (ver) _____

9. que alguien (llamar) _____

10. que las máquinas (funcionar) _____

11. que los ayudantes (helpers) (recibir) _____

12. que ella (levantarse) _____

13. que los niños (sentarse) _____

14. que las mujeres (escribir) _____

15. que nosotros (poder) _____

16. que Tomás y Pancho (querer) _____

17. que María y yo (poner) _____

18. que mi colega (colleague) (venir) _____

19. que él (ir) _____

20. que yo y tú (cumplir) _____

21. que los veteranos (reconocer) _____

22. que el senador (dormir) _____

23. que mis hermanos (calmarse) _____

24. que ellas (sentir) _____

25. que todo el mundo (saber) _____

26. que nadie (pagar) _____

27. que yo (pedir) _____

28. que tú (estar) _____

29. que usted (mirar) _____

30. que Lilia y Guadalupe (comer) _____

EJERCICIOS. Put the infinitive in parenthesis in both the present and imperfect or past subjunctive:

	Present	*Imperfect/Past*
1. que yo (hablar)	_____	_____
2. que tú (levantarse)	_____	_____

3. que usted (ver) _____ _____

4. que él (decir) _____ _____

5. que ella (ir) _____ _____

6. que nosotros (dar) _____ _____

7. que ustedes (leer) _____ _____

8. que ellos (llegar) _____ _____

9. que ellas (poner) _____ _____

10. que yo (buscar) _____ _____

11. que tú (estar) _____ _____

12. que él (poder) _____ _____

13. que ella (subir [to go up]) _____ _____

14. que usted (venir) _____ _____

15. que nosotros (volver) _____ _____

16. que ellos (molestar [to bother]) _____ _____

17. que ellas (querer) _____ _____

18. que ustedes (conocer) _____ _____

19. que tú y él (dormir) _____ _____

20. que María (saber) _____ _____

COMPOUND TENSES IN THE SUBJUNCTIVE

Just as there is a present perfect and pluperfect in the indicative, so there is a present perfect and pluperfect subjunctive. To form the present perfect subjunctive we use the **present subjunctive of _haber_ + past participle.**

Present Perfect Subjunctive

yo	haya	I have	
tú	hayas	you have	
usted		you have	
él	haya	he has	+ cant**ado** (sung), vend**ido** (sold), recib**ido** (received)
ella		she has	
nosotros	hayamos	we have	
ustedes		you have	
ellos	hayan	they have	
ellas		they have	

Pluperfect Subjunctive

To form the pluperfect subjunctive, use the **imperfect subjunctive of _haber_ + past participle.**

yo	hubiera	I had	
tú	hubieras	you had	
usted		you had	
él	hubiera	he had	+ cant**ado** (sung), vend**ido** (sold), recib**ido** (received)
ella		she had	
nosotros	hubiéramos	we had	
ustedes		you have	
ellos	hubieran	they had	
ellas		they have	

THE SUBJUNCTIVE IN NOUN CLAUSES

The subjunctive is used in noun clauses. A noun clause is a dependent clause that functions as the direct object of the main verb. There are *two* conditions that must be fulfilled before the subjunctive is required in noun clauses:

1. The verb in the main clause must express:
   a. an emotion, a wish, a request, a doubt, a denial, an order;

   or

   b. an impersonal expression that implies a wish, an order, an emotion, a doubt, a convenience, or an uncertainty.*

   One way to remember the kinds of verbs that are required in the main clause is to think of the word **WEIRDO**, because each letter stands for one of the categories of verbs:

   Wishing (querer, desear, esperar, preferir, etc.)

   Emotion (estar contento, estar alegre, estar triste, temer, tener miedo, etc.)

   Impersonal (es probable, es una lástima, es preferible, es necesario, etc.)*

   Request (rogar, pedir, suplicar, solicitar, etc.)

   Doubt/**D**enial (dudar, no creer, negar, etc.)

   Ordering (mandar, ordenar, aconsejar, etc.)

2. The subject of the verb in the subordinate clause must be different from the subject and verb in the main clause.

---

* The subjunctive is *not* used in the following impersonal expressions: *es verdad, es evidente, es seguro, es cierto,* etc.

Students of Spanish frequently suffer from *subjunctivitis* when they study the use of the subjunctive in Spanish. That is, they begin to see the subjunctive needed everywhere. Study the chart below so that you may avoid catching this very common malady.

Main Clause	Noun Clause	Explanation
I hope *Yo* espero	that *you* help me. que *usted* me ayude.	The noun clause has a subject (*you*) that is different from the subject in the main clause and the main clause has a *WEIRDO* verb; therefore, the verb in the noun clause will be in the subjunctive. The present subjunctive is used because the action is in the present.
I hope *Yo* espero	that *I* help you. ayudarle.	The noun clause does not have a different subject; therefore, the subjunctive is not required.
I believe *Yo* creo	that *he* helps me. que *él* me ayuda.	The noun clause has a different subject, but the verb in the main clause is not a *WEIRDO* verb; therefore, the verb in the noun clause is in the indicative.
I hoped *Yo* esperaba	that *you* would help me. que *usted* me ayudara.	The noun clause has a subject that is different from the subject in the main clause and the main clause has a *WEIRDO* verb; therefore, the verb in the noun clause is in the subjunctive. It is in the past subjunctive because the action is in the past.
I believed *Yo* creí	that *you* helped me. que *usted* me ayudó.	The noun clause does have a different subject, but the verb in the main clause is not a *WEIRDO* verb; therefore, the verb in the noun clause is in the indicative.

VERBS OF WISHING AND ORDERING

In English verbs of wishing and ordering are frequently followed by a direct object (noun or pronoun) + an infinitive:

I want   John   to initiate   a claim.
(order) (direct object pronoun) +   (infinitive)

In Spanish the conjunction **que** (that) is needed to introduce the noun clause, and the direct object (noun or pronoun) becomes the subject of the clause:

Quiero   que   Juan   inicie*   una demanda.
(order) (conjunction) (subject) (subjunctive)

---

object + infinitive *becomes* **que + subject + subjunctive**

*****iniciar** = initiate.

SEQUENCE OF TENSES IN THE
MAIN AND DEPENDENT (SUBJUNCTIVE) CLAUSES

The sentences below indicate when to use the present subjunctive, the imperfect or past subjunctive, and the compound tenses—the present perfect and pluperfect subjunctive in the noun clauses.

1.	(a)	I *hope* *(present)*	that you	**do** it. *(present)*
	(b)	*Espero* *(present)*	que usted lo	*haga.* *(present)*
2.	(a)	I *hope* *(present)*	that you	**will do** it. *(future)*
	(b)	*Espero* *(present)*	que usted lo	*haga.* *(present)*
3.	(a)	I *hope* *(present)*	that you	**have done** it. *(present perfect)*
	(b)	*Espero* *(present)*	que usted lo	*haya hecho.* *(present perfect)*
4.	(a)	I *hope* *(present)*	that you	**did** it. *(past)*
	(b)	*Espero* *(present)*	que usted lo	*haya hecho.* *(present perfect)* **or** *hiciera* *(past)*
5.	(a)	I *hoped* *(past)*	that you	**did** it. *(past)*
	(b)	*Esperaba* *Esperé* *(past)*	que usted lo	*hiciera.* *(past)*
6.	(a)	I *hoped* *(past)*	that you	**had done** it. *(pluperfect)*
	(b)	*Esperaba* *Esperé* *(past)*	que usted lo	*hubiera hecho.* *(pluperfect)*
7.	(a)	I *had hoped* *(pluperfect)*	that you	**had done** it. *(pluperfect)*
	(b)	Yo *había esperado* *(pluperfect)*	que usted lo	*hubiera hecho.* *(pluperfect)*

Note:
Both the present and the future tenses in the noun clause in English (No. 2 above) are translated by the *present* subjunctive in Spanish.

314

EJERCICIOS. Change the infinitive to the appropriate form of the subjunctive.

1. Los agentes no quieren firmar. Los agentes no quieren que yo _____ .

2. Ella esperaba verlo. Ella esperaba que usted lo _____ .

3. Tú esperas ir. Tú esperas que Juan _____ ahora.

4. Ellos quisieron venir. Ellos quisieron que yo _____ .

5. Es necesario saber. Es necesario que ustedes _____ .

6. Era necesario conocerlo. Era necesario que tú lo _____ .

7. Juanita prefiere hacerlo. Juanita prefiere que él lo _____ .

8. Yo me alegré de estar aquí. Yo me alegré de que ellos _____ aquí.

9. No deseo dormir. No deseo que usted _____ .

10. Nosotros preferimos dárselo. Nosotros preferimos que ella se lo _____ .

11. Ellos querían levantarse. Ellos querían que yo me _____ .

12. No es posible verla. No es posible que yo la _____ .

13. Es importante tener una cláusula de robo (theft).

    Es importante que ustedes _____ una cláusula de robo.

14. Nosotros deseamos comprar la póliza (policy) con protección máxima.

    Nosotros deseamos que tú _____ la póliza con protección máxima.

15. El asegurador (the insurer) deseaba averiguar (to investigate) el accidente.

    El asegurador deseaba que la policía _____ el accidente.

16. Los investigadores no quieren justipreciar el daño (appraise the damage).

    Los investigadores no quieren que nosotros _____ el daño.

17. El agente quería tener seguro contra incendios (fire insurance).

    El agente quería que sus clientes _____ seguro contra incendios.

18. Yo esperaba conseguir seguro de acumulación (endowment).

    Yo esperaba que él _____ seguro de acumulación.

19. No es posible investigar este tipo de demanda (claim). No es posible que el vendedor

    de seguros (insurance salesman) _____ este tipo de demanda.

EJERCICIOS.

Change the infinitive in parenthesis to the appropriate form of the subjunctive.

1. Marta duda que tú (poder) _____ hacerlo.

2. Ellas se alegraron que yo (levantarse) _____ temprano.

3. Ellos quieren que nosotros (ayudarles) _____ .

4. Paco y la señora Ramírez aconsejan que yo (*archivar = to file*) _____ todas las hojas de servicio (service records).

5. Ellos desean que ella lo (hacer) _____ todos los días.

6. La póliza (policy) pide que Vds. (llamar) _____ a la compañía de seguros inmediatamente después del accidente.

7. Es lástima que nosotros no (poder) _____ ayudarle con el alquiler (the rental) del apartamento.

8. Tú esperas que tu esposo (husband) no (ponerse) _____ furioso.

9. Es necesario que ellas (obtener) _____ autorización.

10. Me alegro que la póliza (tener) _____ trece cláusulas.

11. El vice-presidente ordenó que nosotros le (mandar) _____ una copia de la factura (invoice).

12. Las secretarias bilingües insisten (*insistir*) en que ellos solamente les (escribir) _____ _____ a ellas en inglés o en español.

13. El representante de la compañía prefiere que Vd. (ir) _____ a la sucursal (branch office).

14. El gerente general (general manager) dice que es necesario que nuestra correspondencia

    (dar) _____ todos los detalles.

15. Ellos aconsejan que nosotros (buscar) _____ más protección.

16. La consejera quiere que ella (tener) _____ más beneficios.

17. El municipio (the city) les pide que le (entregar [to hand over]) _____ todos los recibos.

18. Nosotros dudábamos que ustedes (hacer) _____ todo el trabajo.

EJERCICIOS. Translate into Spanish.

1. She is happy that we have more protection.

   _____

2. The manager wants you to bring us the receipts (*los recibos*).

   _____

3. It is important that you go to the branch office.

   _____

4. It is necessary that the insurance company have the authorization (*autorización*).

   _____

5. The company representative wants me to give more details.

   _____

6. The general manager ordered them to pay (that they pay).

   _____

7. I am happy that you have all the benefits.

   _____

8. It was necessary that he get a policy with maximum protection.

   _____

9. She wanted César to help her.

   _____

10. They hoped that she was bilingual (*bilingüe*).

    _____

11. We doubt that he will pay more than ($200) two hundred dollars.

    _____

12. It is a pity that you are not able to buy more insurance.

    _____

13. The doctor ordered him to get X-rays.

_____

14. She wants me to pay now.

_____

15. We doubt that they have given him a check.

_____

16. We prefer to have fire insurance.

_____

17. She hopes that you know the truth.

_____

18. They ask that he pay the bill (*la cuenta*).

_____

19. We hoped to sleep well. We hoped that you slept well.

_____

20. They request that the insurer (*el asegurador*) investigate this kind of claim.

_____

21. You fear that they will do it.

_____

22. Do you want to go? Do you want me to go?.

_____

23. She had hoped that I had gone.

_____

24. He hoped that they had believed him.

_____

Diálogo

Empleada	—	Hubiera preferido que usted trajera los originales señor García. Los originales, ¿entiende usted?
Señor García	—	Claro que entiendo. Pero yo no pensaba que fuera necesario **entregarle** los originales. Una copia debería ser suficiente.
Empleada	—	Mire, usted señor, con tantos clientes extranjeros y con el **corre-corre** aquí, el gerente requiere que nos aseguremos de la autenticidad de todos los documentos.
Señor García	—	Mire usted, señorita, yo no vine aquí para que usted me **fastidiara**. Yo había puesto esa información en la planilla, es así porque quien lo hizo fui yo.
Empleada	—	¡No se ponga bravo, señor García! ¡**No se ponga bravo**! Yo no quería que usted **se ofendiera**. Yo sólo quería que usted cumpliera las órdenes de mi gerente.
Señor García	—	Perdón, perdón señorita. Ud. tiene toda la razón. Le ruego que usted me perdone.
Empleada	—	¡Cómo no!, señor García. Ahora, ¿quiere que yo le pase al **jefe** para que él le pueda explicar mejor todo esto?
Señor García	—	¡Cómo no!, muy buena idea ¿dónde está su **despacho**?

VOCABULARIO DEL DIALOGO

entregar	to hand in
corre-corre	the hustle and bustle
fastidiara	would annoy
fastidiar	to annoy
¡No se ponga bravo!	Don't get angry!
se ofendiera	would become offended
jefe	boss
despacho	office

PREGUNTAS SOBRE EL DIALOGO

1. ¿Qué trajo el señor García?

2. ¿Tiene muchos clientes la oficina?

   _____

3. ¿Qué le dice el señor García a la empleada?

   _____

4. ¿Qué le explica la empleada al señor García?

   _____

5. ¿Qué le va a hacer el jefe al señor García?

   _____

Vocabulario del capítulo

COGNATES OR NEAR COGNATES

el agente
la compañía
la copia
la correspondencia
furioso/a
máximo/a
original
el proyecto
el senador

VOCABULARIO

el asegurador	insurer	el gerente	manager
el asunto	matter of business	¿motivo?	why?
la autenticidad	authenticity	la multa	ticket, fine
el beneficio	benefit	la póliza	policy
la cláusula	clause	la sucursal	branch office
la consejera	woman adviser	el sueldo	salary
el estimado	appraisal		

VERBOS

aclarar	to clear up	indignarse	to become indignant
alegrarse	to be glad	justipreciar	to appraise
aguantar	to tolerate	llover	to rain
ampliar	to amplify	matar	to kill
archivar	to file	molestar	to bother
averiguar	to investigate	negar	to deny
comprobar	to substantiate	ofenderse	to become offended
crecer	to grow	recordar	to remember
cuidar	to care for	retirarse	to withdraw
descubrir	to discover	rogar	to beg
explicar	to explain	traficar	to deal in
fastidiar	to bother, to annoy	valer	to be worth
indicar	to indicate		

FRASES

la compañía de seguros	insurance company
¡cómo no!	why not, of course
en cuanto	as soon as
hacer una demanda	to file a claim
hasta que	until
la hoja de servicio	service record
un par	a couple
un par de días	couple of days
el seguro contra incendio	fire insurance
el seguro de acumulación	endowment insurance
la oficina principal	main office

Vocabulario adicional

SOME COMMONLY USED "MANDATOS"

¡Devuélva(n)los/las!	Return them (objects)!
¡Compáre(n)los/las!	Compare them!
¡Confírme(n)lo/la!	Verify/Confirm it!
¡Sáque(n)los/las!	Take them out!
¡Hága(n)melo/la!	Do it for me!
¡Espere(n) un minuto!	Wait a minute!
¡Pague(n) ahora mismo!	Pay right now!

¡Tíre(n)lo/la!	Throw it! Discard it!
¡Entrégue(n)lo/la!	Hand it in!
¡Explíque(n)lo/la!	Explain it !
¡Pída(n)le perdón!	Apologize to him / to her!
¡Pase(n)!	Come in!
¡Tenga(n) la bondad de + infinitive	Would you be kind enough + infinitive
¡No me hable(n) así!	Dont speak to me that way!

EJERCICIOS. Translate into Spanish.

1. Explain it to me (*la póliza*)! ¡ _____ usted!

2. Don't talk to me like that! ¡ _____ ustedes!

3. Pay right now! ¡ _____ usted!

4. Come in! ¡ _____ ustedes!

5. Return them (*los documentos*)! ¡ _____ usted!

6. Take them out (*las cartas*)! ¡ _____ ustedes!

7. Verify it (*la firma*)! ¡ _____ usted!

8. Wait a minute! ¡ _____ ustedes!

9. Do it (*el trabajo*)! ¡ _____ usted!

10. Would you be kind enough to sign!

    ¡ _____ ustedes!

11. Apologize to him! ¡ _____ usted!

12. Compare them (*los clientes*)! ¡ _____ ustedes!

Las diferentes culturas se integran

Capítulo 16
La integración

Lectura

No querríamos que ustedes pensaran que
hemos inventado una fábula romántica
sobre los García.

Por el contrario, todo lo que hemos
escrito **ha sido para que pudieran**   has been so that you could
comprender mejor que esta familia no
es exótica, sino muy común y corriente.

Ahora bien, **sin que** los García   without
se den cuenta, ha comenzado a efectuarse   realizing it
en ellos un intenso proceso de cambio:
comienzan a integrarse.   they are beginning to assimilate
Los García, consciente e inconscientemente,
se están adaptando a las costumbres, al
idioma y a la forma de vida del nuevo país.
Los padres, con mayor intensidad que los
hijos, mantienen y defienden las viejas
formas tradicionales del pasado. Tanto
el señor García como su esposa todavía
se visten de una forma conservadora y   dress
anticuada. Ellos prefieren hablar siempre
español, **a pesar de que** ella habla inglés   despite the fact that

a la perfección y él va aprendiéndolo.

Los hijos, **por lo contrario**, se han
integrado más profundamente a
la cultura de las masas de los Estados Unidos.
A José le fastidia mucho que su hijo
César quiera cambiar cada seis meses
su forma de vestir, mientras que la
señora García está muy **molesta** con la
bárbara dieta que **tanto entusiasma**
a Angel y a Celia: papas fritas y
hamburguesas, refrescos y dulces.
No consigue la señora García, a
pesar de sus múltiples esfuerzos,
que sus hijos **disfruten** de las
comidas chilenas tradicionales.
Los hijos también **han desarrollado**
otra realidad lingüística: hablan
español en casa e inglés en **la calle**,
mientras que en la escuela y en el
trabajo **mezclan** los dos idiomas.
No hay **duda** que el futuro de los
García será bicultural y bilingüe.

on the other hand

popular culture.

It bothers José

annoyed

so excites

does not succeed

enjoy

have developed

the street

they mix

doubt

La gramática

THE SUBJUNCTIVE IN ADJECTIVE CLAUSES

An adjective clause is a dependent clause that modifies a noun or pronoun in the sentence. The relative pronouns *who*, *which*, and *that* frequently introduce the adjective clause.

If the antecedent of the adjective clause is *indefinite* (it does not refer to a particular person or thing),* or *negative*, then the verb of the adjective clause must be in the subjunctive.

Necesito un secretario que **hable** español e inglés.	I need a secretary who speaks Spanish and English. (I have no specific person in mind.)
No conozco a nadie que **haya** sufrido tanto como yo.	I don't know anyone who has suffered as much as I.
No existe ninguno que **sea** más deshonesto que él.	No one exists who is as dishonest as he.
¿Hay alguien que **sepa** más de la situación que ella?	Is there anyone who knows more about the situation than she? (There may not be such a person.)

If the antecedent of the adjective cause is *definite* (refers to a specific person or thing or something known to exist), then the verb of the adjective clause is in the indicative.

Necesito al secretario que **habla** español e inglés.	I need the secretary who speaks Spanish and English. (I have a specific person in mind.)
Sí, conozco a alguien que **ha sufrido** tanto como yo.	Yes, I know someone who has suffered as much as I.
Existen algunos que **son** más deshonestos que él.	There are some who are as dishonest as he.
Hay algunos que **saben** más de la situación que ella.	There are some who know more about the situation than she.

* The indefinite article (*un, una*) usually indicates that it is indefinite.

EJERCICIOS. Change the verb in the indicative to the subjunctive.

1. Queremos la póliza que tiene más opciones.

   Queremos una póliza que _____ más opciones.

2. Ellos prefieren la casa que es de dos pisos (floors).

   Ellos prefieren una casa que _____ de dos pisos.

3. Necesito al médico que es especialista en medicina interna.

   Necesito un médico que _____ especialista en medicina interna.

4. Ella busca al abogado que sabe las leyes de inmigración (immigration laws).

   Ella busca un abogado que _____ las leyes de inmigración.

5. Voy a comprar la cerradura (lock) que da protección máxima.

   Voy a comprar una cerradura que _____ protección máxima.

6. El gerente general conoce a alguien que hace ese tipo de trabajo.

   El gerente general no conoce a nadie que _____ este tipo de trabajo.

7. El agente conoce a alguien que tiene el mismo problema (the same problem).

   El agente no conoce a nadie que _____ el mismo problema.

8. Conocemos a alguien que le puede dar más información.

   No conocemos a nadie que le _____ dar más información.

9. El asegurador (the insurer) conoce a alguien que investiga ese tipo de demanda (claim).

   El asegurador no conoce a nadie que _____ ese tipo de demanda.

10. Conozco a alguien que sabe más que yo.

    No conozco a nadie que _____ más que yo.

11. Hay alguien que está contento con este tipo de protección.

    No hay nadie que _____ contento con este tipo de protección.

12. Hay algo que podemos averiguar.

No hay nada que _____ averiguar.

13. Hay algunos cambios (changes) que son importantes.

No hay ningún cambio que _____ importante.

14. Hay un banco (bank) que queda cerca de aquí.

No hay ningún banco que _____ cerca de aquí.

15. Hay alguien que conoce al gerente.

No hay nadie que _____ al gerente.

EJERCICIOS. Fill in the blank space with the appropriate form of the verb.

1. Buscamos una mujer que (ser) _____ muy trabajadora (hard worker).

2. Necesitamos al joven que (saber) _____ traducir (translate) los documentos.

3. No conocemos a nadie que (comer) _____ tanto como tú.

4. No hay nada que (tener) _____ más importancia que el voto (the vote).

5. ¿Hay alguien que me (*prestar = to lend*) _____ mil dólares?

6. El quiere encontrar una persona que (escribir) _____ bien.

7. ¿Conoce usted a algún estudiante que (ir) _____ a Panamá este verano (summer)?

8. No conocemos a nadie que (tener) _____ tanto dinero como él.

9. Buscan un abogado que (saber) _____ hablar español.

10. No hay nadie que (poder) _____ cambiar nuestra situación.

11. ¿Conoces a alguien que (tocar) _____ el piano?

12. Necesito un hombre que (ser) _____ más alto que yo.

13. Necesitamos a la mujer que (vivir) _____ muy cerca de aquí.

14. Necesitamos una mujer que (vivir) _____ muy cerca de aquí.

15. Busco un ayudante (helper) que (estar) _____ asistiendo a la universidad.

16. Busco al ayudante que (estar) _____ asistiendo a la universidad.

EJERCICIOS

Change the verb form from the present subjunctive to the **present perfect subjunctive**.

Ejemplo:

1. (a) No hay nadie que sepa esto.

   (b) No hay nadie que ___haya sabido___ esto.

2. (a) No conozco a nadie que tenga tanta suerte como tú.

   (b) No conozco a nadie que _____ tanta suerte como tú.

3. (a) El necesita un sicólogo que entienda esa teoría.

   (b) El necesita un sicólogo que _____ esa teoría.

4. (a) Buscamos a alguien que lo vea todos los días.

   (b) Buscamos a alguien que lo _____ todos los días.

5. (a) Necesito un secretario que viva en Manhattan.

   (b) Necesito un secretario que _____ en Manhattan.

6. (a) Estamos buscando a alguien que se acueste muy temprano.

   (b) Estamos buscando a alguien que _____ muy temprano.

7. (a) No hay nadie que no sea izquierdista (leftist).

   (b) No hay nadie que no _____ izquierdista.

8. (a) No hay nadie que se ponga tan nervioso como él.

   (b) No hay nadie que _____ tan nervioso como él.

9. (a) El está buscando un político que no pague por sus votos.

   (b) El está buscando un político que no _____ por sus votos.

SEQUENCE OF TENSES

The past or imperfect subjunctive is generally used when the verb of the main clause is in the past.

No **conocí** a nadie que lo **hiciera**.   I didn't meet anyone who would do it.

EJERCICIOS.
Change the verb form from the present subjunctive to the **past or imperfect subjunctive.**

1. (a) No conozco a nadie que vaya allí.

   (b) No conocí a nadie que _____ allí.

2. (a) El guardia no conoce a nadie que sea más egoísta que él.

   (b) El guardia no conoció a nadie que _____ más egoísta que él.

3. (a) No hay nadie que dé más dinero que ella.

   (b) No había nadie que _____ más dinero que ella.

4. (a) El busca un mecánico que sepa reparar el auto.

   (b) El buscó un mecánico que _____ reparar el auto.

5. (a) ¿Conocen ustedes a alguien que haga tanto ruido (so much noise)?

   (b) ¿Conocieron ustedes a alguien que _____ tanto ruido?

6. (a) No hay nadie que se acueste a esa hora.

   (b) No había nadie que _____ a esa hora.

7. (a) Buscamos a alguien que haya vivido en Miami.

   (b) Buscábamos a alguien que _____ en Miami.

8. (a) Necesito unos empleados que sepan manejar (know how to drive).

   (b) Necesité unos empleados que _____ manejar.

9. (a) La policía está buscando a alguien que viva en aquel barrio.

   (b) La policía estuvo buscando a alguien que _____ en aquel barrio.

ADVERBIAL CLAUSES

Like the adjective clause, the adverbial clause may or may not require the use of a subjunctive verb. If the action referred to in the adverbial clause has not yet taken place (when it refers to an uncertain future outcome), then the subjunctive verb must be used in the adverbial clause.

Cuando **venga** mañana, se lo tendré listo.   When you come tomorrow, I will have it ready for you.

Tan pronto como **termine**, se lo daré.   As soon as I finish, I will give it to you.

The indicative is used if the action is thought of as habitual, as a fact, or as having already taken place.

Cuando **viene** todos los días,   When you come every day,
se lo tengo listo.   I have it ready for you.

Tan pronto como **terminé**, se lo dí.   As soon as I finished, I gave it to you.

The following introduce adverbial clauses:

cuando	when	**mientras**	while, as long as
hasta que	until	**después de que**	after
aunque	although, even though	**siempre que**	provided that
		tan pronto como	as soon as
en cuanto	as soon as, in so far as	**así que; luego que**	as soon as

EJERCICIOS. Change the verb in parenthesis accordingly.

1. (a) Cuando ustedes (terminar) _____, yo saldré.

   (b) Cuando ustedes (terminar) _____, yo salí.

2. (a) Cuando nosotros (llegar) _____, los veremos.

   (b) Todos los días cuando nosotros (llegar) _____los vemos.

3. (a) Tan pronto como nosotros lo (saber) _____, iremos a la corte (court).

   (b) Tan pronto como nosotros lo (saber) _____, fuimos a la corte.

4. (a) No voy a trabajar hasta que ellos me (dar) _____ el permiso (permission).

   (b) No fui a trabajar hasta que ellos me (dar) _____ el permiso.

5. (a) Aunque tú (pagar) _____ la cuenta, yo no le haré el favor.

   (b) Aunque tú (pagar) _____ la cuenta, yo no le hice el favor.

6. (a) Después de que usted nos (traer) _____ los documentos, le daremos el cheque.

(b) Después de que usted nos (traer) _____ los documentos, le dimos el cheque.

7. (a) Mientras ellos (estar) _____ aquí, no le diré la verdad a usted.

(b) Mientras ellos (estar) _____ aquí, no le dije la verdad a usted.

8. (a) Siempre cuando ella (llegar) _____ se pone nerviosa.

(b) Cuando ella (llegar) _____ se pondrá nerviosa.

9. (a) Tan pronto como él (levantarse) _____ se irá.

(b) Tan pronto como él (levantarse) _____ se fue.

10. (a) Aunque (llover[ue]) _____ iré al parque.

(b) Aunque (llover[ue]) _____ fui al parque.

EJERCICIOS. Translate into Spanish.

1. As soon as they hand it in, I will sign (*firmar*) the documents.

_____

2. When he got up, he gave me the work.

_____

3. When we sit down, they will speak to us.

_____

4. They will not be able to do it, even though they have experience.

_____

5. I will work here until they arrive.

_____

6. She will complain until they pay her.

_____

7. I will do it provided that you go with me. .

_____

8. They will go provided that he writes all of the letters.

_____

9. As soon as they left, I began to work.

_____

10. Every day when she sees me, she tells me the same story (*la misma historia*).

_____

11. While (as long as) he is in the house, we will not visit her.

_____

12. I waited here until he saw me.

_____

13. Stay here (*quedarse*) until I call you.

_____

14. They will come early provided that we make the arrangements (*hacer los arreglos*).

_____

ADVERBIAL CONJUNCTIONS AND THE SUBJUNCTIVE

The subjunctive is required when an adverbial conjunction introduces a clause that expresses:
> **(1) purpose**
> **(2) supposition or exception**
> **(3) an unaccomplished result**

The following adverbial conjunctions are always followed by the subjunctive:

con tal que	provided that	**antes de que**	before (that)
para que	in order that, so that	**a menos que**	unless (that)
sin que	without (that)		

1. **Purpose**

   Tengo que terminar este trabajo
   para que él lo *tenga* mañana por la mañana.

   I have to finish this work
   so that he will have it tomorrow morning.

2. **Supposition or Exception**

   No haré nada *a menos que*
   usted me *dé* parte de sus ganancias.

   I won't do anything unless
   you give me part of your profits.

3. **Unaccomplished Result**

   Vaya usted a molestar a su amigo
   antes de que me *enoje*.

   Go bother your friend
   before I get angry.

EJERCICIOS. Fill in the blank spaces with the appropriate form of the verb.

1. (a) Ellos trabajan para que sus hijos (poder) _____ vivir mejor.

   (b) Ellos trabajaron para que sus hijos (poder) _____ vivir mejor.

2. (a) El sale sin que yo lo (ver) _____.

   (b) El salió sin que yo lo (ver) _____.

3. (a) Yo firmo el documento con tal que ustedes (cumplir) _____ con sus deberes.

   (b) Yo firmé el documento con tal que ustedes (cumplir) _____ con sus deberes.

4. (a) Ellos tienen que darnos permiso antes de que nosotros (ir) _____ a la reunión.

   (b) Ellos tuvieron que darnos permiso antes de que nosotros (ir) _____ a la reunión.

5. (a) No podemos hacer eso a menos que ellas nos (dar) _____ permiso.

   (b) No podíamos hacer eso a menos que ellas nos (dar) _____ permiso.

6. (a) Yo te doy el dinero para que no (tener) _____ más problemas.

   (b) Yo te di el dinero para que no (tener) _____ más problemas.

7. (a) Les estoy dando esta información para que ustedes (darse) _____
   cuenta de la situación.

   (b) Les estaba dando esta información para que ustedes (darse) _____
   cuenta de la situación.

8. (a) Se lo digo para que usted (estar) _____ preparado.

   (b) Se lo dije para que usted (estar) _____ preparado.

9. (a) Me pagan antes de que él (volver) _____ .

   (b) Me pagaron antes de que él (volver) _____ .

10. (a) No vamos a ayudarlos a menos que ellos (portarse) _____ bien con mis amigos.

    (b) No íbamos a ayudarlos a menos que ellos (portarse) _____ bien con mis amigos.

IF CLAUSES

When an *if (si) clause* expresses something that is either *contrary to fact at the present time* or something that *might* or *should* happen, the imperfect subjunctive is used in the *if (si) clause* and the conditional or the *ra* form of the imperfect subjunctive* is used in the main clause.

Si yo **estuviera** en casa, lo $\genfrac{}{}{0pt}{}{terminaría}{terminara*}$ más temprano.

If I were at home, I would finish it earlier.

Si yo **hubiera** estado en casa, lo $\genfrac{}{}{0pt}{}{habría}{hubiera*}$ terminado.

If I had been at home, I would have finished it earlier.

When an if (*si*) clause expresses something that is contrary to fact in the past, the pluperfect subjunctive is used in the (*si*) clause and the conditional perfect is used in the result clause.

EJERCICIOS. Fill in the blank space with the appropriate form of the verb.

1. Si yo (estar) _____ en Miami, no estaría contento.

2. Si usted (tener) _____ más tiempo, iría a San Juan.

3. Si nosotros (hacer) _____ caso de sus planes, tendríamos mucho dinero.

4. Si ella (ser) _____ rica, te daría toda su riqueza (wealth).

5. Si yo (ser) _____ usted, no hablaría con ellos.

6. Si tú lo (haber) _____ sabido, no lo habrías hecho.

7. Si ustedes no se (haber) _____ levantado tan tarde, no lo habrían visto.

* The conditional is used far more frequently than the imperfect subjunctive, especially in spoken Spanish. If the imperfect subjunctive is used, then only the *ra* form is permissible.

8. Si usted (tener) _____ más suerte, no estaría en la cárcel.

9. Si ella (estar) _____ en su casa, ellos estarían enojados.

10. Si nosotros (saber) _____ todo esto, no estaríamos lamentando nuestra situación.

11. Si él nos (dar) _____ los papeles, él no tendría tantos problemas hoy.

12. Si nosotros (haber) _____ vendido la casa, ya habríamos ido a Brazil.

13. Si yo (conocer) _____ a tanta gente, estaría muy contento.

EJERCICIOS. Translate into Spanish.

1. I need someone who knows Spanish and English.

   _____

2. Do you need the secretary who has a lot of friends in Washington?

   _____

3. There is nobody who can do that work.

   _____

4. Do you know anyone who is as intelligent as she?

   _____

5. I don't know anyone who is as intelligent as she.

   _____

6. We are looking for the man who sells official documents.

   _____

7. We need the lawyer who has a good knowledge of these laws (*conocimiento de estas leyes*).

   _____

8. We need a lawyer who has a good knowledge of these laws.

   _____

337

9. She needs a man who doesn't complain.

   _____

10. She needs the man who doesn't complain.

    _____

11. Do you know anyone who has done it?

    _____

12. When they sit down, I will speak to them.

    _____

13. When they sat down, I spoke to them.

    _____

14. Although you arrive early, I will not see you.

    _____

15. Although you arrived early, I did not see you.

    _____

16. Wait here until he leaves.

    _____

17. She waited here until he left.

    _____

18. I will be patient (*tener paciencia*) provided that you come early.

    _____

19. As soon as he handed it in, I spoke to him.

    _____

20. As soon as he hands it in, I will speak to him.

    _____

21. After they get up, she will finish her work.

   _____

22. After they got up, she finished her work.

   _____

23. If I were you, I would work more.

   _____

24. If she spoke Spanish, she could communicate with us.

   _____

25. If I were in Arizona, I would not need so much money.

   _____

26. If the letter were written in Spanish, I would understand it.

   _____

27. Please keep quiet so that we can listen to the news (*las noticias*).

   _____

28. They worked a lot so that their children would finish their studies (*estudios*).

   _____

29. She doesn't do anything without my knowing it (without that I know it).

   _____

Diálogo

César	—	Papá, antes de que **me regañe**, perdóneme la demora. Este . . . Flaco se compró unos discos y pasamos un buen rato escuchándolos, y este . . . no me fijé en la hora. Perdón.
Señor García	—	No hay porqué hijo. Los Williams todavía no han llegado.
		(Entran Angel y Celia)
César	—	*Hey "**tigres**" what's happ'nin'?*
Señor García	—	Oyeme, **buen mozo**, eso no te lo perdono. Cuando vengan los Williams hablaremos inglés, mientras tanto español.
César	—	Vale.
Angel	—	Oye, "**Rin**," mamá dijo que no podía comer otra "hamburguesa" a menos que quisiera comer solo. Yo no quiero comer empanadas. ¡Háblale, "Rin"!
Señora García	—	¡Oyeme! ¡Oyeme! Hasta el día que yo no sea la madre de esta **bendita** familia, mis hijos no **comerán basura**.
Angel	—	Pero Julito y Capo comen **lo que les dé la gana**.
Señora García	—	¡Qué lo hagan ellos! Mis hijos comerán comida que **alimente**.
César	—	Si yo fuera tú, yo me callaría. Mamá tiene razón.
Señor García	—	Bueno, hijos, dejemos de **boberías**. César, ¿leíste el periódico del domingo? ¿Te fijaste? **Colo—Colo empató 2—2.**

VOCABULARIO DEL DIALOGO

me regañe	scold me
tigres	wise guys (nonstandard)
buen mozo	good looking young man
"Rin"	abbreviated form of the diminutive of Cesar, "Cesarín."
bendita	blessed
comerán basura	will eat junk food
lo que les dé la gana	whatever they wish
alimente	nourishes
boberías	nonsense
Colo-Colo	Chilean soccer club
empató	tied

PREGUNTAS SOBRE EL DIALOGO

1. ¿Por qué llegó tarde César?

   _____

2. ¿Cómo reaccionó el señor García cuando César habló inglés?

   _____

3. ¿Cómo reaccionó César a la crítica de su papa?

   _____

4. ¿Por qué se quejó Angel?

   _____

5. ¿Qué dijo la señora García?

   _____

Los García en su casa

Vocabulario del capítulo

COGNATES OR NEAR COGNATES

la adaptación	la lingüística
el auto	el método
bicultural	la opción
bilingüe	la perfección
conservador/a	el piano
culinario/a	el plan
la cultura	el político
deshonesto/a	el proceso
el especialista	la protección
exótico/a	la reunión
la fábula	romántico/a
el favor	el secretario
la forma	la situación
formal	la teoría
el futuro	tradicional
la inmigración	la universidad
intenso/a	el voto

VOCABULARIO

anticuado/a	antiquated	los esfuerzos	efforts
la audiencia	hearing	las ganancias	earnings
bárbaro / a	horrible	el gerente	manager
la basura	garbage	el guardia	guard
el cambio	change	las hamburguesas	hamburgers
la cerradura	lock	inconcientemente	unconsciously
concientemente	consciously	inesperado/a	unexpected
la costumbre	custom	la intensidad	intensity
la crítica	criticism	el izquierdista	leftist
el deber	obligation	las masas	masses
la demanda	claim	la merienda	snack
la demora	delay	el parque	park
la dieta	diet	el pasado	past
el disco	record	las papas fritas	French fried potatoes
el egoísta	egotist	el permiso	permission

el piso	floor	sino	but
poderoso/a	powerful	totalmente	completely
la realidad	reality	el valor	value
la riqueza	wealth	el verano	summer
el ruido	noise		

VERBOS

alimentar	to nourish	imponerse	impose
asistir a	to attend	inventar	to invent
conservar	to conserve	investigar	to investigate
defender	to defend	lamentar	lament
disfrutar	to enjoy	llover	to rain
efectuarse	to take hold to take effect	mezclar	to mix
		portarse	to behave
elaborar	to elaborate	prestar	to lend
empatar	to tie	quejarse	to complain
enojarse	to become angry	reaccionar	to react
entusiasmar	to become enthusiastic	recibirse de	to graduate as
		regañar	to scold
fastidiar	to annoy/bother	reparar	to repair
fijarse	to pay attention to to fix, to set	traducir	to translate

FRASES

común y corriente	everyday/ordinary
coger su ritmo	gain momentum
a pesar de que	despite the fact
estar en la onda	to be (with it) in the wave
cumplir con su deber	keep your work (follow up on your obligation)
estar molesto/a	to be annoyed
un buen rato	a good time
es decir	that is to say
hacer los arreglos	make the arrangements
la misma historia	the same story

Vocabulario adicional

SOME COMMONLY USED "MANDATOS"

¡Déje(n)me en paz!	Leave me alone!/in peace!
¡Toque(n)!	Touch!
¡Empuje(n)!	Push!
¡Tire(n)!	Throw!/Pull!/Fire! (weapon)
¡Eche(n)!	Throw!
¡Dé(n) patadas!	Kick!
¡Grite(n)!	Shout!
¡Salte(n)!	Jump!
¡Corra(n)!	Run!
¡Disimule(n)!	Fake it!
¡Encienda(n) la luz!	Turn on the light!
¡Apague(n) la luz!	Turn off the light!

EJERCICIOS. Translate into Spanish.

1. Please leave me alone!   ¡ _____ usted!

2. Please don't touch!   ¡ _____ ustedes!

3. Push!   ¡ _____ usted!

4. Shout!   ¡ _____ ustedes!

5. Jump!   ¡ _____ usted!

6. Fake it!   ¡ _____ ustedes!

7. Pull it!   ¡ _____ usted!

8. Turn off the light!   ¡ _____ ustedes!

9. Run!   ¡ _____ usted!

10. Turn on the light!   ¡ _____ ustedes!

Glossary

SPANISH TO ENGLISH

A

abogada *(la)* lawyer (female)
abogado *(el)* lawyer (male)
abogado defensor *(el)* defense attorney
aborto *(el)* abortion
abrazar to embrace
abrazarse to embrace each other
abrigo *(el)* coat
abril April
abrir to open
abuela *(la)* grandmother
abuelita little, dear grandma
abuelo *(el)* grandfather
aburrido/a bored
acabar de to have just
accidente *(el)* accident
acción judicial *(la)* legal suit
acera *(la)* sidewalk
acercarse to approach
aclarar to clear up
acomodar to make comfortable
aconsejar to advise
acordarse(ue) de to remember
acostarse(ue) to go to bed
acostumbrado/a accustomed
acreditar to authorize
acreedor *(el)* creditor
actitud *(la)* attitude
acusación *(la)* accusation
acusado *(el)* defendant
adaptación *(la)* adaptation
adecuado/a adequate
adelante on ward
además besides
adicional additional
administración *(la)* administration
administrador *(el)* administrator *(male)*
administradora *(la)* administrator *(female)*
administrativo/a administrative

admitir to admit
adulto *(el)* adult
adversario *(el)* adversary
advertir to warn
aflojar relax, loosen
afortunadamente fortunately
agarrar to grab
agencia *(la)* agency
agente *(el)* agent
agente de inmigración *(el)* immigration agent
agente de seguros *(el)* insurance agent
agosto August
agregar to add, to attach
agresivo/a aggressive
agricultura *(la)* agriculture
agua *(el)* water
aguantar to endure, to tolerate (put up with)
ahorrar to save (money, things)
al upon
alcalde *(el)* mayor
alcohólico/a alcoholic
alegrarse de to be happy about
alegre happy
alegría *(la)* happiness
alemán/a German
alfombra *(la)* rug
alguien someone, somebody
alimentar to nourish
aljetreo *(el)* hustle and bustle
almacén (el) department store
alternativa *(la)* alternative
alto/a tall
altura *(la)* height
aluminio *(el)* aluminum
alumna *(la)* female student
alumno *(el)* male student
amar to love
amarillo/a yellow
ambiente *(el)* atmosphere
ambulancia *(la)* ambulance

amenazar to threaten
amiga *(la)* female friend
amigo *(el)* male friend
amor darling, love
amor *(el)* love
ampliación *(la)* enlargement
ampliar to amplify
añadir to add, to join, to exaggerate
ancho/a wide
anciana *(la)* old woman
anillo *(el)* ring
año *(el)* year
anormal abnormal
ansiosamente eagerly
anteayar day before yesterday
anteojos *(los)* eyeglasses
anterior anterior
antes before
antibiótico/a antibiotic
anticuado/a antiquated
anuncio *(el)* announcement
apartado postal *(el)* post office box
apartamento *(el)* apartment
apelación *(la)* appeal
apelar to appeal
apellido *(el)* last name
aplazar to adjourn, to delay
apodo *(el)* nickname
aprender to learn
aquí here
árbol *(el)* tree
archivar to file
archivo *(el)* file
argentina *(la)* the Argentinian woman
argentino *(el)* the Argentinian man
arma *(el)* firearm
arrancar to start
arreglar to arrange
arreglo *(el)* rule, arrangement
arrojar to throw

asaltante *(el)* assailant
asalto *(el)* assault
ascenso *(el)* promotion
asegurador *(el)* insurer
así thus, so, in this way
asignatura *(la)* subject
asimilación *(la)* assimilation
asistente *(el)* assistant
asistir to attend
asistir a la clase to attend class
asociación *(la)* association
áspero/a rough, gruff, harsh
astuto/a astute, smart
asunto *(el)* matter
ateo *(el)* the atheist
atleta *(el)* athlete
atractivo/a attractive
atraer to attract
atreverse a to dare
atropellar to run over, to strike, to hit
audiencia *(la)* hearing
aumento *(el)* increase
autenticidad *(la)* authenticity
auto *(el)* auto
autobús *(el)* bus
automaticamente automatically
autopista *(la)* turnpike
autoridad *(la)* authority
auxilio *(el)* aid, help
avergonzado/a embarrassed
averiguar to investigate, to find out
aviso *(el)* announcement
ayuda *(la)* help
ayudante *(el)* assistant
ayudar to help
azul blue

B

bajo/a short, low, under
bañar to bathe someone
bañarse to bathe oneself
banco *(el)* bench, bank
bandera *(la)* flag
banquero *(el)* banker
barato/a inexpensive
bárbara horrible
barbaridades *(las)* atrocities, horrors
barrio *(el)* the neighborhood
basta enough
bastante enough
basura *(la)* garbage
basurero *(el)* garbage collector
bebé *(el)* baby
beber to drink

bebida *(la)* drink
bebidas alcohólicas alcoholic beverages
béisbol *(el)* baseball
bendito blessed
beneficiario *(el)* beneficiary
beneficio *(el)* benefit
biblioteca *(la)* library
bicultural bicultural
bien well
billete de entrada *(el)* entrance ticket
billetera *(la)* wallet
biográfico/a biographic
blanco/a white
boberías nonsense
bodeguero *(el)* grocer
bolígrafo *(el)* ballpoint pen
boliviana *(la)* the Bolivian woman
boliviano *(la)* *the Bolivian man*
bolsillo *(el)* pocket
bombero *(el)* fireman
bondad *(la)* kindness
bonito/a pretty
borracho/a drunk
borrador *(el)* eraser
boticario *(el)* druggist
bracero *(el)* contract laborer from Mexico
brazo *(el)* arm (body)
buenas noches good evening
buenas tardes good afternoon
bueno/a good
buenos días good day
bufanda *(la)* scarf
bufete *(el)* lawyer's office
burocracia *(la)* bureaucracy
burócrata *(el)* bureaucrat
burocrático/a bureaucratic
buscar to look for

C

cabeza *(la)* head
cablegrama *(el)* cablegram
cada each
café *(el)* cafe
cafetería *(la)* cafeteria
cajón *(el)* the drawer
cajoncito *(el)* the little drawer
cálculo *(el)* calculation
calentar to heat
calificación *(la)* grade
callado/a taciturn, silent
calle *(la)* the street
calmante *(el)* sedative
calmar to calm down
calor *(el)* heat

caluroso/a hot
cama *(la)* bed
cambiar to change
cambio *(el)* change
camillero *(el)* stretcher-bearer
caminar to walk
camión *(el)* truck
camionero *(el)* truckdriver
campo de juego *(el)* playground
cansado/a tired
cantidad *(la)* amount
cara *(la)* face
cárcel *(la)* jail
cardiólogo *(el)* cardiologist
cariño *(con)* affection
carpeta *(la)* folder, portfolio
carta *(la)* the letter
cartero *(el)* the mailman
casa *(la)* house
casado/a married
casarse to get married
casero *(el)* landlord, housing agent
casi almost
caso *(el)* case
casualmente by chance
catarro *(el)* cold (illness)
católico/a Catholic
causa *(la)* cause
centro *(el)* downtown
cerca near
cerradura *(la)* lock
cerrar(ie) to close
certificado *(el)* certificate
chaqueta *(la)* jacket
charla *(la)* chat, talk
cheque *(el)* cheque
chilena *(la)* the Chilian woman
chileno *(el)* the Chilian man
chocolate *(el)* chocolate
chófer *(el)* driver
choque *(el)* crash, accident
cirujano *(el)* surgeon
cita *(la)* appointment
citar to quote, to summon
ciudad *(la)* the city
claro of course
clase *(la)* class
cláusula *(la)* clause
clemencia *(la)* clemency
cliente *(el)* customer
clínica *(la)* clinic
cobrar to charge
coche *(el)* car
cocina *(la)* kitchen
cocinera *(la)* cook
codicia *(la)* greed
coger to catch, to seize, to get, to grab

cola *(la)* line
colega *(el)* colleague
colombiana *(la)* the Colombian
  (female)
colombiano *(el)* the Colombian
  (male)
combate *(el)* combat
comenzar to begin
comer to eat
comerciante *(el)* businessman
comerciar to trade
comestibles *(los)* food
comida *(la)* food, dish, meal
comité *(el)* committee
cómodo/a comfortable
compañera *(la)* companion
  (female)
compañero *(el)* companion
  (male)
compañía *(la)* company
competente competent
completamente completely
completar to fill out
complicado/a complicated
compra *(la)* purchase
comprar to buy
comprender to undrstand
comprensión *(la)*
  understanding
comprobar to prove,
  to corroborate,
  to substantiate
compulsivo/a compulsive
computadora *(la)* computer
común common
comunicar to communicate
comunicarse con
  to communicate with
comunidad *(la)* community
con with
concientemente consciously
condición *(la)* condition
conducir to drive
conductor *(el)* conductor
conferencia *(la)* conference
confidencial confidential
conflicto *(el)* conflict
congreso *(el)* congress
conocer to know
conocimiento *(el)* knowledge
consciente conscientious
conseguir to obtain, to get
consejera *(la)* counselor
  (female)
consejero *(el)* counselor *(male)*
conserje *(el)* janitor,
  maintenance man
conservador/a conservative
conservar to conserve, save
considerar to consider

consulta *(la)* consultation
consumidor *(el)* consumer
contador *(el)* accountant
contento/a happy
contestar to answer
contrario *(al)* on the other hand
contrato *(el)* contract
contribución *(la)* contribution,
  tax
contribuyente *(el)* taxpayer,
  contributor
control *(el)* control
controlar to control
convencer to convince
conveniente convenient
conversar to converse, to chat
convertirse to become
convicto *(el)* convict
convidado *(el)* guest
copa *(la)* alcoholic drink
copia *(la)* copy
coraje *(el)* courage
correo *(el)* the mail
correr to run
correspondencia *(la)*
  correspondence
corto/a short
corte *(la)* court
cortinas *(las)* the curtains
cosa *(la)* thing
costar(ue) to cost
costumbre *(la)* the custom
crecer to grow
crédito *(el)* credit
creer to believe
crimen *(el)* crime
criminal criminal
criticar to criticize
cruzar to cross
cuaderno *(el)* notebook
cuadra *(la)* block
cuadrado/a square
cuanto *(en)* as soon as
cuarta vez fourth time
cuartel *(el)* police precinct,
  police station
cuarto *(el)* room, quarter
cubana *(la)* the Cuban *(female)*
cubano *(el)* the Cuban *(male)*
cubiertos *(los)* silverware
cuchillo *(el)* knife
cuello *(el)* the neck
cuenta *(la)* bill
cuerpo *(el)* body
cuestionario *(el)* questionnaire
cuidadano/a citizen
cuidarse to care for oneself
culinario/a culinary
culpa *(la)* blame
culpar to blame

cultura *(la)* culture
cura *(el)* priest
curso *(el)* course

D

dar to give
dar de alta to release
  (a patient)
datos *(los)* data
de from, of
deber *(el)* obligation
débil weak
decano *(el)* dean
décima vez tenth time
decir to say, to tell
declaración conjunta *(la)* joint
  declaration
declaración de salario *(la)* wage
  and tax return
declaración jurada *(la)*
  deposition, sworn statement
declarar to declare
dedicado/a dedicated
dedo *(el)* finger
deducción *(la)* deduction
deducción normal *(la)*
  standard deduction
defender(ie) to defend
defraudar to defraud, to rob
delegado *(el)* delegate
delgado/a thin
deliberar to deliberate
delincuente *(el/la)* delinquent
demanda *(la)* claim
demanda legal *(la)* legal claim
demás *(los)* the rest
demasiado too much
demócrata *(el)* democrat *(male)*
demócrata *(la)* democrat
  (female)
demora *(la)* lateness, delay
dentista *(el/la)* dentist
denunciar to denounce
dependiente *(el/la)* clerk,
  'dependent
derecho/a right
desahucio *(el)* eviction
desanimado/a disheartened,
  discouraged
desánimo *(el)* discouragement
desarrollar to develop
desarollo *(en)* developing
desastre *(el)* disaster
descanso *(el)* recess, break
desconfiar to have doubts,
  to mistrust
descorazonarse to get
  discouraged

descubrir to discover
desde...hasta from...to
desear to wish, to want
desempleado (el) unemployed person
desempleo (el) unemployment
desgraciadamente unfortunately
deshonesto/a dishonest
desmayarse to faint
desorientar to disorient
despacho (el) office
despacio slowly
despertar(ie) to awaken someone
despertarse(ie) to wake oneself up
después after
destreza (la) skill
desventaja (la) disadvantage
desvestirse(i) to undress oneself
detalle (el) detail
detective (el) detective
detener to detain
detenido/a arrested, detained
devolución (la) refund
devolver to return (an object)
día (el) day
diagnóstico (el) diagnosis
dicho (el) saying
diciembre December
diente (el) tooth
dieta (la) diet
difícil difficult
difunto/a deceased
diligencia (la) errand
dinero (el) money
Dios God
dirección (la) address, management, administration
director (el) male director
directora (la) female director
dirigirse a to address
disco (el) record
discurso (el) speech
discutir to argue
disfrutar to enjoy
distrito (el) district
divorciado/a divorced
doctor (el) doctor (male)
doctora (la) doctor (female)
documentación (la) documentation
documento (el) document
dólar (el) dollar
dolor (el) pain
domingo (el) Sunday

dominicana (la) the Dominican woman
dominicano (el) the Dominican man
dormir(ue) to sleep
dormirse(ue) to fall asleep
drástico/a drastic
droga (la) drug
drogadicto (el) drug addict
durante during
durar to last

E

económico/a economic
edificio (el) building
efectuarse to take hold, to take effect
eficiente efficient
egoísta (el/la) egotist
elaborar to elaborate
elegantemente elegantly
emborracharse to become drunk
emergencia (la) emergency
emigración (la) emigration
emigrar to emigrate
empatar to tie
empleada (la) employee (female)
empleado (el) employee (male)
empleo (el) employment, job
encontrarse(ue) to find oneself
encrucijada (la) trap, bind, crossroads
endrogarse to become drugged
enemigo (el) enemy
enero January
enferma (la) sick woman
enfermarse to become ill
enfermedad (la) illness
enfermera (la) female nurse
enfermero (el) male nurse
enfermo (el) sick man
enfermo/a ill
enfrentarse to confront
enloquecer to become mad, to enrage
enloquecerse to become insane
enojado/a angry
enojarse to become angry
enseñar to teach
entender(ie) to understand
entrada (la) entrance
entre between, divided by
entregar to hand in
entregarse to turn oneself in
entrenador (el) coach

entrevista (la) interview
entusiasmar to become enthusiastic
enviar to send
epidemia (la) epidemic
epiléptico (el) epileptic
equipo (el) equipment, team
equivocarse to make a mistake, to be wrong
error (el) error
erupción (la) rash
escalera (la) stairway
escalpelo (el) scalpel
escándalo (el) scandal
escoger to choose
escribir to write
escritorio (el) desk
escuchar to listen to
escuela (la) school
esencial essential
esforzarse to make an effort
esfuerzo (el) effort
espalda (la) the back
España Spain
español (el) the Spanish man
española (la) the Spanish woman
español/a Spanish (adj.)
especial special
especialista (el/la) specialist
esperanza (la) hope
esperar to wait for, to hope, to expect
espiritual spiritual
esposa (la) wife
esposo (el) husband
esquina (la) corner
estacionar to park
estaciones (las) the seasons
Estados Unidos (los) United States
estatuto (el) statute
estimado (el) appraisal
estómago (el) stomach
estorbar to disturb
estropear to spoil, to damage
estudiante (el/la) student
estudiar to study
estudio (el) study
estufa (la) stove
evidencia (la) evidence
evitar to avoid
exactamente exactly
examen (el) exam
excelente excellent
exótico/a exotic
experiencia (la) experience
experto (el) expert
explicar to explain

extensión *(la)* extension
extranjero *(el)* foreigner
extraño/a strange

F

febrero February
fábrica/factoría *(la)* factory
fábula *(la)* fable
facilidades *(las)* facilities
fácil easy
fácilmente easily
factura *(la)* bill
falso/a false
falta *(la)* absence
faltar to cut, to miss
familia *(la)* family
familiar familiar
famoso/a famous
fanático/a fanatic
fantástico/a fantastic
farmacéutico *(el)* pharmacist
farmacia *(la)* pharmacy
fastidiar to bother, to annoy
fastidioso/a annoying
favor *(el)* favor
favorito/a favorite
federal federal
felicidades *(las)* congratulations
feo/a ugly
fiador *(el)* bailbondsmen
fianza *(la)* bail
figura *(la)* figure
fijarse to set, to fix
fila *(la)* row
final final
finalmente finally
firmar to sign
física *(la)* physics
fisiología *(la)* physiology
fisioterapista *(el/la)* physiotherapist
foco *(el)* focus
folleto *(el)* booklet
forma *(la)* form
formal formal
fotografía/foto *(la)* photograph
fotógrafo *(el)* photographer
frenar to stop
frío *(el)* cold
frío/a cold
frustrado/a frustrated
fuerte harsh, strong
fumar to smoke
funcionar to work
funcionario *(el)* public employee
furioso/a furious
fútbol *(el)* football
futuro *(el)* the future

G

ganancias *(las)* earnings
ganar to earn, to win
garaje *(el)* garage
garantizar to guarantee
gastar to spend
gemelo *(el)* twin
generalmente generally
gente *(la)* people
gentío *(el)* crowd
geografía *(la)* geography
gerente *(el)* manager
gimnasio *(el)* gymnasium
ginecólogo *(el)* gynecologist
gobierno *(el)* government
golpe *(el)* punch, blow
gordo/a fat
gracias thank you
gracias *(las)* thanks
grande large, great
grave grave
grito *(el)* shout, scream
grueso/a thick
grupo *(el)* group
guante *(el)* glove
guardar to guard, to look after
guardia *(el)* guard
guardia *(la)* collective bodyguards
guerra *(la)* war

H

hábil able, capable
habitante *(el)* inhabitant
hablador/a talkative
hablar to speak
hacer to do
hacia towards
hallar to find
hamburgesas *(las)* hamburgers
hecho *(el)* deed, fact
herido *(el)* injured person
hermana *(la)* the sister
hermano *(el)* brother
hierro *(el)* iron
hígado *(el)* liver
hija *(la)* daughter
hijo *(el)* son
hijos *(los)* children
hipertenso *(el)* hypertensive person
hipocondríaco *(el)* hypochondriac
hispana *(la)* Hispanic female
hispano *(el)* Hispanic male
histérico/a hysterical
historiador *(el)* historian

hoja *(la)* page, leaf sheet (of paper)
hombre *(el)* man
honesto/a honest, modest
hora *(la)* hour
horrible horrible
hospital *(el)* hospital
hostil hostile
hoy today
huella digital *(la)* fingerprint
huérfano *(el)* orphan
humillante humiliating

I

idea *(la)* idea
identidad *(la)* identity
identificación *(la)* identification
idioma *(el)* language
impacto *(el)* impact
impermeable *(el)* raincoat
imponer to impose
imponerse impose
importante important
imposible impossible
impuesto *(el)* tax
incapacitado *(el)* handicapped person
incapaz incompetent
incendio *(el)* fire
incidente *(el)* incident
inconcientemente unconsciously
incorporarse to sit up
independiente independent
indicado/a indicated
indicar to indicate
indignarse to become indignant
indocumentado *(el)* illegal alien
inesperado/a unexpected
infección *(la)* infection
infierno *(el)* hell
información *(la)* information
informe *(el)* report
ingeniero *(el)* engineer
inglés English
ingreso *(el)* income
iniciar to begin, initiate
injusticia *(la)* injustice
inmediatamente immediately
inmigración *(la)* immigration
inmovilizado/a immobilized
inquietud *(la)* restlessness, anxiety
inquilino *(el)* tenant
inscribir to register
insinuación *(la)* insinuation

inspección *(la)* inspection
institución *(la)* institution
instructor *(el)* instructor
intensidad *(la)* intensity
intenso/a intense
interesante interesting
interno *(el)* intern
interrogar to interrogate
inválido *(el)* invalid
inventar to invent
investigación *(la)* investigation
investigador *(el)* investigator
investigar to investigate
invierno *(el)* winter
invisible invisible
ir to go
irracional irrational
irse to leave
izquierdista *(el/la)* leftist
izquierdo/a left

J

jefa *(la)* female boss
jefe *(el)* male boss
joven young *(adj.)*
joven *(el)* young man
joven *(la)* young woman
judía *(la)* Jew *(female)*
judío *(el)* Jew *(male)*
judío/a Jewish
juego *(el)* game
jueves *(el)* Thursday
juez *(el)* the judge
jugador *(el)* player, gambler
juguete *(el)* toy
juicio *(el)* judgment, decision
julio July
junio June
junto/a together
jurar to swear
justicia *(la)* justice
justipreciar to appraise
justo/a just
juzgado *(el)* court
juzgar to judge

L

laboratorio *(el)* laboratory
ladrillo *(el)* brick
ladrón *(el)* thief
lamentar lament
lámpara *(la)* lamp
lápiz *(el)* /**lápices** *(los)* pencil/
   pencils
largo/a long
lástima *(la)* pity

lastimado/a injured/hurt
latina *(la)* Latin *(female)*
latino *(el)* Latin *(male)*
lavandero *(el)* laundry man
lavar to wash oneself
lección *(la)* lesson
leche *(la)* milk
leer to read
lejos far
lesión *(la)* lesion
levantar to get up, to lift
levantarse to get oneself up
ley *(la)* law
librería *(la)* bookstore
libro *(el)* book
licencia *(la)* licence
limpiar to clean
línea *(la)* line
lingüística *(la)* linguistics
lío *(el)* mess
listo/a smart, ready
llamada *(la)* call
llamar to call someone
llamarse to be named
llegada *(la)* arrival
llenar to fill, to fill out
llevar to carry
llover to rain
lógico/a logical
lograr to succeed
lotería *(la)* lottery
luego then
lugar *(el)* place
lunes *(el)* Monday

M

madera *(la)* wood
maduro/a mature, ripe
maestro *(el)* the man teacher
maestra *(la)* the woman teacher
malgastar to waste
malo/a bad, ill
mamá *(la)* mother, mamma
mañana tomorrow
mandamiento *(el)* warrant
mandar to send
mandona *(la)* a pushy woman
manejar to drive, to work
manejo *(el)* ability to handle,
   the handling
manicomio *(el)* mental
   institution
manifestaciones *(las)*
   manifestations, protests
mano *(la)* hand
maquillaje *(el)* make-up
máquina *(la)* machine

máquina de escribir *(la)* typewriter
máquina de revelar *(la)* the
   developer
maravilla *(la)* wonder, marvel
marcharse to go
marido *(el)* husband
martes *(el)* Tuesday
marzo March
más more
masas *(las)* masses
matar to kill
materia *(la)* material
matrícula *(la)* registration,
   matriculation
matricularse to enroll,
   to matriculate
mayo May
mayor older
mayoría *(la)* majority
mecánico *(el)* mechanic
mediano/a medium height
médica *(la)* female physician
medicina *(la)* medicine
médico *(el)* male physician
medida *(la)* measure
mejorar to improve,
   to get better
memorizar to memorize
menor younger
mensualmente monthly
mentir to lie
mentira *(la)* lie
mercachifle *(el)* the peddler
mercader *(el)* merchant
mercancía *(la)* merchandise
merienda *(la)* snack
mes *(el)* month
mesa *(la)* table
metadona *(la)* methadone
método *(el)* method
metro *(el)* meter
metropolitano/a metropolitan
mexicana *(la)* Mexican woman
mexicano *(el)* Mexican man
mezclar to mix
miembro *(el)* member
mientras while
miércoles *(el)* Wednesday
mil veces a thousand times
militar military
mirar to look at
misma *(la)*/**mismo** *(el)* /
   the same
mismo *(lo)* the same thing
moda *(la)* style
molestar to bother, to annoy
molesto/a estar bothered,
   annoyed

momento *(el)* moment
montar to mount
montón *(el)* pile
moreno/a dark
morir to die
motocicleta *(el)* motorcycle
motor *(el)* motor
motorista/automovilista *(el)* motorist
muchacha *(la)* young woman
muchacho *(el)* young man

muchas veces many times
muchedumbre *(la)* crowd
mucho much, a lot, many
muerte *(la)* death
mujer *(la)* woman
muletas *(las)* crutches
multa *(la)* fine
multiplicado por multiplied by
mundo *(el)* world
municipal municipal
municipio *(el)* municipality, city
murmurar to mumble
música *(la)* music
musulmán *(el)* Muslim
mutilado/a mutilated
muy very
muy poco very little

N

nacionalidad *(la)* nationality
naipe *(el)* playing cards
necesitar to need
negar to deny
negocio *(el)* business
negro/a Negro, black
nervioso/a nervous
neurótico *(el)* neurotic
nevar to snow
nieve *(la)* snow
niña *(la)* little girl
niño *(el)* little boy
noche *(la)* night
nocturno/a nocturnal, nightly
nombre *(el)* name
normal normal
norteamericana *(la)* North American *(female)*
norteamericano *(el)* North American *(male)*
nota *(la)* grade
novena vez ninth time
noviembre November

O

obrera *(la)* worker *(female)*
obrero *(el)* worker *(male)*
obtener to get, to obtain
ocasión *(la)* occasion
octava vez eighth time
octubre October
ocupado/a busy
odiar to hate
ofenderse to become offended
oferta *(la)* offer
oficial *(el)* official
oficina *(la)* office
oficinista *(el/la)* clerk
ofrecer to offer
oír to hear
ojo *(el)* eye
olvidarse to forget
omitir to omit
ómnibus *(el)* bus
opción *(la)* option
operación *(la)* operation
oportunidad *(la)* opportunity
óptico *(el)* optician
optimista *(el/la)* optimist
orden *(la)* order
orientar to guide, to familiarize
original original
oscuridad *(la)* darkness
otoño *(el)* autumn
otro/a another, other
oxígeno *(el)* oxygen
oyente *(el)* auditor

P

paciencia *(la)* patience
paciente *(el)* patient *(male)*
paciente *(la)* patient *(female)*
pagar to pay
pago *(el)* payment
país *(el)* country
palido/a pallid
pantalones *(los)* pants
papá *(el)* father, papa
papel *(el)* paper
papeleo *(el)* paper work, red tape
paquete *(el)* package
par *(un)* a couple
parabrisas *(el)* windshield
paralítico/a paralytic
parar to stop
pararse to stand
parecer to appear, to seem
pareja *(la)* the couple
pariente *(el)* relative

parque *(el)* park
participar to participate
partido *(el)* political party
partir to leave
pasado *(el)* past
pasajero *(el)* passenger
pasaporte *(el)* passport
pasar to happen, to pass
pasillo *(el)* hallway, corridor
pastel *(el)* cake
patólogo *(el)* pathologist
patrullero *(el)* patrol car
peatón *(el)* pedestrian
pecho *(el)* chest
pedir to ask for
pelear to fight
peligrar to be in danger
peligroso/a dangerous
pelo *(el)* hair
pequeño/a small
perdido/a lost
perfección *(la)* perfection
perfume *(el)* perfume
periodista *(el)* journalist
permiso *(el)* permission
permitir to permit
pero but
perro *(el)* dog
persona *(la)* person
peruana *(la)* Peruvian *(female)*
peruano *(el)* Peruvian *(male)*
pesar to weigh
pesimista *(el/la)* pessimist
pesquisa *(la)* investigation
petición *(la)* request
piano *(el)* piano
pie *(el)* foot
pierna *(la)* leg
píldora *(la)* pill
piso *(el)* floor
pistola *(la)* pistol
pizarra *(la)* blackboard
placas *(las)* the X-ray plates
plan *(el)* plan
planilla *(la)* application
planilla *(el)* form
plástico/a plastic
plato *(el)* dish, plate
playa *(la)* beach
pleito *(el)* law suit, litigation
pluma *(la)* pen
población *(la)* population
pobre poor
pobreza *(la)* poverty
pocas veces a few times
poco little
poder(ue) to be able
poderoso/a powerful

policía *(el)* individual policeman
policía *(la)* police force
policía de tránsito *(el)*
    traffic policemen
político *(el)* politician
póliza *(la)* policy
pomada *(la)* ointment
ponerse to become
por fin finally
porque because
¿por qué? why
portarse to behave
portátil portable
posibilidad *(la)* possibility
posible possible
posición *(la)* position
postal postal
predilecto/a favorite
preferir(ie, i) to prefer
pregunta *(la)* question
prender to grasp
prendero *(el)* pawnbroker
prensa *(la)* press (newspaper)
preocupado/a worried
preocuparse to worry
preparación *(la)* preparation
presidente *(el)* president
presidiario *(el)* convict
prestar to lend
presumido/a presumptuous
presupuesto *(el)* budget
prever to foresee
previo/a prior, previous
prima *(la)* cousin *(female)*
primario/a primary
primavera *(la)* spring
primera vez first time
primero *(el)* first
primo *(el)* cousin *(male)*
principal main
principiante *(el)* beginner
prisionero *(el)* prisoner
privado *(en)* in private
probar to try, prove
problema *(el)* problem
proceso *(el)* trial,
    legal proceedings
producir to produce
producto *(el)* product
profesión *(la)* profession
profesional professional
profesor *(el)* professor *(male)*
profesora *(la)* professor
    (female)
profundo/a profound
prohibir to prohibit
prometer to promise
pronto soon
propaganda *(la)* advertisement,

propaganda
propietario *(el)* the landlord
propina *(la)* tip
propio/a own
protección *(la)* protection
proteger to protect
protegerse to protect oneself
protestante *(el)* Protestant
    (male)
protestante *(la)* Protestant
    (female)
protestar to protest
provincia *(la)* province
próximo/a next
proyecto *(el)* project
pruebas *(las)* the tests
público/a public
pueblo *(el)* town, people
puerta *(la)* door
puertorriqueña Puerto Rican
    woman
puertorriqueño Puerto Rican
    man
pues well *(pause word)*
puesto *(el)* job, position
pulso *(el)* pulse

Q

queja *(la)* complaint
quejarse to complain
    (reflexive)
querer to want, to wish
    to desire, to love
que who, which,
    that *(relative pronoun)*
¿qué? what? *(interrogative*
    pronoun)
¡qué + a noun what (a or an)...!
quedar to remain
quedarse to stay, remain; to be,
    be left *(reflexive)*
¿quién(es)? who? whom?
quirófano operating room
quitar to take away, to remove
quitarse *(el)* to remove,
    to take off (clothes) *(reflexive)*

R

radio *(la)* the radio
radiografía *(la)* X-ray
radiología *(la)* radiology
radiólogo *(el)* radiologist
rápidamente rapidly
raro/a strange
ratito a little while
rayos X *(los)* X-rays
reaccionar to react
realidad *(la)* reality

realmente really
recepcionista *(la)* receptionist
receso *(el)* recess
receta *(la)* recipe
rechazar to reject
recibir to receive
recibo *(el)* receipt
recién recently
reclamate *(el)* claimant
reclamar to demand, to file a
    complaint, to sue
recobrar to get back, recover
recoger to pick up
recompensa *(la)* compensation
recordar(ue) to remember
rectangular rectangular
recuerdo *(el)* memory
recuperarse to recuperate
redondo/a round
referencia *(la)* reference
refrán *(el)* refrain saying
refrigerador *(el)* refrigerator
regalo *(el)* gift
regañar to scold, to chide,
    to quarrel
regresar to return
religión *(la)* religion
rellenar to fill out
reparar to repair
repaso *(el)* review
reporte *(el)* report
reportera *(la)* female reporter
reportero *(el)* male reporter
republicano *(el)* republican
residente *(el)* the resident
resolver to resolve
respeto *(el)* respect
responder to respond, to answer
responsabilidad *(la)*
    responsibility
responsable responsible
respuesta *(la)* response, answer
resto *(el)* the rest
resultado *(el)* result
retirarse withdraw
retrasado mental *(el)* retarded
    person
reunión *(la)* meeting, reunion
reunir to unite, to get together,
    to gather
reunirse con get together with
revisar to revise, to review
revista *(la)* magazine
revólver *(el)* revolver
rico/a rich, delicious
riqueza *(la)* wealth
rodear to surround
rogar to beg
rojo/a red

romántico/a romantic
romper to break
ropa *(la)* clothing
roto/a broken
ruido *(el)* noise
rumbo *(el)* route

S

sábado *(el)* Saturday
saber to know
sabor *(el)* flavor
sabroso/a delicious
sacar to take out, to get
sacerdote *(el)* priest
sacudir to shake
sala *(la)* room
salir to leave
saloncito *(el)* small room
salud *(la)* health
saludar to greet
saludarse to greet one another
sanatorio *(el)* sanatorium
sandalia *(la)* sandal
sangrar to bleed
sangre *(la)* the blood
santo *(el)* saint
secretaria *(la)* secretary
    (female)
secretario *(el)* secretary *(male)*
seguida *(en)* at once
segunda vez second time
seguro/a safe
seleccionar to choose
semáforo *(el)* light, signal
semestre *(el)* semester
señor *(el)* sir, Mr.
sentado/a seated
sentarse(ie) to sit down
sentirse (ie) to feel
separado/a separated
septiembre September
séptima vez *(la)* seventh time
serie *(la)* the series
servicio *(el)* service
servicio de impuestos internos
    (el) Internal Revenue Service
sexo *(el)* sex
sexta vez *(la)* sixth time
sicológico/a psychological
sicólogo *(el)* psychologist
sicótico *(el)* psychotic
siempre always
silla *(la)* chair
sino but
sirena *(la)* siren
sitio *(el)* place, location
situación *(la)* situation
sobornar to bribe

soborno *(el)* bribe
sobre on, upon
sobrevivir to survive
sobrina *(la)* niece
sobrino *(el)* nephew
socialista *(el/la)* socialist
solamente only
soldado *(el)* soldier
solicitar to apply for
sólo only, solely
solo/a alone
solución *(la)* solution
solucionar to solve
sordo *(el)* deaf person
sótano *(el)* basement, cellar
suavemente softly
subir to ascend, to go up
subterráneo *(el)* subway
sucio/a dirty
suegra *(la)* mother-in-law
suegro *(el)* father-in-law
sueldo *(el)* salary
suelo *(el)* ground
suerte *(la)* luck
suéter *(el)* the sweater
suficiente sufficiently
sufrimiento *(el)* suffering
sufrir to suffer
sugerencia *(la)* suggestion
suicidarse to commit suicide
supervisor *(el)* male supervisor
supervisor *(la)* female
    supervisor
surgir to appear, to arise

T

tabla *(la)* schedule
tablilla *(la)* bulletin board
tal, tales such
tal vez perhaps
también also, too
tanque *(el)* tank
tarde *(la)* afternoon
tarea *(la)* assignment
tarifas legales *(las)* legal
    proceedings
tarjeta *(la)* card
tarjeta de residencia *(la)*
    residency card
taxi *(el)* taxi
técnico *(el)* technician
telefónico/a telephone
teléfono *(el)* telephone
televisión *(la)* television
televisor *(el)* television set
temperatura *(la)* temperature
temprano early
tener que to have to, must

teoría *(la)* theory
terapista *(el)* therapist
tercera vez *(la)* third time
término *(el)* term
tesoro *(el)* treasure, dearest
testamento *(el)* will
testigo *(el)* witness
testigo ocular *(el)* eyewitness
testimonio *(el)* testimony,
    affidavit
tiempo *(el)* time
tiempo libre free time
tienda *(la)* store
timo *(el)* fraud
tipo *(el)* type
tiza *(la)* chalk
todavía still, yet
todito every little thing
todo everything
todo/a all, every
tomar to take, to eat, to drink
totalmente completely
trabajador social *(el)* social
    worker *(male)*
trabajadora social *(la)* social
    worker *(female)*
trabajador/a hard worker
trabajar to work
tradición *(la)* tradition
traducir to translate
traer to bring
traficar to deal in
tráfico *(el)* traffic *(colloquial)*
trámite *(el)* the carrying on of
    business
tramposo *(el)* cheater
tranquilizante *(el)* tranquilizer
tranquilizar to calm down
tranquilo/a tranquil, calm
transformarse to be transformed
tránsito *(el)* traffic
transportación *(la)*
    transportation
tratar de to try to
tratarse to deal with, be about
tremendo/a tremendous
tren *(el)* train
tribunal *(el)* court
triste sad
truco *(el)* trick

U

último/a last
único/a only
universidad *(la)* university
universitario/a university *(adj.)*
urgente urgent
urólogo *(el)* urologist

usar to use
útil useful

V

vacaciones *(las)* vacation
vagabundo *(el)* vagabond
valer to be worth.
valor *(el)* value
vándalo *(el)* vandal
vano *(en)* in vane
vecindario *(el)* neighborhood
vecino *(el)* neighbor
velocidad *(la)* speed
vendedor *(el)* salesman
vender to sell
venezolana *(la)* the Venezuelan woman
venezolano *(el)* the Venezuelan man
venir to come
ventaja *(la)* advantage

ventana *(la)* window
ventanilla *(la)* window (ticket office, bankteller, etc.)
ver to see
verano *(el)* summer
verdad *(la)* truth
verde green
verificar to verify
verse to appear, to seem to be
vestirse(i) to dress oneself
viaje *(el)* trip
vino *(el)* wine
violador *(el)* rapist
violar to violate, to rape
violento/a violent
vitamina *(la)* vitamin
vivir to live
volante *(el)* steering wheel
voluntario/a voluntary
volver(ue) to return
voto *(el)* vote
voz *(la)*, voces *(las)* voice, voices

Y

y and
ya already, now; *(sometimes used for emphasis only:* ¡Ya lo creo! of course!
yo I

Z

zapato *(el)* shoe
zero zero

Glossary

A

ability to handle, the handling el manejo
able, capable hábil
abnormal anormal
abortion el aborto
about, concerning acerca de
about (reference to time) a eso de
absence la falta
accident el accidente
accountant el contador
accusation la acusación
accustomed acostumbrado/a
adaptation la adaptación
to add, to join, to exaggerate añadir
to add, to attach agregar
additional adicional
to address dirigirse a
address, management, adminis-tration la dirección
adequate adecuado/a
to adjourn, to delay aplazar
administrator (female) la administradora
administrator (male) el administrador
administration la administración
administrative administrativo/a
to admit admitir
the adult el adulto
advantage la ventaja
adversary el adversario
advertisement, propaganda la propaganda
to advise aconsejar
affection el cariño
affectionately con cariño
after después
afternoon la tarde
agency la agencia
agent el agente
aggressive agresivo/a
to agree on quedar
agriculture la agricultura

aid el auxilio
alcoholic alcohólico/a
alcoholic beverages bebidas alcohólicas
alcoholic drink la copa
all todo/a
almost por poco, casi
alone solo/a
alphabetical order el orden alfabético
also, too también
alternative la alternativa
aluminum el aluminio
always siempre
ambulance la ambulancia
amount la cantidad
to amplify ampliar
angry enojado/a
to become angry estar enojado
announcement el aviso, el anuncio
to annoy fastidiar
annoying fastidioso/a
answer la respuesta
to answer contestar, responder
antibiotic el antibiótico
antiquated anticuado/a
apartment el apartamento
apparently por lo visto
appeal (legal) la apelación
to appeal apelar
to appear parecer
application la planilla
to apply for solicitar
appointment la cita
appraisal el estimado
to appraise justipreciar
to approach acercarse
April abril
Argentinian el argentino (male), la argentina (female)
to argue discutir
to arise (figurative) surgir
arm (body) el brazo
to arrange arreglar

arrangement el arreglo
arrested detenido/a
to be arrested estar detenido
arrival la llegada
to ascend subir
to ask for pedir(i)
to ask questions hacer preguntas
assailant el asaltante
assault el asalto
assignment la tarea
assimilation la asimilación
assistant el ayudante, el asistente
association la asociación
as soon as en cuanto
astute astuto/a
the atheist el ateo
athlete el atleta
at least por lo menos
atmosphere el ambiente
at once en seguida
to attract atraer
attractive atractivo/a
atrocities las barbaridades
to attend asistir a
to attend class asistir a la clase
attitude la actitud
auditor el oyente
August agosto
authenticity la autenticidad
authority la autoridad
to authorize acreditar, autorizar
automatically automáticamente
autumn el otoño
to avoid evitar
to awaken someone despertar(ie)

B

baby el bebé
back la espalda
bad, ill malo/a (estar)

bad, evil malo/a (ser)
bail la fianza
bailbondsman el fiador
ballpoint pen el bolígrafo
bank el banco
banker el banquero
baptismal certificate
    la fe de bautismo
baseball el béisbol
basement el sótano
to bathe oneself bañarse
to bathe someone bañar
bathroom el cuarto de baño
    (el servicio, el retrete,
    el inodoro, el excusado)
beach la playa
because porque
to become ponerse
bed la cama
before antes
before the appointment antes de
    la cita
to beg rogar
to begin comenzar, iniciar
beginner el principiante
to behave portarse
to believe creer
bench el banco
beneficiary el beneficiario
benefit el beneficio
besides además
between, divided by entre
bicultural bicultural
bilingual bilingüe
bill la factura
biographic biográfico/a
black negro/a
blackboard la pizarra
'to blame culpar
to bleed sangrar
blessed bendido/a
blood la sangre
block la cuadra
blow el golpe
blue azul
body el cuerpo
Bolivian el boliviano (male),
    la boliviana (female)
book el libro
bookkeeper el tenedor de libros
booklet el folleto
bookstore la librería
bored aburrido/a
boss el jefe (male),
    la jefa (female)
to bother molestar, fastidiar
bothered, annoyed, to be
    annoyed molesto/a,
    estar molesto/a

branch office la sucursal
break (rest) el descanso
to break romper
to bribe sobornar
brick el ladrillo
to bring traer
broken roto/a
brother el hermano
budget el presupuesto
building el edificio
bulletin board la tablilla
bureaucracy la burocracia
bureaucrat el burócrata
bureaucratic burocrático/a
burn la quemadura
bus el ómnibus
business el negocio
businessman el comerciante
busy ocupado/a
but sino
to buy comprar
by chance casualmente

C

cablegram el cablegrama
cafeteria la cafetería
cake el pastel
calculation el cálculo
call la llamada
to call someone llamar
to calm down calmar,
    tranquilizar
capable hábil
car el auto, el coche
card la tarjeta
cardiologist el cardiólogo
to care for oneself cuidarse
to carry llevar
carrying on of business
    el trámite
case el caso
to catch coger
Catholic católico/a
cause la causa
cellar el sótano
certified certificado/a
chair la silla
chalk la tiza
change el cambio
to change cambiar
to charge cobrar
chat la charla
cheater el tramposo
check el cheque
chemistry la química
chest el pecho
children los hijos

Chilian el chileno (male),
    la chilena (female)
chocolate el chocolate
to choose seleccionar, escoger
citizen el ciudadano (male),
    la ciudadana (female)
city la ciudad
claim la demanda
claimant el reclamante
class la clase
clause la cláusula
to clean limpiar
to clear up aclarar
clemency la clemencia
clerk el oficinista
clerk el/la dependiente
clinic la clínica
to close cerrar(ie)
clothing la ropa
coach el entrenador
coat el abrigo
coffee el café
cold el frío
cold (illness) el catarro,
    el resfriado
colleague el colega
Columbian el colombiano (male),
    la colombiana (female)
combat el combate
to come venir
comfortable cómodo/a
to commit suicide suicidarse
committee el comité
common común
to communicate comunicar
to communicate with
    comunicarse con
community la comunidad
company la compañía
companion el compañero (male),
    la compañera (female)
compensation la recompensa
competent competente
complaint la queja
to complain quejarse
to file a complaint reclamar
complete completo/a
completely completamente,
    totalmente
complicated complicado/a
compulsive compulsivo/a
computer la computadora
concerning acerca de
condition la condición
conductor el conductor
conference la conferencia
confidential confidencial
conflict el conflicto

to confront confrontar, enfrentarse
congratulation felicitación
congress el congreso
conscientious concienzudo/a
consciously concientemente
consequence la consecuencia
conservative conservador/a
to conserve conservar
to consider considerar
consultation la consulta
consumer el consumidor
contract el contrato
contribution la contribución
control el control
to control controlar
convenient conveniente
to converse conversar
convict el presidiario
to convince convencer
cook el cocinero (male), la cocinera (female)
copy la copia
corner la esquina
correspondence la correspondencia
correspondence course el programa de correo
corridor el pasillo
to cost costar (ue)
counselor el consejero (male), la consejera (female)
country el país
couple (people) la pareja, un par de + object (a couple of)
courage el coraje
course el curso
court la corte, el juzgado, el tribunal
cousin el primo (male), la prima (female)
crash (accident) el choque
crazy loco/a
to become crazy enloquecer, volverse loco/a
credit el crédito
creditor el acreedor
creole dish el plato criollo
crime el crimen
criminal criminal
to criticize criticar
to cross cruzar
crowd la muchedumbre, el gentío
crutch la muleta
Cuban el cubano (male), la cubana (female)
culinary culinario/a
culture la cultura

curtain la cortina
custom la costumbre
customer el cliente
to cut (to miss) faltar

D

to damage estropear, dañar
to be in danger peligrar
dangerous peligroso/a
to dare atreverse a
dark moreno/a
darkness la oscuridad
darling mi amor
data los datos
daughter la hija
day el día
day before yesterday anteayer
deaf person el sordo
to deal in traficar
to deal with tratarse
dean el decano
dear querido/a
death la muerte
deceased (person) el difunto (male), la difunta (female)
December diciembre
to declare declarar
deduction la deducción
deed, fact el hecho
to defend defender
defendant el acusado
defense attorney el abogado defensor
to defraud defraudar
delay la demora
to delay aplazar
delegate el delegado
to deliberate deliberar
delicious sabroso/a, rico/a
delinquent el delincuente
to demand reclamar
democrat el/la demócrata
to denounce denunciar
dentist el/la dentista
to deny negar
department store el almacén
dependent el/la dependiente
deposition (sworn statement) la declaración jurada
desk el escritorio
despite a pesar de
detail el detalle
detailed paperwork el fastidioso papeleo
to detain detener
detective el detective

to develop desarrollar
developer la máquina de revelar
diagnosis el diagnóstico
to die morir(ue)
diet la dieta
difficult difícil
director el director (male), la directora (female)
dirty sucio/a
disadvantage la desventaja
disaster el desastre
discouraged, disheartened desanimado/a
to discover descubrir
dish, plate el plato
dishonest deshonesto/a
to disorient desorientar
district el distrito
to disturb estorbar
divorced divorciado/a
to do hacer
doctor el doctor (male), la doctora (female)
document el documento
documentation la documentación
dog el perro
to do harm hacer daño
dollar el dólar
Dominican el dominicano (male), la dominicana (female)
door la puerta
downtown el centro
drastic drástico/a
drawer el cajón
to dress oneself vestirse(i)
drink la bebida
to drink beber, tomar
to drive conducir, manejar
driver el chófer
drug la droga
drug addict el drogadicto
to become drugged endrogarse
druggist el boticario
drunk borracho/a
to become drunk emborracharse
during durante

E

each cada
early temprano
to earn ganar
earnings las ganancias
easily fácilmente
to eat comer, tomar
economic económico/a
efficient eficiente

effort el esfuerzo
egotist el/la egoísta
eighth time la octava vez
to elaborate elaborar
elegantly elegantemente
embarrassed avergonzado/a
to embrace abrazar
emergency la emergencia
emergency room la sala de emergencia
to emigrate emigrar
emigration la emigración
employee el empleado (male); la empleada (female)
employment el empleo
to endure aguantar
enemy el enemigo
engineer el ingeniero
English inglés/a
to enjoy disfrutar, gozar
enlargement la ampliación
enough basta
to enroll matricularse
to enter entrar
to become enthusiastic entusiasmar
entrance la entrada
entrance ticket el billete de entrada
epidemic la epidemia
epileptic el epiléptico
equipment el equipo
eraser el borrador
errand la diligencia
error el error
essential esencial
everybody todo el mundo
everything todo
every afternoon todas las tardes
every day todos los días
every evening todas las noches
everywhere en todas partes
every little thing todito
eviction el desahucio
evidence la evidencia
exactly exactamente
exam el examen
excellent excelente
exotic exótico/a
to expect esperar
experience la experiencia
expert el experto
to explain explicar
extension la extensión
eye el ojo
eyeglasses los anteojos
eyewitness el testigo ocular

F

fable la fábula
face la cara
facilities las facilidades
fact el hecho
factory la fábrica, la factoría (not standard)
to faint desmayarse
to fall caer
to fall asleep dormirse(ue)
false falso/a
familiar familiar
family la familia
family doctor el médico de cabecera
family planning la planificación familiar
famous famoso/a
fantastic fantástico/a
far lejos
fat gordo/a
father el papá
father-in-law el suegro
favor el favor
favorite favorito/a
February febrero
federal federal
Federal Government el gobierno federal
to feel sentirse(ie)
fifth time la quinta vez
to fight pelear
figure la figura
to file archivar
to file a claim hacer una demanda
to fill llenar
to fill out completar, llenar, rellenar
final final
finally por fin
to find hallar, descubrir
to find oneself encontrarse(ue)
to find out averiguar, descubrir, saber (in preterite only)
fine la multa
finger el dedo
fingerprint la huella digital
fire el incendio
firearm el arma
fire insurance el seguro contra incendio
fireman el bombero
first primero
first name el nombre de pila
first time la primera vez
flag la bandera

flavor el sabor
floor el piso
focus el foco
folder la carpeta
food la comida, los comestibles
foot el pie
football el fútbol
foreigner el extranjero (male), la extranjera (female)
to foresee prever
forever para siempre
to forget olvidarse
form la planilla
formal formal
former anterior
fortunately afortunadamente
fourth time la cuarta vez
fraud el timo, el fraude
free time el tiempo libre
French fried potatoes las patatas fritas
Friday el viernes
friend el amigo (male), la amiga (female)
from de
from ... to desde ... hasta
from where de dónde
frustrated frustrado/a
furious furioso/a
future el futuro

G

game el juego
garage el garaje
garbage la basura
garbage collector el basurero
to gather reunir, recoger
generally generalmente
gentleman el señor
geography la geografía
German alemán/a
to get back recobrar
to get discouraged descorazonarse
to get (to grab) coger, obtener
to get oneself up levantarse
to get up (lift oneself) levantarse
gift el regalo
to give dar
glove el guante
God Dios
to go marcharse, irse
to go shopping ir de compras
to go to bed acostarse(ue)
to go up subir
good bueno/a
good afternoon buenas tardes

good day buenos días
good evening buenas noches
good news buenas noticias
government el gobierno
to grab agarrar, coger
grade la nota
grade school la escuela primaria
to graduate as recibirse de
grandfather el abuelo
grand jury el gran jurado
grandmother la abuela
to grasp prender
grave (serious) grave
greed la codicia
green verde
to greet saludar
to greet one another saludarse
grocer el bodeguero
gross income los ingresos brutos
ground el suelo
group el grupo
to grow crecer
gruff áspero/a
guard el guardia,
     la guardia (a collective body)
to guarantee garantizar
to guard guardar
guest el convidado
to guide orientar
gymnasium el gimnasio
gynecologist el ginecólogo

H

hair el pelo
hallway el pasillo
hamburger la hamburguesa
hand la mano
handicapped person
     el incapacitado
to hand in entregar
to happen pasar
happiness la alegría
happy alegre
happy contento/a
to be happy about alegrarse
hard worker trabajador/a
harsh fuerte
to hate odiar
to have tener
to have to tener que
to have doubts desconfiar
to have just acabar de
head la cabeza
health la salud
to hear oír
hearing la audiencia
heat el calor

to heat calentar
height la altura
hell el infierno
help la ayuda, el auxilio
to help ayudar
here aquí
high school la escuela secundaria
Hispanic el latino (male),
     la latina (female)
historian el historiador
home la casa
honest honesto/a
hope la esperanza
to hope esperar
horrible horrible, bárbara
hour la hora
hospital el hospital
hostile hostil
house la casa
Housing Authority
     El Deparatamento de Vivienda
hot caluroso/a
how(?) ¿cómo?
humiliating humillante
husband el esposo
hustle and bustle el aljetreo
hypertensive man el hipertenso
hypochondriac el hipocondríaco
hysterical histérico/a

I

idea la idea
identification la identificación
ill enfermo/a
to become ill enfermarse
illegal alien el indocumentado
illness la enfermedad
immediately inmediatamente
immigration la inmigración
immigration agent el agente de
     inmigración
immobilized inmovilizado/a
impacto el impacto
important importante
to impose imponer
impossible imposible
to improve mejorar
in en
incident el incidente
income el ingreso
incompetent incapaz
increase el aumento
independent independiente
to indicate indicar
indicated indicado/a
to become indignant indignarse
inexpensive barato/a
infection la infección

to inform poner al tanto,
     informar
information la información
inhabitant el habitante
injustice la injusticia
injured, hurt lastimado/a,
     herido/a
in private en privado
to become insane enloquecerse
insinuation la insinuación
inspection la inspección
instead of en vez de
institution la institución
instruction la instrucción
instructor el instructor
insurance agent el agente de
     seguros
insurance company
     la compañía de seguros
insurer el asegurador
intense intenso/a
intensity la intensidad
interesting interesante
intern el interno
Internal Revenue Service el
     Servicio de Impuestos Internos
to interrogate interrogar
interview la entrevista
invalid el inválido
to invent inventar
to investigate investigar
investigation la pesquisa,
     la investigación
investigator el investigador
invisible invisible
iron el hierro
irrational irracional

J

jacket la chaqueta
jail la cárcel
janitor el conserje
January enero
Jew el judío (male),
     la judía (female)
Jewish judío/a
job (position) el puesto,
     el trabajo, el empleo
joint declaration la declaración
     conjunta
journalist el periodista
judge el juez
to judge juzgar
judgment el juicio
July julio
to jump out saltar de
     + direct object

June junio
just justo/a
justice la justicia

K

to kill matar
kindness la bondad
kitchen la cocina
knife el cuchillo
to know saber *(a fact)*,
   conocer *(a person)*
knowledge el conocimiento

L

laboratory el laboratorio
labor union el sindicato
ladder la escalera
to lament lamentar
lamp la lámpara
landlord el propietario, el casero
language el idioma, la lengua
large grande
last último/a
to last durar
last straw *(limit)* el colmo
lateness la demora
laundry el lavadero,
   la lavandería
law la ley
law suit el pleito
lawyer el abogado *(male)*,
   la abogada *(female)*
lawyer's office el bufete
to leave irse, partir, salir
to learn aprender
left izquierdo/a
leftist el/la izquierdista
leg la pierna
legal claim la demanda legal,
   el pleito
legal proceedings las tarifas
   legales
legal suit la acción judicial
to lend prestar
lesion la lesión
lesson la lección
letter la carta
library la biblioteca
license la licencia
lie la mentira
to lie mentir
life la vida
to lift levantar
light *(signal)* el semáforo,
   la luz
line la línea

line *(of people)* la cola
linguistic lingüística
to listen to escuchar
little poco
little boy el niño
little drawer el cajoncito
little girl la niña
to live vivir
little *(dear)* **grandma**
   la abuelita *(colloquial)*
liver el hígado
lock la cerradura
logical lógico/a
to look at mirar
to look for buscar
long largo/a
lost perdido/a
lottery la lotería
love el amor
to love amar, querer
luck la suerte;
   bad luck la mala suerte

M

machine la máquina
magazine la revista
mail el correo
mailman el cartero
majority la mayoría
main principal
main office la oficina principal
to make manifest poner de
   manifiesto
to make a mistake equivocarse
to make an effort esforzarse
to make comfortable acomodar
make-up el maquillaje
man el hombre
management la dirección
manager el gerente
manifestations
   las manifestaciones
many mucho
many times muchas veces
March marzo
married casado/a
to get married casarse
masses las masas
material la materia
matter el asunto
mature maduro/a
May mayo
mayor el alcalde
meal la comida
meanwhile mientras tanto
measure la medida
mechanic el mecánico
medicine la medicina

medium height mediano/a
member el miembro
to memorize memorizar
memory el recuerdo
mental institution el manicomio
merchandise la mercancía
merchant el mercader
mess el lío
meter el metro
methadone la metadona
method el método
metropolitan metropolitano/a
Mexican el mexicano *(male)*,
   la mexicana *(female)*
military militar
milk la leche
to mistrust desconfiar
to mix mezclar
moment el momento
Monday el lunes
money el dinero
month el mes
monthly mensualmente
more más
Moslem el musulmán
mother la mamá, la madre
mother-in-law la suegra
motor el motor
motorcycle la motocicleta
motorist el/la motorista,
   automovilista
much mucho/a
multiplied by multiplicado por
to mumble murmurar
municipal municipal
municipal ordinance
   la ordenanza municipal
municipality el municipio
music la música
mutilated mutilado/a

N

name el nombre
   last name el apellido
to be named llamarse
nationality la nacionalidad
natural science las ciencias
   naturales
near cerca
neck el cuello
to need necesitar
neighbor el vecino
neighborhood el vecindario,
   el barrio
neither . . . nor ni . . . ni
nephew el sobrino
nervous nervioso/a
neurotic el neurótico

news las noticias
next próximo/a
next project el próximo proyecto
next semester el semestre que
    viene, el próximo semestre
next week la semana que viene,
    la próxima semana
next year el año que viene,
    el próximo año
nickname el apodo
niece la sobrina
night la noche
night shift el turno de noche
ninth time la novena vez
nocturnal nocturno/a
noise el ruido
nonsense las boberías
normal normal
North American
    el norteamericano (male),
    la norteamericana (female)
notebook el cuaderno
to nourish alimentar
November noviembre
nurse el enfermero (male),
    la enfermera (female)

O

obligation el deber
to obtain conseguir, obtener
occasion la ocasión
October octubre
of de
of course claro, seguro,
    por supuesto
to become offended ofenderse
to offer ofrecer
office el despacho
official el oficial
ointment la pomada
old viejo/a
old woman la anciana
older mayor
to omit omitir
on (upon) sobre
on the other hand al contrario
only (adj.) único/a
only (adv.) solamente
onward adelante
to open abrir
operating room el quirófano
operation la operación
opportunity la oportunidad
opportunity to work
    la oportunidad de trabajar
optician el óptico
optimist el/la optimista
option la opción

order (command) la orden,
    (order, class, group) el orden
original original
orphan el huérfano
other el otro, la otra
own propio/a
own language el propio idioma
oxygen el oxígeno
oxygen tank el tanque de oxígeno

P

package el paquete
pain el dolor
page la hoja
pale pálido/a
pants los pantalones
paper el papel, la hoja
paperwork el papeleo
paragraph el párrafo
paralyzed paralítico/a
to park estacionar
park el parque
to participate participar
to pass pasar,
    salir bien (an exam)
passenger el pasajero
passport el pasaporte
past el pasado
pathologist el patólogo
patience la paciencia
patient el/la paciente
patrol car el patrullero
pawnbroker el prendero
to pay pagar
pay raise aumento de sueldo
payment el pago
peddler el mercachifle
pedestrian el peatón
pen la pluma
pencil el lápiz
people la gente, el pueblo
perfection la perfección
perfume el perfume
perhaps tal vez
permission el permiso
to permit permitir
person la persona
Peruvian el peruano (male),
    la peruana (female)
pessimist el/la pesimista
pharmacist el farmacéutico
pharmacy la farmacia
photograph la fotografía, la foto
photographer el fotógrafo
physician el médico (male),
    la médica (female)
physician el médico (male),
    la médica (female)

physics la física
physiology la fisiología
physiotherapist
    el/la fisioterapista
piano el piano
to pick up recoger
pile el montón
pill la píldora, la pastilla
pistol la pistola
pity la lástima
place el lugar, el sitio
plan el plan
plastic plástico/a
player el jugador
playground el campo de juego
playing card el naipe
please por favor
pocket el bolsillo
police force la policía
policeman el policía
police precinct el cuartel
policewoman la mujer policía
policy la póliza
political party el partido
political science la ciencia
    política
politician el político
poor pobre
population la población
portable portátil
position la posición
possibility la posibilidad
possible posible
postal postal
postcard la tarjeta postal
post office la oficina de correos
post office box el apartado postal
poverty la pobreza
powerful poderoso/a
to prefer preferir(ie,i)
preparation la preparación
president el presidente (male),
    la presidenta (female)
press (newspaper) la prensa
presumptuous presumido/a
pretty bonito/a
priest el sacerdote, el cura
primary primario/a, primero
prior previo/a
prisoner el prisionero
in private en privado
probably a lo mejor,
    probablemente
problem el problema
process el proceso
to produce producir
product el producto
professional profesional

professor el profesor (*male*),
la profesora (*female*)
profound profundo/a
to prohibit prohibir
project el proyecto
to promise prometer
promotion el ascenso
to protect proteger
to protect oneself protegerse
protection la protección
to protest protestar
Protestant el/la protestante
to prove comprobar
province la provincia
psychological sicológico/a
psychologist el sicólogo
psychotic el sicótico
public público/a
in public en público
public employee el funcionario
Puerto Rican
el puertorriqueño (*male*),
la puertorriqueña (*female*)
pulse el pulso
punch, blow el golpe
purchase la compra
pushy woman la mandona
put up with aguantar

Q

quarter el cuarto
question la pregunta
questionnaire el cuestionario
to quote citar

R

radio la radio
radiology la radiología
radiologist el radiólogo
to rain llover
raincoat el impermeable
rapidly rápidamente
rapist el violador
rash la erupción
to react reaccionar
to read leer
ready listo/a, preparado/a
reality la realidad
to realize darse cuenta de
really realmente
receipt el recibo
to receive recibir
recently en estos días,
recién
receptionist la recepcionista
recess el receso, el descanso
recipe la receta

record el disco (*music*)
rectangular rectangular
to recuperate recuperarse
red rojo/a
reference la referencia
refrain el refrán
refrigerator el refrigerador
refund la devolución
to register inscribir
registration la matrícula
to reject rechazar
relative el pariente
relax aflojar
to release (*a patient*) dar de alta
religion la religión
to remain quedarse
to remember acordarse(ue) de,
recordar(ue)
to repair reparar
report el informe, el reporte
reporter el reportero (*male*),
la reportera (*female*)
republican el republicano (*male*),
la republicana (*female*)
request la petición
residence card el carnet,
la tarjeta de residencia
resident el/la residente
to resolve resolver
respect el respeto
to respond responder
response la respuesta
responsibility la responsabilidad
responsible responsable
rest los demás, el resto
result el resultado
as a result of a consecuencia
retarded person el retrasado
mental
restlessness la inquietud
to return volver(ue), regresar
to return (*an object*) devolver
reunion la reunión
review el repaso
to review revisar
to revise revisar
revolver el revólver
rich rico/a
right derecho/a
ring el anillo
ripe maduro/a
romantic romántico/a
room la sala, el cuarto
round redondo/a
route el rumbo
row la fila
rug la alfombra
to run correr
to run over atropellar

S

sad triste
safe seguro/a
safety belt el cinturón de
seguridad
saint el santo
salary el sueldo
same mismo/a, lo mismo
salesman el vendedor
sanatorium el sanatorio
sandal la sandalia
Saturday el sábado
to save (*money, things*) ahorrar,
conservar
to say decir
saying el dicho
scalpel el escalpelo
scandal el escándalo
scarf la bufanda
schedule la tabla
school la escuela
to scold regañar
search warrant el orden de
registro
seasons las estaciones
seated sentado/a
second time segunda vez
secretary el secretario (*male*),
la secretaria (*female*)
sedative el calmante
to see ver
to seem verse, parecer
to seize coger
to sell vender
semester el semestre
to send mandar, enviar
separated separado/a
September septiembre
series la serie
service el servicio
service record la hoja de
servicio
to set fijarse
seventh time la séptima vez
sex el sexo
to shake sacudir
shoe el zapato
short (*size*) bajo/a, corto/a
shout el grito
sick man el enfermo
sick woman la enferma
sidewalk la acera
to sign firmar
silk blouse la blusa de seda
silverware los cubiertos
siren la sirena
sister la hermana
to sit down sentarse(ie)

to sit up incorporarse
situation la situación
sixth time la sexta vez
skill la destreza
to sleep dormir(ue)
slowly despacio
small pequeño/a
Small Claims Court el Tribunal
    de Reclamaciones
small room el saloncito
smart listo/a (ser)
to smoke fumar
snack la merienda
snow la nieve
to snow nevar
social sciences las ciencias
    sociales
social worker
    el trabajador social *(male)*,
    la trabajadora social (female)
socialist el/la socialista
softly suavemente
soldier el soldado
solution la solución
to solve solucionar
somebody, someone alguien
son el hijo
soon pronto
Spain España
Spanish español/a
to speak hablar
special especial
specialist el/la especialista
speech el discurso
speed la velocidad;
   high speed la velocidad alta
to spend gastar
spiritual espiritual
to spoil estropear, dañar
spring la primavera
square cuadrado/a
stairway la escalera
to stand pararse
standard deduction
    la deducción normal
to start *(a machine)* arrancar
statute el estatuto
steering wheel el volante
still todavía
stomach el estómago
to stop parar, frenar
store la tienda
stove la estufa
strange raro/a,
    extraño/a
street la calle
stretcher la camilla
stretcher-bearer el camillero
to strike atropellar

to stroll dar paseos
strong fuerte
student el/la estudiante
to study estudiar
study estudio
subject la asignatura
to substantiate comprobar
to substantiate claims
    comprobar las declaraciones
subway el tren subterráneo
to succeed lograr
such tal, tales
suddenly de repente
to sue reclamar
to suffer sufrir
suffering el sufrimiento
sufficient, enough bastante
suggestion la sugerencia
summer el verano
to summon citar
Sunday el domingo
supervisor el supervisor *(male)*;
    la supervisora (female)
surgeon el cirujano
surrogate judge el juez de
    testamentarías
to surround rodear
to survive sobrevivir
to swear jurar
sweater el suéter

T

table la mesa
taciturn *(silent)* callado/a
to take tomar
to take care of oneself cuidarse
to take hold *(to take effect)*
    efectuarse
take off *(remove)* quitarse
to take out sacar
talkative hablador/a
tall alto/a
tank el tanque
tax el impuesto, la contribución
taxi el taxi
taxpayer, contributor
    el contribuyente
to teach enseñar
teacher el maestro *(male)*,
    la maestra *(female)*
team el equipo
technician el técnico
telephone el teléfono
telephonic telefónico/a
television set el televisor
to tell decir
temperature la temperatura
tenant el inquilino

tenth time decima vez
term el término
test la prueba
testimony el testimonio
thank you gracias
that which lo que
that que
then luego
theory la teoría
therapist el/la terapista
thick grueso/a
thief el ladrón
thin delgado/a
thing la cosa
third time tercera vez
a thousand times mil veces
to threaten amenazar
to throw arrojar
Thursday el jueves
thus *(so, in that way)* así
ticket *(fine)* la multa
to tie *(a score)* empatar
time el tiempo
tip la propina
tired cansado/a
today hoy
together junto/a
to tolerate aguantar
tomorrow mañana
tomorrow afternoon
    mañana por la tarde
tomorrow evening
    mañana por la noche
tomorrow morning
    mañana por la mañana
too también
too much demasiado
tooth el diente
towards hacia
town el pueblo
toy el juguete
to trade comerciar
tradition la tradición
traffic el tránsito
traffic policeman el policía de
    tránsito
train el tren
tranquil tranquilo/a
tranquilizer el tranquilizante
to be transformed transformarse
to translate traducir
transportation la transportación
trap *(bind)* la encrucijada
travel agent el agente de viajes
treasure el tesoro
tree el árbol
tremendous tremendo/a
trial el proceso
trick el truco

trip el viaje
truck el camión
truckdriver el camionero
truth la verdad
to try to tratar de
to try probar
Tuesday el martes
to turn oneself in entregarse
turnpike la autopista
twin el gemelo
type tipo/a
typewriter la máquina de
    escribir

U

ugly feo/a
unconsciously
    inconcientemente
to understand entender(ie),
    comprender
understanding, comprehension
    la comprensión
to undress oneself desvestirse(i)
uneasiness la inquietud
unemployed person
    el desempleado
unemployment el desempleo
unemployment agency
    la agencia de desempleo
unexpected inesperado/a
unfortunately desgraciadamente,
    por desgracia
to unite reunir
United States los Estados Unidos
university la universidad
university (adj.) universitario/a
until hasta que
upon al
urgent urgente
urologist el urólogo
to use usar
useful útil

V

vacation las vacaciones
vagabond el vagabundo

value el valor
vandal el vándalo
Venezuelan el venezolano (male),
    la venezolana (female)
to verify verificar
very muy
very little muy poco
victim la víctima
vigilance la vigilancia
violent violento/a
vitamin la vitamina
voice, voices la voz, las voces
voluntary voluntario/a
vote el voto

W

wage and tax return
    la declaración de salario
to wait for esperar
to wake oneself up
    despertarse(ie)
to walk caminar
wallet la billetera, la cartera
to want querer(ie)
to want querer(ie)
war la guerra
to warn advertir
warrant el mandamiento
to wash oneself lavarse
to waste malgastar
water el agua
wealth la riqueza
Wednesday el miércoles
to weigh pesar
well bien
well (pause word) pues
what? ¿qué?
wheelchair la silla de ruedas
where(?) ¿dónde?
wherever dondequiera
which(?) ¿cuál?,
    que (relative pronoun)
while mientras
white blanco/a
who quien,
    que (relative pronoun),
    ¿quién? (interrogative)

whose ¿de quién?
wide ancho/a
wife la esposa
will el testamento
to win ganar
window (ticket office, bank
    teller, etc.) la ventanilla
windshield el parabrisas
wine el vino
winter el invierno
to wish desear
with con
to withdraw retirarse
witness el testigo
woman la mujer;
    old woman la anciana
wood la madera
work el trabajo
to work (function) funcionar,
    trabajar
work schedule el turno de
    trabajo
worker el obrero (male),
    la obrera (female)
world el mundo
worried preocupado/a
to worry preocuparse
to be worth valer
write escribir

X

X-ray los rayos X,
    la radiografía
X-ray plates las placas

Y

year el año
yellow amarillo/a
yet todavía
young joven
young man el joven
young woman la joven
younger menor

Verb Chart

REGULAR VERBS

Infinitive

ayudar	comer	recibir
to help	*to eat*	*to receive*

Present Participle

ayudando	comiendo	recibiendo

Past Participle

ayudado	comido	recibido

THE SIMPLE TENSES

INDICATIVE MOOD
Present Tense

ayudo	como	recibo
ayudas	comes	recibes
ayuda	come	recibe
ayudamos	comemos	recibimos
(ayudáis)*	(coméis)*	(recibís)*
ayudan	comen	reciben

Imperfect Tense

ayudaba	comía	recibía
ayudabas	comías	recibías
ayudaba	comía	recibía
ayudábamos	comíamos	recibíamos
(ayudabais)	(comíais)	(recibíais)
ayudaban	comían	recibían

Preterite Tense

ayudé	comí	recibí
ayudaste	comiste	recibiste
ayudó	comió	recibió
ayudamos	comimos	recibimos
(ayudasteis)	(comisteis)	(recibisteis)
ayudaron	comieron	recibieron

Future Tense

ayudaré	comeré	recibiré
ayudarás	comerás	recibirás
ayudará	comerá	recibirá
ayudaremos	comeremos	recibiremos
(ayudaréis)	(comeréis)	(recibiréis)
ayudarán	comerán	recibirán

Conditional Tense

ayudaría	comería	recibiría
ayudarías	comerías	recibirías
ayudaría	comería	recibiría
ayudaríamos	comeríamos	recibiríamos
(ayudaríais)	(comeríais)	(recibiríais)
ayudarían	comerían	recibirían

SUBJUNCTIVE MOOD
Present Tense

ayude	coma	reciba
ayudes	comas	recibas
ayude	coma	reciba
ayudemos	comamos	recibamos
(ayudéis)**	(comáis)**	(recibáis)**
ayuden	coman	reciban

Imperfect Tense (-ra form)

ayudara	comoera	recibiera
ayudaras	comieras	recibieras
ayudara	comiera	recibiera
ayudáramos	comiéramos	recibiéramos
(ayudarais)	(comierais)	(reciberais)
ayudaran	comieran	recibieran

Imperfect Tense (-se form)

ayudase	comiese	recibiese
ayudases	comieses	recibieses
ayudase	comiese	recibiese
ayudásemos	comiésemos	recibiésemos
(ayudaseis)	(comieseis)	(recibieseis)
ayudasen	comiesen	recibiesen

IMPERATIVE†

ayuda (tú)	come (tú)	recibe (tú)
ayudad (vosotros)	comed (vosotros)	recibid (vosotros)

* Forms in parentheses correspond to the **vosotros, vosotras** form.

** For the negative **tú** and **vosotros** command forms, and for both affirmative and negative **usted, ustedes,** and **nosotros** command forms, the corresponding subjunctive forms are used.

THE COMPOUND TENSES

Perfect Infinitive	haber ayudado (comido, recibido), *to have helped (eaten, received)*
Perfect Participle	habiendo ayudado (comido, recibido), *having helped (learned, received)*

INDICATIVE MOOD

Present Perfect		Pluperfect		Preterit Perfect	
he		había		hube	
has		habías		hubiste	
ha	ayudado	había	ayudado	hubo	ayudado
hemos	comido	habíamos	comido	hubimos	comido
(habéis)	recibido	(habíais)	recibido	(hubisteis)	recibido
han		habían		hubieron	

Future Perfect		Conditional Perfect	
habré		habría	
habrás		habrías	
habrá	ayudado	habría	ayudado
habremos	comido	habríamos	comido
(habréis)	recibido	(habríais)	recibido
habrán		habrían	

SUBJUNCTIVE MOOD

Present Perfect		Pluperfect (-ra and -se forms)	
haya		hubiera, hubiese	
hayas		hubieras, hubieses	
haya	ayudado	hubiera, hubiese	ayudado
hayamos	comido	hubiéramos, hubiésemos	comido
(hayáis)	recibido	(hubierais, hubieseis)	recibido
hayan		hubieran, hubiesen	

IRREGULAR VERBS

Class I *(-ar, -er)*

cerrar*(ie)*   *to close*

Present Indicative	**cierro, cierras, cierra,** cerramos, (cerráis), **cierran**
Present Subjunctive	**cierre, cierres, cierre,** cerremos, (cerréis), **cierren**
Command (tú)	**cierra, no cierres**

Like **cerrar:** atravesar, *to cross;* empezar, *to begin;* despertar(se), *to awaken, wake up;* negar, *to deny;* pensar, *to think;* recomendar, *to recommend;* sentar(se), *to sit down.*

perder*(ie)*   *to lose*

Present Indicative	**pierdo, pierdes, pierde,** perdemos, (perdéis), **pierden**
Present Subjunctive	**pierda, perdas, pierda,** perdamos, (perdáis), **pierdan**
Command (tú)	**pierde, no pierdas**

Like **perder:** defender, *to defend;* entender, *to understand.*

encontrar(ue) to find

Present Indicative	**encuentro, encuentras, encuentra,** encontramos, (encontráis), **encuentran**
Present Subjunctive	**encuentre, encuentres, encuentre,** encontremos, (encontréis), **encuentren**
Command (tú)	**encuentra, no encuentres**

Like **encontrar:** acordarse, *to remember;* acostarse, *to go to bed;* almorzar, *to have lunch;* contar, *to count;* demonstrar, *to demonstrate;* mostrar, *to show;* probarse, *to try on;* recordar, *to remember;* rogar, *to beg, ask;* sonar, *to sound, ring;* volar, *to fly.*

volver(ue) to return

Present Indicative	**vuelvo, vuelves, vuelve,** volvemos, (volvéis), **vuelven**
Present Subjunctive	**vuelva, vuelvas, vuelva,** volvamos, (volváis), **vuelvan**
Command (tú)	**vuelve, no vuelvas**

Like **volver:** devolver, *to return (something);* doler, *to ache;* envolver, *to wrap up;* jugar, to play (a game); llover, *to rain;* mover, *to move.*

Class II *(-ir)*

sentir(ie) to feel

Present Participle	**sintiendo**
Present Indicative	**siento, sientes, siente,** sentimos, (sentís), **sienten**
Present Subjunctive	**sienta, sientas, sienta,** sintamos, (sintáis), **sientan**
Command (tú)	**siente, no sientas**
Preterite	sentí, sentiste, **sintió,** sentimos, (sentisteis), **sintieron**
Past/Imperfect Subjunctive	**sintiera,** etc. **sintiese,** etc.

Like **sentir:** advertir, *to warn;* convertir, *to convert;* divertir(se), *to amuse (oneself);* preferir, *to prefer;* referir, *to refer.*

dormir(ue) to sleep

Present Participle	**durmiendo**
Present Indicative	**duermo, duermes, duerme,** dormimos, (dormís), **duermen**
Present Subjunctive	**duerma, duermas, duerma,** durmamos, (durmáis), **duerman**
Command (tú)	**duerme, no duermas**
Preterite	dormí, dormiste, **durmió,** dormimos, (dormisteis), **durmieron**
Past/Imperfect Subjunctive	**durmiera,** etc. **durmiese,** etc.

Like **dormir:** morir, *to die.*

Class III *(-ir)*

pedir(i) to ask

Present Participle	**pidiendo**
Present Indicative	**pido, pides, pide,** pedimos, (pedís), **piden**
Present Subjunctive	**pida, pidas, pida,** pidamos, (pidáis), **pidan**
Command (tú)	**pide, no pidas**
Preterite	pedí, pediste, **pidió,** pedimos, (pedisteis), **pidieron**
Past/Imperfect Subjunctive	**pidiera,** etc. **pidiese,** etc.

Like **pedir:** conseguir, *to get;* despedirse, *to take leave;* repetir, *to repeat;* seguir, *to follow;* servir, *to serve;* vestir, *to dress.*

OTHER IRREGULAR VERBS

In the following list, we have included only the tenses which have one or more irregular form. The subjunctive tenses are not given unless a particular verb varies from the general rule.

andar *to walk, go*

Preterite	**anduve, anduviste, anduvo, anduvimos, (anduvisteis), anduvieron**

caber *to fit*

Present Indicative	**quepo,** cabes, cabe, cabemos, (cabéis), caben
Future	**cabré, cabrás,** etc.
Conditional	**cabría, cabrías,** etc.
Preterite	**cupe, cupiste, cupo, cupimos, (cupisteis), cupieron**

caer *to fall*

Participles	**cayendo, caído**
Present Indicative	**caigo,** caes, cae, caemos, (caéis), caen
Preterite	caí, **caíste, cayó, caímos,** (caísteis), **cayeron**

decir *to say, tell*

Participle	**diciendo, dicho**
Present Indicative	**digo, dices, dice,** decimos, (decís), **dicen**
Preterite	**dije, dijiste, dijo, dijimos, (dijisteis), dijeron**
Future	**diré, dirás,** etc.
Conditional	**diría, dirías,** etc.
Command (tú)	**di, no digas**

estar *to be*

Present Indicative	**estoy, estás, está,** estamos, (estáis), **están**
Present Subjunctive	**esté, estés, esté,** estemos, erstéis), **estén**
Preterite	**estuve, estuviste, estuvo, estuvimos, (estuvisteis), estuvieron**

haber *to have*

Present Indicative	**he, has, ha, hemos,** (habéis), **han**
Present Subjunctive	**haya, hayas, haya, hayamos, (hayáis), hayan**
Preterite	**hube, hubiste, hubo, hubimos, (hubisteis), hubieron**
Future	**habré, habrás,** etc.
Conditional	**habría, habrías**

hacer *to do, make*

Past Participle	**hecho**
Present Indicative	**hago,** haces, hace, hacemos, (hacéis), hacen
Preterite	**hice, hiciste, hizo, hicimos, (hicisteis), hicieron**
Future	**haré, harás,** etc.
Conditional	**haría, harías,** etc.
Command (tú)	**haz, no hagas**

incluir   to include

Present Participle	**incluyendo**
Present Indicative	**incluyo, incluyes, incluye,** incluimos, (incluís), **incluyen**
Preterite	incluí, incluiste, **incluyó,** incluimos, (incluisteis), **incluyeron**

Like **incluir:** construir, *to construct;* contribuir, *to contribute;* distribuir, *to distribute;* huir, *to flee;* sustituir, *to substitute*

ir   to go

Present Participle	**yendo**
Present Indicative	**voy, vas, va, vamos,** (vais), **van**
Present Subjunctive	**vaya, vayas, vaya, vayamos,** (vayáis), **vayan**
Imperfect Indicative	**iba, ibas, iba, íbamos,** (ibais), **iban**
Preterite	**fui, fuiste, fue, fuimos,** (fuisteis), **fueron**
Command (tú)	**ve, no vayas**

oír   to hear

Participles	**oyendo, oído**
Present Indicative	**oigo, oyes, oye,** oímos, (oís), **oyen**
Preterite	oí, **oíste, oyó,** oímos, (oísteis), **oyeron**

poder   to be able

Present Participle	**pudiendo**
Present Indicative	**puedo, puedes, puede,** podemos, (podéis), **pueden**
Preterite	**pude, pudiste, pudo, pudimos,** (pudisteis), **pudieron**
Future	**podré, podrás,** etc.
Conditional	**podría, podrías,** etc.

poner   to put, place

Past Participle	**puesto**
Present Indicative	**pongo,** pones, pone, ponemos, (ponéis), ponen
Preterite	**puse, pusiste, puso, pusimos,** (pusisteis), pusieron
Future	**pondré, pondrás,** etc.
Conditional	**pondría, pondrías,** etc.
Command (tú)	**pon, no pongas**

producir   to produce

Present Indicative	**produzco,** produces, produce, producimos, (producís), producen
Preterite	**produje, produjiste, produjo, produjimos,** (produjisteis), **produjeron)**

Like **producir:** traducir, *to translate*

querer   to want; to love

Present Indicative	**quiero, quieres, quiere,** queremos, (queréis), **quieron**
Preterite	**quise, quisiste, quiso, quisimos** (quisisteis), **quisieron**
Future	**querré, querrás,** etc.
Conditional	**querría, querrías,** etc.

saber *to know*

Present Indicative	**sé**, sabes, sabe, sabemos, (sabéis), saben
Present Subjunctive	**sepa, sepas, sepa, sepamos, (sepáis), sepan**
Preterite	**supe, supiste, supo, supimos, (supisteis), supieron**
Future	**sabré, sabrás**, etc.
Conditional	**sabría, sabrías**, etc.

salir *to leave, go out*

Present Indicative	**salgo**, sales, sale, salimos, (salís), salen
Future	**saldré, saldrás**, etc.
Conditional	**saldría, saldrías**, etc.
Command (tú)	**sal, no salgas**

ser *to be*

Present Indicative	**soy, eres, es, somos, (sois), son**
Present Subjunctive	**sea, seas, sea, seamos, (seáis), sean**
Imperfect Indicative	**era, eras, era, éramos, (erais), eran**
Preterite	**fui, fuiste, fue, fuimos, (fuisteis), fueron**
Command (tú)	**sé, no seas**

tener *to have*

Present Indicative	**tengo, tienes, tiene**, tenemos, (tenéis), **tienen**
Preterite	**tuve, tuviste, tuvo, tuvimos, (tuvisteis), tuvieron**
Future	**tendré, tendrás**, etc.
Conditional	**tendría, tendrías**, etc.

traer *to bring*

Participles	**trayendo, traído**
Present Indicative	**traigo**, traes, trae, traemos, (traéis), traen
Preterite	**traje, trajiste, trajo, trajimos, (trajisteis), trajeron**

valer *to be worth*

Present Indicative	**valgo**, vales, vale, valemos, (valéis), valen
Future	**valdré, valdrás**, etc.
Conditional	**valdría, valdrías**, etc.

venir *to come*

Present Participle	**viniendo**
Present Indicative	**vengo, vienes, viene**, venimos, (venís), **vienen**
Preterite	**vine, viniste, vino, vinimos, (vinisteis), vinieron**
Future	**vendré, vendrás**, etc.
Conditional	**vendría, vendrías**, etc.
Command (tú)	**ven, no vengas**

ver *to see*

Past Participle	**visto**
Present Indicative	**veo**, ves, ve, vemos, (veis), ven
Imperfect Indicative	**veía, veías, veía, veíamos, (veíais), veían**

Index